hip hop in american cinema

PETER LANG
New York • Washington, D.C./Baltimore • Bern
Frankfurt am Main • Berlin • Brussels • Vienna • Oxford

Melvin Donalson

hip hop in american cinema

PETER LANG
New York • Washington, D.C./Baltimore • Bern
Frankfurt am Main • Berlin • Brussels • Vienna • Oxford

Library of Congress Cataloging-in-Publication Data

Donalson, Melvin Burke.
Hip hop in American cinema / Melvin Donalson.
p. cm.
Includes bibliographical references and index.
1. Hip-hop in motion pictures. 2. Motion pictures—United States. I. Title.
PN1995.9.H46D66   791.43'611—dc22   2006035075
ISBN 978-0-8204-6345-2

Bibliographic information published by **Die Deutsche Bibliothek**.
Die Deutsche Bibliothek lists this publication in the "Deutsche
Nationalbibliografie"; detailed bibliographic data is available
on the Internet at http://dnb.ddb.de/.

Cover design by Joni Holst

© 2007 Peter Lang Publishing, Inc., New York
29 Broadway, 18th floor, New York, NY 10006
www.peterlang.com

Printed in the United States of America

With much love,
for my brother, Brian,
and
my son, Derek,
and their hip-hop generations

Contents

Preface

At 50 plus years, I am an unlikely interpreter of the hip-hop youth movement. However, my personal and professional experiences have brought me in close contact with those who have lived with hip hop as an integral part of their lives.

I first became interested in hip hop through my brother, Brian. Fifteen years my junior, Brian was a member of a break dancing crew, called The Young Generation, in the early 1980s. They performed in and around Boston and our hometown area of Cape Cod, Massachusetts, including a gig as an opening act for the emerging pop group, The New Edition. By the late 1980s, Brian joined me in southern California, pursuing a solo career as a rapper, calling himself Sweets-the-MC. Eventually, I became one of his managers which was unfortunate for him. My minimal skills as a manager were never close to his talents and creativity as an MC. In 1988, with his single "What's Up?" we did a mini-tour playing clubs in Santa Barbara, Los Angeles, Boston, Cape Cod, and Chicago. Since the mid-1990s, Brian has been working the other side of the microphone as a music producer, though he still has a captivating flow as a rapper.

From those years with Brian, and other hip-hop performers, I was witness to the liberating effects of hip hop—from anger and frustrations—and the inspiring aspects of hip hop—for dreams and imagination. On stage and in the studio, as Brian rapped into the mic, it was a mesmerizing experience of rhymes, rhythms, and spontaneous inventiveness.

By the year 2000, my son, Derek, was thirteen, and as a father, I was dealing with a teenager who grew up with hip hop during its controversial and commercial decade. Years before he became a teen, I made a point of initiating conversations about hip-hop lyrics, video images, and gender messages. Those discussions continued during his high school years as hip hop provided Derek with an outlet for adolescent attitudes and a connection to his peers. My efforts to encourage his appreciation of r&b, jazz fusion, and classic rock had a measurable effect as we took turns listening to one another's music while traveling, eating, and "hanging" together.

From my brother's experiences to my son's adolescent years, hip hop grew in its appeal and influence in society while becoming an integral part of American popular culture. Although the changes in forms and performers have been many, hip hop's presence in the entertainment, trends, and commerce of American life continues to be significant.

From the late 1990s to the 2005, as an academic and writer, I traveled to various foreign locations, including London, Paris, Amsterdam, Geneva, Vancouver, and the South African cities of Johannesburg, Pretoria, and Capetown. In various degrees of display, hip hop manifested itself in all of those cities. The once local neighborhood novelty had reached far beyond its Bronx origins and touched young people across nationalistic, cultural, and racial lines. Those attributes of endurance and relevance have continually fascinated me as a professional educator and author.

Consequently, when approaching a third area of critical study on film, following my books *Black Directors in Hollywood* and *Masculinity in the Interracial Buddy Film*, the opportunity to examine the junction between hip hop and American cinema was difficult to resist. The hope of this book is that it informs those readers who may not have knowledge of hip-hop culture and its evolution within the framework of American feature films. At the same time, for those hip-hop aficionados who may read the book, I trust that the exploration and assessment here will be comprehensive enough to attain a nod of approval—if not for its success, then at least for its efforts.

Finally, my desire is that *Hip Hop in American Cinema* will encourage an understanding and appreciation for the ways in which popular culture expressions touch all of us, revealing perspectives about who we are individually and as a society.

Acknowledgments

In the time it has taken to research and write this book, I have been able to interact with numerous people who have assisted my approach to the book's content. From students to professional writers, the numerous statements, opinions, and ideas about hip hop informed me about the value that hip hop holds for so many, both young and old.

With that stated, I must recognize three individuals who were ongoing resources for me in thinking through my exploration of hip hop: Dan White Hodge, Melina Abdullah, and Bakari Kitwana. In particular, Bakari's friendship and discussions were of great assistance in my completion of the manuscript. Through Bakari and his celebrated Rap Sessions Tour, I was able to benefit from meeting and listening to numerous hip-hop scholars and journalists, including Davy D, Cheryl Keyes, Adam Mansbach, Joan Morgan, Mark Anthony Neal, Ernie Paniccioli, Raquel Rivera, Tracy Sharpley-Whiting, and Oliver Wang.

In providing their feedback and recommendations about hip-hop performers and film titles I have to thank Brian Donalson and Derek Donalson.

For taking time from his work to read my manuscript, I have to give my deep thanks to film scholar Andrew Gordon.

In the detailed-oriented work of improving the manuscript, I am indebted to Dr. Heidi Burns and her editing skills. In addition, helping with the completion of this book, I appreciate all of the assistance that Brittany Schwartz, Allison Faust, and Linda Webster have provided.

Once again, I received expert support from the librarians and staff at the Motion Picture Academy's Margaret Herrick Library in Beverly Hills, California. At the same time, the financial assistance from the Katherine Carter Fund of the English Department at California State University-Los Angeles was quite helpful.

Finally, for all of her patient listening, encouragement, and insightful perspectives, I am extremely grateful to my wife, Beverly A. Tate. Our many discussions about hip hop, feature films, and youth movements both shaped and sustained my critical approach to this book.

Introduction

When considering the many youth movements of the twentieth century, hip hop ranks as the most enduring and pervasive cultural milestone. As with other such complex phenomena, it did not develop in a vacuum. Over the first six decades of the century, a number of discernible youth movements occurred that collectively contributed to the emergence of hip hop.

First, the 1920s brought the age of the flapper and the "lost generation." The flapper was an irreverent challenge to traditional images of womanhood, as women dressed in revealing fashions (showing necks, arms, thighs, legs, and ankles); smoking cigarettes in public; dancing wildly in public; and going out unchaperoned with men in the new invention called the automobile. At the same time, the lost generation was a label attributed to young white writers, such as Ernest Hemingway, F. Scott Fitzgerald, and William Faulkner, who criticized American values, wealth, and racism, respectively. In addition, the 1920s fostered the New Negro movement where young black writers, such as Langston Hughes, Countee Cullen, Wallace Thurman, and Zora Neale Hurston, embraced their African American past, grass root communities, and literary aesthetics to proclaim the Harlem Renaissance. Augmenting the literary achievements, other Negro artists were integrated into the Harlem Renaissance collection of talents: Paul Robeson and Josephine Baker on stage; Aaron Douglas and Meta Fuller in painting and sculpture; and Louis Armstrong, Bessie Smith, and Duke Ellington in music. The social changes, altered attitudes, and creative energy of the 1920s youth movement was halted by the formidable arrival of the Depression era.

In the late 1940s, the emergence of the beats, or beatniks—young people who stepped away from the mainstream standards to embrace Negro music, Negro language, performance poetry, sandals, loose-fitting clothing, goatees, and marijuana as part of their lifestyles—brazenly rejected the traditional family structure, corporate employment, and Christian ethics. The beats lingered into the fifties with the writing of Jack Kerouac, Alan Ginsberg, and William Burroughs, but the defiant attitudes were absolved into the dominant musical movement of the 1950s—rock-n-roll.

Young people in the 1950s saw the rock-n-roll music as symbolic of a new way of looking at life—freedom to release emotions in public, freedom to enjoy suggestive dancing, freedom to speak a unique vernacular, freedom to celebrate Negro culture, and freedom to lose oneself in the ecstasy of the moment. With the 1950s youth movement personified through Elvis Presley and Little Richard in music and James Dean in movies, the validation of the rock era endured through its absorption into mainstream culture.

In the late 1960s, the student movement across the country at various universities and colleges assumed a political aspect in anti-war rallies, black power protests, brown power statements, environmental sermons, and women's rights campaigns. At the same time, the hippie movement, with less political emphasis, attempted to exalt "love" (often meaning uncommitted and frequent sexual trysts), "flower power," "anti-establishment attitudes," and hallucinogenic drugs as the pursuits in life.

As each of these movements defined a specific historical era in American society, they all reflected the manner in which young people, organized by age and attitude more than any formal agenda, chose to respond and behave in contrast to the status quo shaped by adults. These movements affirmed the younger perspectives on traditions and conventional standards, i.e., the rebellion against the established norms.

Notably, these movements must be assessed for their bond to racial dynamics, as black American culture continually affected and, in some cases, composed the essence of the creativity and stylings of the movements. In particular, the many forms of black music have drawn nonblack listeners of all ages, but the younger nonblack audience has embraced black cultural expressions in a dedicated, unapologetic fashion. As cultural critics Sonia Maasik and Jack Solomon state, "in the last fifty years or so, white teens have identified with the African American subculture, viewing the music of black America as an authentic medium for the expression of their own resentments and desires....Today, the carefully scripted anger and hostility that can be found in many hip-hop numbers is embraced by white teens as an expression of their own anger—against their parents, against rules and restrictions, against any form of authority at all."[1] This reaching across racial lines by white youths functions as one step in a dialectical process that eventually synthesizes, or co-opts, black cultural expressions into what is typically labeled as mainstream society.

However, hip hop possesses the unique distinction of being a movement that has gone beyond black and white teens as its primary constituency. Unlike other movements, from its earliest years, hip hop contained conspicuous intercultural aspects. Specifically, during its birth in the Bronx, New York, teens from African American, black Caribbean, and Puerto Rican backgrounds participated in hip hop's various forms. Additionally, the techniques of Asian and Brazilian martial arts fed into dance techniques, later followed by the insertion of white rock and pop music ingredients.

Although a convincing argument could be made that "rap" has its origins and development within black culture, hip hop expressions have been shaped by various racial, ethnic, and cultural contributors. Perhaps, the openness to interracial relationships springs from some optimistic aspect within youth movements, with hip hop exemplifying the contemporary possibilities of racial tolerance. Perhaps, in a parallel fashion to hip hop in the 1980s and 1990s, the concept of multiculturalism promoted inclusiveness as a progressive facet within American society. Regardless, the multiracial composition of the hip-hop movement remains a significant, measurable component. As scholar S. Craig Watkins concludes, hip hop "has always been multiracial, multicultural, and multilingual. Those qualities formed a movement that has defied all attempts to impose the strict racial definitions and caricatures that endeavor to limit its potential reach and influence."[2]

When searching for the initial origins of hip hop, the mid-to-late 1970s provided the time frame that fostered the movement within inner-city neighborhoods. The term, "hip hop," covered as a broad category of modes, including graffiti writing, DJ-ing, break dancing, MC-ing (rapping), street language, clothing, and defiant-and-sexual attitudes.

As discussed in chapter 1, more than one source was credited for coining the term "hip hop," but graffiti writing, break dancing, and rapping surfaced as the most visible expressions during the movement's early years. The novelty of those expressions announced a different type of youthful creativity, while instantly provoking a dismissive scorn by older voices. Of the three expressions, break dancing offered the most comfortable zone for both young and old, as it celebrated raw physical expression without political accusations against the prevailing social structure. Seizing the opportunity to capture the inventiveness of graffiti, break dancing, and rap, in the mid-1980s Hollywood courted the younger audience with movies that highlighted all three elements. In turn, the big screen presentation brought the novelty of hip hop to a mass audience, and with long history of producing musical and dance films, Hollywood merely added hip-hop music and dance to its inventory.

However, it soon became evident that "rap" usurped the dominant status in the hip-hop marketplace. Chapter 2 follows that evolution, particularly as gangsta rap snarled its way into public debates. Using the "hood films" of the early 1990s as a strategy for delivering gangsta rap to audiences, Hollywood took advantage of the close association between gangsta rap's violence, profanity, and hypermasculinity in the traditional action and gangster film genres.

By the late 1990s, the gangsta rap image had been thoroughly exploited in music and in Hollywood, prompting the search for fresh expressions that could still connect with younger audiences. In music, hip hop began to have more subgenres and trends, while Hollywood acknowledged the black urban professionals who maintained their links to the hip-hop movement even as they worked mainstream jobs. Chapter 3 considers those films being produced at the turn of the century, as the hip-hop generation broadened in age, interests, and pursuits.

As a method of examining rappers and the significant Hollywood's ongoing interaction with hip hop, two chapters provide a case study of MCs who attained pivotal status in both the music and film arenas. Chapter 4 assesses the central role of Tupac Shakur as an architect of gangsta rap in the 1990s. Simultaneously, his screen roles earned him a status as a talented actor moving toward superstardom. Chapter 5 evaluates the singular position that Queen Latifah created for herself in the male-dominated world of rap. Then with an impressive list of film credits, she delivers an Oscar-nominated performance and achieves a lead actress status.

In addition to examining the above expressions and MCs, throughout all of the chapters, the importance of language, clothing, and attitudes of the hip-hop generation is underscored, as movies absorbed those elements to denote authenticity of the movement. As for language, hip-hop terminology has been typically transitory and changeable as with any other popular culture entity. Often esoteric and remote to the mainstream, hip-hop phraseology was presented and contextualized for mass audiences through Hollywood films. With an inextricable link to the black oral tradition, the hip-hop lexicon takes meaning from the spelling, enunciation, and setting at the time of use. In its rebellious, non-standard English structure, scholar Kermit E. Campbell states of hip-hop language: "parents, political leaders, and the like may have some cause for concern…about their suburban world being turned upside down. If anything, rap is exposing suburban youth to the rich African American vernacular rhetorical tradition, to the game [survival skills] that urban youth have in spite of the dominant culture's damaging characterization of them and their 'degenerate' surroundings."[3] Eventually, hip-hop argot became associated with profane, sexist, and violent language, prompting various sources to organize campaigns to censure hip-hop lyrics. On its part, Hollywood seized the controversy about the pejorative language and presented it as an inextricable element of hip-hop culture.

Although less daunting than hip-hop language, clothing and generational attire held its own particular status. From the late 1970s to the late 1980s, athletic suits, leather suits, untied name-brand sneakers, and assorted accessories, such as eyeglasses, chains, jewelry, and hats represented the "look" of the performing MCs that influenced the dressing styles of the fans. Then, by the 1990s and the ensuing years, oversized pants and shirts, thick bomber jackets, untied work boots, and assorted accessories, such as knitted caps, baseball caps, sunglasses, flashy jewelry, and grills (teeth ornamentation) provided the "look" of the hard-edged MC and hip hopper. This latter "look" incited harsh criticisms from those outside of hip hop, particular as many made connections among baggy hip-hop apparel, street gang membership, and prison inmate attire. With the "hood film" cycle of the early 1990s, Hollywood depicted that plausibility, often sending a mixed message about the relationship between black youths and criminal behavior.

In regard to hip-hop attitudes, any effort to simplify that aspect would be problematic. Within each generation, the aspiration toward being "cool," i.e., having an affected, detached air, functions as an operative shaper of behavior. Specifically, within hip hop, a marked shifting to the hard-edged attitude among performers occurred with Run-D.M.C. during the 1980s; then, with the advent of gangsta rap, a group such as N.W.A. modeled a more aggressive, potentially violent disposition. In the early twenty-first century, a successful performer such as Kanye West positioned himself as a streetwise MC with middle-class sensibilities. Regardless of the attitude, the bottom line has been an image which can connect with a fan base, as hip hoppers pick and choose their preferred posturing. Even more challenging in evaluating attitude, a generation's ethos is identified which often leads to an incorrect assumption that hip hoppers are a monolithic group. Certainly, the way that hip-hop youths perceive their world—in regard to matters such as values, morality, sexuality, education, and so on—displays some common points, but generalizations labeled as facts can be faulty. Hollywood, never motivated by fairness or logic, has played an ongoing role in reducing hip hoppers to a homogeneous group, with only a few rare cinematic exceptions.

For over twenty-five years, hip hop and Hollywood intersected in a manner that benefited both in regard to the attainment of financial success in entertainment field. Although numerous critics have argued that Hollywood distorted the "authenticity" or "realness" of urban street life and the black male image, the link between hip hop and Hollywood continues to exemplify the reigning power of capitalism to merge seemingly antithetical entities. In its unashamed positioning for the highest financial returns, Hollywood sidestepped questionable images, contradictory messages, and ethical issues about hip hop to reach the ultimate goal of a maximum profit for the least amount of investment. As audiences turned out to view hip hop in American cinema, Hollywood assumed a fundamental role as the interpreter of the youth movement. More than any other medium, Hollywood mainstreamed hip-hop culture, shaping its expressions as acceptable and dynamic forms of entertainment. Hollywood gave audiences access to the environments, vernacular, clothing, and attitudes that framed hip hop, making it palatable to the wider audience that was unfamiliar with its elements. As chapter 6 discusses, the indissoluble relationship between hip-hop themes, music, and performers and profitable box office returns was motive enough for the corporate greenlighting and marketing of films and soundtracks.

Hip Hop in American Cinema charts the progression of the hip-hop movement and Hollywood's role in promoting and approbating that movement between 1984 and 2005. In examining and discussing over sixty films, the text focuses upon the content of feature films, excluding documentaries, concert films, animation, straight-to-video, and/or made for television movies. Although the excluded categories of films would certainly contribute to appreciating hip hop's significance in American cinema, Hollywood's feature films serve as the central sources in this book because those movies have been marketed to and have reached the largest mainstream audience. Consequently, feature films provide evidence of the types of movies that make their way into the neighborhood theaters, urban and rural, and into the thoughts and reflections of audiences across racial, gender, class, and age lines. *Hip Hop in American Cinema* reveals the representation and depiction of a pervasive youth movement and, at the same, demonstrates the manner in which popular culture, economic practices, political traditions, and gender patterns coalesced to affirm and maintain the ideologies and institutions of American society.

1

Representin' in the Beginnin': The 1980s

In *Breakin'* (1984), the energetic Turbo (Michael "Boogaloo Shrimp" Chambers) represents hip-hop creativity as he flashes his dynamic break dancing skills.

More than any other medium, Hollywood movies introduced mainstream America to hip-hop culture in the 1980s. In particular, Hollywood seized upon the visual and aural dynamics of three expressions of the youth culture to showcase: graffiti writing, break dancing, and rapping. The presentation of hip-hop culture was not based upon an altruistic concern to reveal the environmental, economic, and social challenges of inner city communities, but was connected instead to a more basic goal—profits. Although urban background grit and grime often served as a realistic backdrop of hip-hop-related films, the studio objectives remained linked to the commercial appeal of the exotic and foreign, rather than provoking and stirring social activism.

For Hollywood in the 1980s, hip-hop culture possessed dynamics that were compatible with the established musical genre and its variations. Popular music and movies enjoyed a lengthy, interrelated relationship since the era of talkies began in the late 1920s. Popular music functioned as a significant aspect of movies by shaping the mood and tone of a sequence, or serving as the selection heard and responded to by characters within the film. Although popular music never strengthened the case for "film-as-art" arguments, it nonetheless sparked the appeal to audiences that Hollywood could market.

In the 1930s, the catchy tunes of a Busby Berkeley musical, such as *Babes in Arms* (1939), connected with the positive and optimistic story lines of the films. Likewise in later decades, a musical like *Stormy Weather* (1942) and a biopic, such as *The Glenn Miller Story* (1953), displayed the manner in which popular songs from ballrooms to radio found their way into Hollywood movies. When Hollywood met rock music in the 1950s, there was a distinctive change that signaled the inextricable role of popular music for decades to come. With movies that exploited the rock craze, such as *Rock Around the Clock* (1956), other movies went beyond showcasing the music and into exploring the teenage angst that led to rock music's generational appeal. Popular works, such as *Blackboard Jungle* (1955) and *Rebel Without a Cause* (1955) explored the behavioral and psychological factors that motivated teenage attitudes and rock music's ability to connect to youth.

As soul, r&b, and funk permeated the stories that were based in black experiences but aimed at a mainstream audience in the late 1960s and early 1970s, Hollywood began to appreciate the market value of the movie soundtrack. With urban action films such as *Shaft* (1972) and *Super Fly* (1972) on the one hand, and dramas such as *Lady Sings the Blues* (1972), *Mahogany* (1975), and *Cooley High* (1975) on the other, the intersection of commercial music and movie merchandising became evident. The *Shaft* soundtrack led to composer Isaac Hayes' academy award, and the *Super Fly* soundtrack, composed by r&b legend Curtis Mayfield, contained several songs that made it to the top charts of popular songs.

In the decade of the 1980s, the newness of hip hop was adapted via music-dance films into a marketable entertainment form for mainstream audiences. These hip-hop-related movies, however, did not exist in a vacuum, but rather they sustained themselves within an existing trend and cycle of movies, such as *Saturday Night Fever*, *Staying Alive* (1979), *All That Jazz* (1979), *Flashdance* (1983), *Purple Rain* (1984), *Footloose* (1984), and *A Chorus Line* (1985), to name some.

Two of the aforementioned films proved to be box-office milestones for movies featuring popular music. In the late 1970s, the film *Saturday Night Fever* both recognized and escalated the popularity of disco music, dance, and trendy clothing. The musical soundtrack, performed in part by the pop group the Bee Gees, became the highest grossing soundtrack at that time, and several of the singles—"How Deep is Your Love," "Night Fever," and "Disco Inferno"—rose to financial success in mainstream music. *Saturday Night Fever* demonstrated the profitable manner in which a short-lived music form could enjoy a meteoric ascendancy via Hollywood marketing. Then, the 1984 success of *Purple Rain* even surpassed *Saturday Night Fever* in merging American cinema with the pop music world. The hard rock and funk of Prince's music, along with his screen performance, led to an impressive 13.5 million soundtrack copies being sold; an academy award nomination for best original song score;[1] and over 68 million dollars at the box office.[2]

With this historical marriage between popular music and movies, Hollywood remained open to the next trend that could garner profits and could lead to the next phenomenon in merchandising. The studios eventually found that golden goose in the various expressions of hip-hop culture.

By the end of the 1980s rap would serve as hip hop's major cinematic element. However during the early years of the decade, break dancing and graffiti art were the popular phenomena. By the late 1970s in the Bronx, black and Latino teenaged "b-boys" developed breaking as part of their individual, group, and neighborhood expression and identity. One cultural critic explains that the "word 'b-boy' is derived from 'break-boy', the term [DJ] Herc used for those who hit the dance floor during the 'break' segments [in the music]....The word eventually became common urban vernacular to describe any devoted hip hopper."[3] As author Sally Banes notes: "The intensity of the dancer's physicality gives breaking a power and energy even beyond the vitality of graffiti and rapping.... Breaking is a competitive display of physical and imaginative prowess, a highly codified dance form that in its early stages served as an arena for both battles and artistic invention and that allowed for cracking open the code to flaunt personal inventiveness."[4] Unique and distinctive in its execution and kinetic style, this east coast street dancing with its acrobatic, body-torquing set of movements made its way from New York to Chicago and into Los Angeles. By then, the incorporation of "locking" emphasized more jerky, machine-line, popping body movements while the "Electric Boogie [was] a mimelike movement of the entire body, full of wiggles and robotic head turns...."[5] While break dancing required the dancer to physically go to the sidewalk or surface to complete the choreography, the locking and electric boogie required the dancer to maintain an upright position. Combining the movements into one routine resulted in a rather novel and captivating visual style. Accompanied by taped music, often instrumental, blaring from a portable player, or boom box, the break dancer and poplocker perceived the streets as a wide canvas of creativity.

For the graffiti writer, the surfaces of the environment itself served as a canvas for self-expression. However, the self-expression was viewed as vandalism by many in the public, particularly in New York City, where city officials waged an ongoing legal battle from the early 1970s to the early 1980s against the popularity of graffiti writing throughout the city.[6] As aptly assessed by journalist Jeff Chang: "Roaming through gang turfs, slipping through the long arms and high fences of authority, violating notions of property and propriety, graffiti writers found their own kind of freedom....They were just what they were, a strike against their generation's invisibility....They were doing it to be known amongst their peers, to be recognized for their originality, bravado, daring, and style."[7]

One of the first films that captured this counterculture was *Wild Style* (1983), an independent fictional movie that was shot by a documentary filmmaker in 16mm and then transferred to 35mm for theatrical release.[8] Although scripted, the nonprofessional performers plucked from the streets often improvised their lines in what one critic at the time called "the truest cinematic look at that world."[9] Containing its "basic young-artist-finds-himself-and-true-love" plot, critic Ellin Stein succinctly capsulizes the film: "The term 'wild style' refers to a jagged, broken form of lettering that replaced the more balloonlike look of early graffiti. The film is a celebration of hip hop, expressed visually in graffiti, musically in rapping, and physically in the dance style known as 'breakin'."[10]

However, *Wild Style*'s low-budget, unpolished techniques failed to reach a large audience, but it did suggest to Hollywood, along with the growing popularity of break dancing, that a movie presenting those visual aspects of hip-hop culture could find an audience. In 1983, Hollywood's successful dance movie, *Flashdance* (1983), included break dancing in a pivotal scene. As Alex (Jennifer Beals) prepares for stressful audition to enter a noted dance institute, she observes and later incorporates the extemporaneous break dancing moves performed on a street corner (by the popular Rocky Steady dance crew). Fusing her classical, modern, and break dancing methods, Alex displays a street-influenced routine that wins her acceptance.

By the summer of 1984, Hollywood committed to several films that presented the urban world of hip-hop culture to a general audience. The film, *Beat Street* ambitiously sought to capture the expressions of break dancing, graffiti, and rap, while *Breakin'* and *Breakin' 2: The Electric Boogaloo* (1985) highlighted the urban dance craze in its many forms.

Beat Street approached hip hop as a counterculture that was a creative and curious territory to be consumed by mainstream America. As a way of showing the distinctive musical form, cameo performances were sprinkled throughout the movie by then-popular and pioneering acts, including Grandmaster Melle Mel and the Furious Five, Afrika Bambaataa, the Treacherous Three, Tina B., and Brenda Starr. In some of the its segments, the movie referenced street life and urban hardships that confronted the black and Latino characters pursuing dreams of success in suffocating neighborhood environments. However, the film avoided extended social commentary, spotlighting graffiti art, break dancing, and rapping, while including the significance of hip-hop language, clothing, and attitudes.

In the movie's storyline, Kenny (Guy Davis) and Chollie (Leon W. Grant) are two African American friends who love rap music, and they bond with Ramon (Jon Chardiet), a Puerto Rican graffiti writer who has had a baby with his girlfriend, Carmen (Saundra Santiago). Kenny's younger brother, Lee (Robert Taylor) is a break dancer who hangs with a group of fellow dancers and who develops a friendship with Tracy (Rae Dawn Chong), a college student who studies music and dance forms.

With all of these areas covered, the story submerges the audience into a world of anger, rebellion, and inventiveness, as the characters intersect at their mutual love for creative expression. The dramatic crisis in the movie occurs when Ramon is killed in a subway after confronting another tagger who has been defacing Ramon's graffiti murals. Ramon's death becomes a catalyst for bringing all of the characters together in a commemorative celebration on New Year's Eve where rap, gospel, modern dance, and break dancing are performed at a club event.

With noted actor-activist Harry Belafonte as the film's co-producer, and a respectful budget that reached $9.5 million,[11] *Beat Street* attempted to entertain while informing the audience about characters and an environment that were alien from the mainstream. Belafonte insists that the film is "about people who make up hip-hop culture. It's not going to be a frivolous look at undulating bodies, but a look at the cultural phoenix that has risen out of the ashes of the South Bronx....There is no doubt about our commercial intentions, but there is also no doubt that we have tried to be uncompromising in terms of the social-political power of the text...."[12]

As an introduction into the hip-hop world, this film effectively gives the audience a glimpse of the various expressions and tensions intrinsic in the music, styles, and argot of the young counterculture. Importantly, by showing the urban milieu and the intercultural dynamics shaping hip hop, the movie does justice to the origins and foundations of the youth movement. Although the movie retains the traditional Hollywood ending, where all things work out in an upbeat manner, the characterizations and story are intent upon revealing hip hop as a nonthreatening and creative force.

Making its way into New York movie theaters one month before *Beat Street*,[13] *Breakin'* , as the title suggests, highlights what its press kit heralded as "a new form of street dancing...from the core of the nation's inner cities...spreading to street corners, shopping malls and school yards everywhere...breakdancing is crossing over into the mainstream of American performing arts after nearly a decade as a strictly urban phenomenon."[14]   The obvious intentions of these notes were to position break dancing as a legitimate mainstream activity, safely evolved from its inner-city origins. These intentions emerge conspicuously in the film's familiar story line and innocent tone, as one critic concludes that "[a]miable and well-paced, [*Breakin'*] exudes a beach party ambience and a mild exoticism...."[15]   However, the movie connected with an audience as it grossed $30 million in just a few weeks[16] on a budget of "under $2 million to make."[17]

As *Breakin'* celebrates poppin', lockin', break dancing, and uptempo music, the movie does not pretend to explicate the financial pressures, urban blight, or countercultural viewpoints about the status quo. The film follows the similar genre patterns and themes of dance-based movies, such as *Staying Alive* and *Flashdance,* as it shifts its production design and dialogue to the urban streets of Los Angeles rather than New York.

Kelly (Lucinda Dickey), a young white waitress who studies modern dance and aspires for a professional career, meets two street dancers: a Latino whose street name is Ozone (Adolfo "Shabba-Doo" Quinones) and a black youth whose street name is Turbo (Michael "Boogaloo Shrimp" Chambers). Although Kelly comes from a classically trained background—a point emphasized by Franco (Ben Lokey), her sexually aggressive dance instructor—Ozone and Turbo create from their innate talents and street smarts. Soon, the three dancers become a trio, as their dance techniques win break dancing battles at the local club; audiences on the streets of Venice, California; and finally a dance competition for a major stage production. Although Kelly, nicknamed Special K, and Ozone have an obvious romantic attraction, they both stay true to the pure emotions and vitality of their dancing, which ultimately helps the three to be selected as the marquee stars of the show, "Street Jazz."

Director Joel Silberg tries hard to pull a mainstream audience into the upbeat and benign elements of the film's hip-hop dance. With very little rappin'—though popular Ice-T performs on stage at the local club—and very little hip-hop argot—though expressions such as "fresh," "bag on us," wacked," and "buggin'" emerge—the movie submerges the audience into the high-energy, hyper-kinetic world of youths who find passion and purpose in dance. These main characters—who refrain from drugs, alcohol, profanity, and sex—are dancing fools, who recognize their class differences. For example, Kelly lives in a big house while Ozone and Turbo share a garage, but they never allow those distinctions or their ethnic contrasts to interfere with worshipping the beat of the music. Instead of this movie being a story that has dance, it is actually a visual dance show that allows a story to surface between the long dance sequences.

From the opening credits to the final freeze frame, the camera focuses upon upper body movements, such as finger pointing, snapping wrists, tilting heads, and twisting torsos, and lower body dynamics, such as gyrating hips, undulating butts, stepping feet, and spinning on sides, backs, and heads. Some dance sequences, whether solo performances or ones choreographed for two or three, seem more like an instructional video where the audience can pick up techniques on popping and locking. Although most of the music is given a source within the movie, be it via a boom box, cassette tape, or recorded studio music, the film still has that tone of fantasy. It is a movie where teens don't have parents and where minimum-wage jobs allow teens to afford fancy outfits, dance lessons, music cassettes, living quarters, and gas to fill their cars.

Two of the film's major stars, Adolfo "Shabba-Doo" Quinones and Michael "Boggaloo Shrimp" Chambers, had gained recognition in breakdancing prior to the film. Both had been, at one time, members of the dance troupe called "The Lockers," a group that accentuated poplocking after the dance movements were showcased in the 1970s on the television show *Soul Train*.[18] Their thinly written characters in the film maintain the story's connection to hip hop's streetwise sensibilities, but their urban ethnic edge suffocates under the white wholesomeness of Kelly's character.

The sequel, *Breakin' 2: Electric Boogaloo* (1985) brings back the three main characters, who are dealing with life after the close of their big show. Kelly, dancing as a chorus girl, feels her life is a bit stale. She returns home to stay with her rich parents, who become important characters in this sequel, but she quickly spends all of her time with Ozone and Turbo, who share a garage in East Los Angeles and teach at a neighborhood community center called "Miracles." When a greedy business man conspires to tear down the center in order to build a mall on the space, the trio has to raise $200,000 to save the center from being demolished. With that well-worn plot in place, the three characters are off to raise funds through their hip-hop dance and attitudes.

The sequel attempts to deal with more ethical and political concerns than the first installment, as Kelly's father displays his disdain for "street people"; as the businessman uses his influence and legal maneuverings at city hall; and as the responsibility for urban youths becomes a major issue. However, the tone remains on the same level as the initial film, with sequences that move even more into fantasy. For example, when Ozone and Turbo take Kelly through the neighborhood to see the community center, the three erupt into dance while music comes up from no apparent source, and as they gyrate along the streets, various neighborhood characters, of diverse cultural backgrounds, join them in dance: yard workers, the mailman, phone man, old women, kids, and a police officer. It becomes a Disneyland main street parade where harmony and goodwill dominate. This opening guarantees that there'll be a happy ending, despite the bumps and clashes along the way.

The significant aspect of this sequel is that, like its predecessor, the world of hip hop is represented as a healing agent within families and in the community. In particular, break dancing and poplocking function as catalysts for inspiring people to lose themselves in music and movement in order to find an inner joy that affects others in a domino effect. Hip hop is shown as a youth movement that could reconcile differences of any kind if only given the opportunity to do so.

A reviewer for *Box Office* barely tolerates the film when writing that "[i]f you've seen even one Judy Garland/Mickey Rooney/hey-gang-let's-put-on-show musical, you know how it turns out...'Breakin 2' also presents an admirably rosey, upbeat, ethnically harmonious view of life in which people from all walks of life can solve their problems through dance...even the story's most cynical villains become okay guys by the end."[19]

With the popular response to *Beat Street*, *Breakin'*, and *Breakin' 2: The Electric Boogaloo*, the novel aspects of hip hop, particularly break dancing, signaled a entirely new area that Hollywood could develop for addicting a younger audience to its trappings. However, as Jeff Chang notes, the meteoric obsession with break dancing began to wane by the middle of the 1980s. He writes: "After 'Beat Street', every kid across the country wanted to breakdance and every city council and shopping mall official wanted to ban it. But the only thing that put a stop to the dance was its marketing overkill."[20] Illustrating break dancing's trendy appeal, the dance form and/or various dancing crews appeared at numerous, disparate events: the 1984 summer Olympic Games in Los Angeles; at the Lincoln Center; at President Reagan's second inauguration; on toys, wristbands, shoes, and how-to books; and television commercials.[21]

By the mid-1980s, break dancing had migrated into the various corners of American society and saturated popular culture. Once a novelty, it began to seem cliché. Emblematic of the overkill of break dancing was yet another movie, *Body Rock* (1984), which failed to connect with audiences. Similar to *Breakin'* films, *Body Rock* focuses a white protagonist named Chilly, played by Lorenzo Lamas who starred on television's serial drama *Falcon Crest*.

Chilly is the "leader of a group known as The Body Rock Crew" whose "claim to fame is its public graffiti murals, though [they're] equally at home on the dance floor where members perform some rather astounding break-dance and jazz-style maneuvers."[22] Due to his dancing skills, Chilly gains an entree into high society and possible stardom, but he soon finds that the street life and his crew are more valuable than the "shallow and pretentious" world of fame.[23] Although the movie was perhaps well intentioned, critic Elvis Mitchell couldn't resist lowering rather scathing comments, concluding that "'Body Rock' appears to be nothing more than a hip version of 'Sesame Street'. Apparently, the film's premise came about when someone said, 'Hey, let's make a breakdance movie with a bunch of rhythmless white people'....'Body' turns breakdancing and rap into a joke."[24]

Appearing in the following year, *Fast Forward* (1985) utilizes dancing as a vehicle for achieving dreams. Directed by Sidney Poitier, the movie follows eight high school dancers from Ohio who pool their resources and talents to journey and compete in New York City. The group, calling themselves the "Adventurous Eight," contains boys and girls from a variety of ethnic groups, who are forced to dance on the street for survival money; soon they confront another break dancing crew working the same streets. The eight adapt the break dancing moves of their rivals into their more modern-interpretive routines, eventually defeating the street dancers in a dance-off battle and winning a televised competition.

Fast Forward's objective is not to bring an audience deep into the hip-hop culture and the significance of break dancing within that urban world. Instead, the film maintains a kinship to the conventional Hollywood musical, as "the movie at times calls for a suspension of reality," and "at its heart, the film affirms the American myth that everyone—regardless of race, gender, or class—can fulfill their dreams it they remain true to those dreams."[25]

Just as break dancing began to ebb as the premier element of hip hop by the mid-1980s, rapping took its place in the spotlight and has dominated ever since. Viewed by some critics as part of the continuum of generations of folk tradition, doo-wop, soul, funk, and poetry, rap music surfaced in New York City neighborhoods as early as 1974. Used as a form of entertainment at house parties, rap was a collection of rhyming words recited above turntable mixing of vinyl records.[26] Journalist David Samuels observes that though "much is made of rap as a kind of urban streetgeist, early rap had a more basic function: dance music" as it "quickly spread from New York to Philadelphia, Chicago, Boston, and other cities with substantial black populations."[27]

The Sugar Hill Gang's tune, "Rapper's Delight" gained radio airtime in 1979; the lyrics of this tune are credited with offering up the term "hip hop" from the opening, rhythmic ad-libbed line.[28] Still, other sources refer to various rapping DJs as the possible originators of the term. One such celebrated figure was DJ Hollywood, known for taking the Jamaican style of banter and "orchestrating a merger of black street wit, the latest dance hits, and turntable technology to drive a crowd of tough-to-please New York dancers into total ecstasy."[29]

Regardless of the origin of the term, the song "Rapper's Delight," which "unexpectedly sold 2 million copies...created a vast audience for rap around the country, and unleashed a mad scramble of MC groups looking for record contracts."[30] By 1982 with "The Message," by Grandmaster Flash and the Furious Five, rap music had established itself as an emissary for the younger urban generation which accepted the overall label of hip hop to identify their street culture.

Even so, hip hop refused to be just an urban craze among Black Caribbean, African American, and Latino youths. Despite little radio airtime, the underground word-of-mouth activity maintained the musical form, as it modified the language and verbal expressions. Significantly, scholar. Paula Massood observes that the "release of the early hip-hop films closely coincides with the launch of MTV in 1981.... But while MTV was responsible for bringing rap to mainstream attention with its 1981 broadcast of Debbie Harry's 'Rapture', the reality was that the network was reluctant to integrate hip-hop into its video rotation....rap was added to MTV's format—in a segregated manner—through "Yo! MTV Raps" and "Fade to Black."[31] In a complementary perspective, noted professor Tricia Rose argues: "By 1989, MTV began playing rap music on a relatively regular basis, and multi-million unit rap sales by the Beastie Boys, Tone Loc, M.C. Hammer and Vanilla Ice convinced music industry executives that rap music, for all of its 'blackness' in attitude, style, speech, music, and thematics, was a substantial success with white teenagers."[32] Rose and other critics go on to conclude that the crossover to white youths was merely another example, of many, in which the appeal of black cultural expressions served as forms of rebellion, identity, and creativity for white youngsters. Rap—with its human beat-box noises, record scratching, sampling of other tunes, and breathless pacing—had carved its way into the airwaves by the end of the 1980s.

Beat Street delivered rap to movie audiences as an integral ingredient of hip hop culture, but *Krush Groove* (1985) extended the emphasis on the musical form in a more pronounced manner. Directed by Michael Schultz, the premier black director of the 1980s, *Krush Groove* was inspired by the experiences of one of hip hop's most significant moguls—Russell Simmons. In the movie, the protagonist, Russell (Blair Underwood) struggles to get his brother Run (Joseph Simmons) and partners DMC (Daryl McDaniels) and Jam Master Jay (Jason Mizell) into the competitive music world. When Russell borrows money from a local gangster and becomes romantically linked to the same woman as his brother, complications occur until they're appropriately resolved by the film's end.

However, the weighty matters of the plot do not prevent the movie from engaging the audience with the performances by both established and up-and-coming hip hop artists. With a generous supply of settings in night clubs, stage contests, recording studios, and concerts, the movie hosts an array of talents. In a subplot, famed rapper Kurtis Blow (as himself) plays a promoter for Run-D.M.C. and the Fat Boys (as themselves). Blow gets the chance to perform "If I Ruled the World," while the Fat Boys do a humorous turn with the tune "All You Can Eat." Additionally, playing the romantic interest, Sheila E. (as herself) remains dubious of rap's musical aspects as she constantly extols the virtues of her funk-R&B roots. She energetically performers two of her hits: "Love Bizarre" and "Holly Rock." Augmenting these major performers, the movie also adds a sequence at a contest, allowing short glimpses of the other performers, including the New Edition, the Beastie Boys, and LL Cool J.

More polished than its predecessors, *Krush Groove* displays hip hop in a more complex fashion, as it provides a view of the music business, the crime connections, and the older versus younger hip-hop performers. As noted in the *Village Voice*, the film "is arguably the best of the hip-hop flicks," as it avoids the "schlocky battles for aesthetic respectability. The off-stage life of the budding rappers here is the business of show business—cash flow, contracts, management turf wars...."[33] At the same time, never losing sight of its priority to entertain the audience, the movie's ensemble cast of performers blends effectively, and the movie's pacing contains the same brisk energy as the rap tunes it features. By presenting rappers as being similar to any other aspiring talents, the movie encourages viewers to relate on a fundamental level with the characters. Despite the hip-hop terminology and attitudes, the rappers emerge as just regular urban kids attempting to find jobs based on their passions and seeking expression in a form that holds their fervor.

Similar to previous movies, the images from *Krush Groove* suggests that hip hop as a counterculture is accessible to mainstream population. The movie basically presents rap as a youth-oriented arena that offers opportunities for creative expression and emotional release. The conventional bad guys here are the gangsters who loan and then threaten the young entrepreneur who has a dream. As such, the story doesn't venture into a presentation of rap music as an intensive political or sociological weapon against society's ills and barriers. Instead, the movie has a particular innocence about it, and seems more of a homage to older Hollywood films that emphasized popular music as merely a companion expression to adolescent growing pains.

Unlike the dramatic turns that make up *Krush Groove*, the movie *Rappin'* (1985), also directed by Joel Silberg, veered in a different direction. More intent upon capturing the whimsical nuances of rap, the movie cavalierly shapes the verbal stylings as an outer expression of inner feelings. Inspired by the legend of Robin Hood and his Merry Men, this movie urbanizes the legend by presenting John Rappin' Hood and his Wild Men.

The story focuses on John (Mario Van Peebles) who returns from a stretch in jail to his old neighborhood to live with his religious grandmother (Edye Byrde) and younger brother Allan (Leo O'Brien). While inside, John obviously worked out in the gym and kept his hair well coiffured, as he appears in the opening credits looking very much like a print ad model with his smooth, handsome features, tight abs, and pleasant demeanor. In the old neighborhood, he connects with his crew (the Wild Men) which includes Ice (Eric LaSalle) and Moon (Kardeem Hardison). At the same time, he has an ongoing confrontation with an old nemesis, Dwayne (Charles Flohe), who is now dating John's former romantic interest, Dixie (Tasia Valenza). As a subplot, a greedy developer, led by Cedric Wilson (Rony Clanton), strategizes to take over rental properties of the neighborhood in order to tear them down for more lucrative business development.

Like the old musicals from the 1930s and 1940s, *Rappin'* has its characters abruptly bursting into song—that is to say, rap—at various places in the story. The rapping becomes an extension of the emotional moment or thoughts of a given character, disrupting the realistic tone of the movie, and transforming it into a fanciful vehicle. In that illusionary mode, the urban decay and unemployment are visible, but they are never scrutinized as ominous factors. In John's hood—a carefully constructed mix of various ethnic characters—people peacefully interact and co-exist, always looking out for one another and connected by their respect for John and his crew, who have been known to help the weak and needy with food, heat, and other necessities.

At its best, *Rappin'* legitimizes street talk, celebrating rap as an individual articulation and entertaining form, harmless and beneficial all at once. Rap exists primarily as a rhyming mode that offers personal feelings to be heard through an infectious, exhilarating form. By the end credits, with its happy ending, all the major characters are literally rapping with John and his Wild Men who traverse their neighborhood that's been saved from the greedy developer by John's leadership. At the movie's end, the economic conditions are still apparent, but John, who has gained a record deal through Dixie's efforts, believes that as long as he can rap freely and spontaneously, life will always remain on a positive tip. In a *Los Angeles Times* review, one critic confesses that "'Rappin'...may make you groan, but it never makes you fidget....The movie is chock-full of absurdities...but absurdity, after all, is the stock-in-trade of many good musicals. And the last scene is its high point: a vast under-the-credit unison rap by nearly the entire cast, a little urban ethnic melting pot, joined by the bonds of doggerel."[34]

By today's standards, *Rappin'* appears simplistic, clumsily crafted, and humorous in its rap techniques. Even the brief cameo performances by Ice-T and Full Force fail to give an edge to the proceedings. Instead, it has a quickly made, low-budget aspect to it, and the innocent tone and happy-ever-after storyline hit a false note for a contemporary audience aware of urban realities and political conflicts. Given the commercial intentions of the filmmakers, the movie also accentuates language, rhyming, and free-style form that provides early rap music its distinctiveness. By minimizing the very economic, political, and cultural issues that inspired many rappers assured its accessibility to a broad mainstream audience.

Even as *Rappin'* received mixed responses from mainstream critics, two other hip hop-related films fared worse. Although boasting a cast of popular white actors—Timothy Hutton, Robert Urich, Kim Cattrall, and Robert Culp—*Turk 182* (1985) misfires when incorporating graffiti writing as a topic. Avoiding the cultural and social elements that shaped graffiti and tagging, the movie "tells what happens when a Little Guy in...metropolis makes the Big Guy stand up and take notice. The underdog is Mr. Hutton's Jimmy Lynch, who becomes a renegade graffiti artist to avenge the injustices done to his brother Terry (Robert Urich), an injured fireman."[35] Compared more with the underdog-becomes-champion theme of *Rocky* (1976) than with hip hop, the film exploits the urban conflict between graffiti writers and city officials, particularly the well publicized New York City multi-million-dollar, anti-graffiti campaign between 1971 and 1981.[36]

Following in 1986, the movie *Delivery Boys* suffers more severe dismissals from critics and uninterested audiences. The movie follows the comical episodes of three break dancers who earn money by working as pizza delivery boys. With Caribbean, Puerto Rican, and white characters, the movie attempts to connect to a cross-section of viewers,[37] but it falls short in its content. One *Variety* review concludes that " the 'Porky's'-style grossout humor is uninspired, as are the performances....[the] music is weak and dance choreography repetitive."[38]

By the time the movie *The Disorderlies* (1987) arrives to the screen, hip hop had found recognition in American popular culture. For almost a decade, the radio airwaves, record sales, music magazines, and television music-format shows positioned rap music as a prevalent form making its way from the urban street corners into suburban neighborhoods. With a wider audience in place, the potential for *The Disorderlies* was evident, but the film failed to augment the achievements of the hip hop-influenced movies that came before.

Fashioned as a showcase vehicle for the popular rap trio, The Fat Boys, who appeared as supporting characters in the earlier *Krush Groove, The Disorderlies*—although directed by Michael Schultz who also helmed *Krush Groove*—never gets above a cartoonish atmosphere and does little to promote hip-hop cultural expressions. The basic premise has the Fats Boys—Markie (Mark Morales), Buffy (Darren Robinson), and Kool (Damon Wimbley)—employed by a sinister nephew attempting to kill his rich uncle via their incompetent caretaking techniques. As Buffy and Kool proceed to carelessly complete their duties, Markie consistently chases the maid about the premises of the uncle's estate. Eventually, the uncle becomes affectionate to the three and grows healthier, undermining the nephew's plans of a quick demise for the inheritance.

Although slapstick and sight gags can work effectively on the screen, they are overused in this movie, resulting in a level of humor similar to *Car Wash* (1976). In contrast to that film though, as well as *Krush Groove*, the poignant moments and interesting character traits never emerge to give balance to the movie's efforts at humor. Instead, the movie serves up a cute triteness, as when the white conservative uncle accepts the hip-hop manners of The Fat Boys, eventually using words such as "homeboy" and "illin'." In general, the rapping remains a collection of silliness, and hip-hop culture disappears into one-liners. As cultural critic Donald Bogle concluded, this movie "was an out and out embarrassment."[39]

The 1988 film, *Tougher Than Leather*, brought a different type of tone in its depiction of hip hop and evoked negative responses by those who position themselves as guardians of cinematic taste. Indicative of the changes occurring within rap by the late 1980s, the movie and its stars, Run-D.M.C., were vilified for violent images and messages. Given credit by many as the rap group that "made music that was as hard as New York pictured itself," in 1983, "Run-DMC's first single 'It's Like that/Sucker MCs'...completely changed hip-hop. Previously, hip-hop records were pretty much party jams," but "'Sucker MCs' redefined the b-boy as all attitude: a hard rock with his arms crossed, a scowl...untied sneakers."[40]

Although the trio, Run (Joseph Simmons), D.M.C. (Darryl McDaniels), and DJ Jam Master Jay, lived outside of the Bronx in a middle-class environment, they would "shout" words above a "hard beat" with an "aggressive" force in a "rhyming style [that wasn't] singsongy, suave, or part of any known continuum."[41] For many, Run-D.M.C. established a new hip hop cool attitude as "[t]hey looked street in their matching Adidas suits...big Cazal eyeglasses, and those weird black fedoras. Sometimes they wore matching black leather suits."[42] Even as the hard image inspired other rappers, it attracted equally aggressive audiences at concerts, and to the irritation of an older generation, Run-D.M.C. became "the first rap group to break through to the white audience" with its third album, *Raising Hell*, that contained the remake of Aerosmith's "Walk This Way," selling "3 million copies" along with a "U.S. concert tour [that] was a box-office smash."[43]

When planning on starring in their first movie, Run-D.M.C. wanted to bring their aggressive style to the screen. According to Rick Rubin, the co-owner of Def Pictures, record producer, and director of *Tougher Than Leather*: "We wanted to show what it's really like on the streets—and that it's not another Hollywood fantasy like 'Krush Groove.'"[44] Consequently, as journalist points out, "[a]s a rap picture, it bears scant resemblance to 'Krush Groove'...or other modern movies about nice kids finding expression through black street culture. Here we have machine guns, knife fights and crack."[45] Basically, a revenge-themes movie, Run-D.M.C. portray themselves in a story has one of their friends getting murdered, with the crime "dismissed as simply another casualty of the worlds of crack and rap. So, Run-D.M.C. set out to clear their friend's name by finding the people responsible."[46] One source stated that with the film "rated R for violence, nudity and non-stop profanity," *Tougher Than Leather*'s "violent, sexist bent harken[ed] defiantly and perhaps embarrassingly back to the 'blaxploitation' era of the '70s." At the same time that critics attacked the movie's content and images, theaters dealt with additional aspects of screening the film. "Following weekend violence that left one person dead and several injured," five theaters in the Detroit area stopped showing the movie,"[47] while on Long Island, New York, the film was pulled from theaters when a fan was stabbed to death at a rap concert.[48] Even before the release of the movie, the members of Run-D.M.C. were already defending themselves to be positive role models after a 1986 Long Beach, California, concert where "41 people were injured during gang violence."[49] Presaging the impending decade of controversy about the link between rap and violent behavior, Run justified *Tougher Than Leather* by arguing: "Kids will understand [the violence]. Parents will, too. After all, they loved 'Rambo,' didn't they? They loved '48 HRS,' didn't they?"[50] Neither the fans nor the critics appreciated the movie, as it went down as a failure at the box office.

In the wake of the disappointing responses to *The Disorderlies* and *Tougher Than Leather*, director Spike Lee made certain that his film, *Do the Right Thing* (1989), effectively integrated the dynamics of the hip-hop youth culture, interracial conflict, and urban politics. With his independent filmmaking background and a commitment to explore racial politics—as indicated by his two earlier films, *She's Gotta Have It* (1986) and *School Daze* (1988)—Lee avoids the Hollywood, sanitized approach to hip hop. The filmmaker coalesces hip-hop expressions with the daily struggle to survive and find validation in an economically challenged, urban neighborhood. Film historian Ed Guerrero observes that the movie "depicts a broad, polyphonic, social landscape of varied characters, subplots, political outlooks, and racial groupings, all contending and coexisting in [a] racially tense, stagnant atmosphere."[51]

In the opening sequence, choreographer-actress Rosie Perez demonstrates the moves, attitude, and sexuality intrinsic to hip hop. As the credits roll, she dances to Public Enemy's "Fight the Power," an assertive anthem to black cultural pride and a rejection of white heroes. This tune works as a foundation for the urban personalities simmering with anger throughout the film, but in particular to one character, Radio Raheem (Bill Gunn). An African American young man who commands respect, Radio Raheem walks his neighborhood with his boom box blaring "Fight the Power." Although he does not own the buildings and vehicles crowding his streets, Radio Raheem owns the neighborhood. As he crosses the paths of Puerto Rican, Caucasian, Korean, and black inhabitants, Raheem's hip-hop music, like a superhero's theme song, announces and validates his presence "on the block." Later, when confronting Sal (Danny Aiello), the Italian owner of the local pizza parlor, Raheem explodes into physical fighting when his boom box and music are destroyed by Sal. Raheem is inseparable from his music, and to be without his tune renders him out of control and later, a victim, of a choke hold by the arriving police. For Raheem, and his generation, the music isn't a form of entertainment, but an expression of identity and existence.

Spike Lee shows this urban neighborhood as a contemporary quilt of cultural expressions with hip hop being one of the significant forms. Hip hop is pervasive and visible, not only for the black characters but to the other ethnic groups who comprehend its meaning to Radio Raheem and the larger youth movement. As a director, Lee extends the efforts made by Stan Lathan and Michael Schultz, in *Beat Street* and *Krush Groove*, respectively. By integrating the dress, vernacular, and music, the world of hip hop takes shape as a viable, substantive presence, not just an entertaining diversion.

At the same time, *Do the Right Thing* accomplishes an objective missing from earlier hip-hop related films of the previous decade. Without the need to "introduce" viewers to hip hop culture, the film presents the aspects of the culture—language, dress, attitude, music—in a realistic context and significantly the political and social malaise feeding into hip-hop culture. The film displays the "signs of the effects of economic shifts, such as rising rates of unemployment among African American men, an increasing association of criminality with black youths, the growing influence of rap music…, an escalating feeling of helplessness and lack of agency (often interpreted as nihilism)," as well as "the tensions and anger generated by these conditions."[52] The film comments on the depths and severity of the inner city's jungle-like maze that many were navigating with the help of hip hop culture and rap's expressive form. These same neighborhoods would become the setting for a host of films, images, and hip- hop expressions as the cycle of "hood films" surfaces in the 1990s.

When assessing all of the movies mentioned here, hip hop in varying degrees maintained its youth connection and anti-establishment sensibilities. At the same time, the movies mentioned here were indicators of two issues that would later emerge as crucial points of debate with hip hop. First of all, the movies, for various reasons, presented hip hop as a multi-ethnic and multiracial youth movement during its earliest years. Arguably, this factor serves the perspective that hip hop, despite its black youth origins, has encouraged an interracial understanding and inclusion in American society. In his book, *Why White Kids Love Hip Hop* (2005), author Bakari Kitwana commends the hip-hop generation for avoiding the "old racial politics" of racial polarization for more racially progressive viewpoints and efforts.

Second, the crucial point about gender emerges in these films in a more subtle manner. The male dominance in hip-hop expressions—particularly graffiti writing, break dancing, and rap—reflects, for some, the often troubling aspect of gender inequality, even misogyny, surfacing within hip-hop culture. In a 1984 *Ms.* magazine review of *Beat Street* and *Breakin'*, critic Martha Nelson reflects on the male dominance in hip hop, citing the discrepancy in female representation in the films. She questions: "Why don't women breakdance? Is it because girls have a separate-but-equal street art in their intricate Double-Dutch jump-rope routines and competitions?... Women, in that world [break dancing] are consigned to the sidelines where they play worshipful cheerleaders, keeping time to the beat."[53] These comments merely presage later condemning perspectives about hip hop's lyrical messages and video images of women.

In the 1980s, hip hop's journey from its urban roots and into the lifestyles and imaginations of suburban youths became a major cultural and commercial migration. Inevitably, that transference beyond hip hop's origins made the youth culture an irresistible harvest for Hollywood's voracious appetite for box office profits. However, due to the presence of an underground network of hardcore rappers and the rise of gangsta rap in the next decade, hip hop maintained its distinctive label as an urban youth movement, even as it was continually embraced by mainstream listeners.

2

Chillin' and Killin': Hood Rats and Thugs, 1990–1999

Merging gangsta rap and gangster movie action, rapper Ice-T, right,
portrays undercover cop Scotty Appleton who partners with Detective
Nick Peretti (Judd Nelson) in *New Jack City* (1991).

During the 1990s, hip hop in its many expressions permeated popular
culture, making its impact unavoidable in urban and rural America. In
particular, rap music, often used in the media as a synonym for hip hop,
assumed the spotlight as the primary expression. For some, "rap" and
"music" appear paradoxical considering the former identifies speaking
rapidly and rhythmically as opposed to singing and instrumentation.
However, a younger generation connected to the naturalness and

accessibility of rap, allowing anyone the possibility of being an MC (Microphone Controller). At the same time, the vocal qualities that distinguish rappers could be detected by the experienced fan, with the more skillful and unique rapper gaining adulation. As cultural critic Toure observes: "To be a great MC you must have a hypnotizing flow—a cadence and delivery that get inside the drum and bass patterns and create their own rhythm line. You must have a magnetic voice...but it must be a compelling sound...you must say rhymes with writerly details, up-to-the-minute slang, bold punch lines...."[1]

As rap music developed in the 1990s, it splintered into various forms and subgenres, including commercial, gangsta, and conscious rap. Commercial rap included those performers and stylings that found radio and television airtime, proclaiming its purpose for partying, dancing, and freestyle expression—performers such as DJ Jazzy Jeff and the Fresh Prince, LL Cool J, and De La Soul. By the early twenty-first century, however, commercial rap would be identified much differently, as a musical form overflowing with graphic, sexually explicit content. Noting gangsta rap, the form emerged as one of the most debated, criticized subgenres in the early part of the decade, serving as the source of rejection from an older generation in the mainstream audience. In its late 1980s infancy, gangsta rap targeted the malevolence and oppression of inner-city Philadelphia (rapper Schooly D) and, in particular, Los Angeles (rap groups N.W.A. and The Geto Boys).[2] In Chicago in the early 1990s, Conscious rap (the performer Common), often underground and less promoted, articulated the cultural, political, and artistic efforts in content and form.

Interestingly, these three rap tributaries that diverged from hip-hop culture did not weaken rap's appeal; instead, through creative evolution, controversy, and continual mainstreaming, rap increased in its popularity. As one source emphasizes: "In 1998, for the first time ever, rap outsold what previously had been America's top-selling format, country music."[3] Indisputably, hip hop was more than a transitory fad, leaving music historian David J. Szatmary to conclude that "[b]y the end of the 1990s, hip-hop pop had become the new music for a new generation."[4]

The proliferation of hip hop in the 1990s can be traced to a number of sources that in a short span of time converged, sometimes unintentionally, across commercial, political, and cultural lines. Magazines such as *Source* and *Vibe* both catered to and created a hip-hop audience across racial lines. Music video programs on MTV and BET fostered the notable rap performers, while introducing new talents for consumption. The successful network situation comedy, *The Fresh Prince of Bel Air* (1990-1996), brought hip hop, black characters, and class issues into primetime programming. Journalists and cultural critics, such as Bakari Kitwana, Nelson George, and Toure, assessed hip hop for its crucial connections between American youth culture and popular perspectives. At the same time, scholars, such as Tricia Rose, Michael Eric Dyson, Cornel West, Henry Louis Gates, and Todd Boyd connected academic analysis and cultural theories to the pervasiveness and authenticity of hip hop to American society. In an oppositional position, the ongoing criticisms about the violence, obscenity, and sexism in rap lyrics earned national attention through three particular voices: Tipper Gore, social activist and co-founder of the Parents Resource Music Center, a media-watch organization; C. Delores Tucker, a civil rights activist, politician, and co-founder of the National Congress of Black Women; and William Bennett, the Secretary of Education for the Ronald Reagan administration in the 1980s and the Director of Drug Policy for the George H.W. Bush administration in the early 1990s. With so many sources and agendas targeting hip hop, it remained quite visible in the public's attention and imagination.

Without question, American cinema served as a vital medium for promoting and sustaining hip hop in the 1990s for mainstream consumption as the many aforementioned influences fostered its significance. Some movies, such as *Just Another Girl on the I.R.T.* (1993), *Squeeze* (1997), and *Ride* (1998) highlighted hip-hop youth culture through music soundtracks, language, and dress codes in order to position those films as trendy and contemporary. Still other films, during the decade, such as *Friday* (1995), *Phat Beach* (1996), *Fakin' Da Funk* (1997), and *I Got the Hook-Up* (1998), integrated well-known rap personalities into cameo roles and/or supporting fictional characters within their stories. As one critic notes: "Rap's impact on the Hollywood film industry has also been significant. Across the spectrum, rap has found its way into the soundtrack and themes of movies both big and small…. Hollywood has been willing to produce…these types of films for a very simple reason: with a relatively small investment there is the potential for large returns."[5]

Two hip hop-flavored films, *House Party* (1990) and *House Party 2* (1991), began the decade in a fashion reminiscent to the movies of the 1980s. In these two films, hip hop was clean, palatable, and just another expression of teenage growing pains. With the lead characters being played by two New York rappers known as Kid 'N Play, the *House Party* films were upbeat and fun. As one critic observes: "not since 'Cooley High' (1975) has a feature film given black adolescents so much equal opportunity to hang loose and be themselves—without being perceived as threatening sociopaths."[6]

The first film follows Kid (Christopher Martin) who slips out of the house to party at the home of his friend, Play (Christopher Martin). While breaking his father's restrictions to socialize with his peers, Kid becomes captivated by two girls, Sharane (A.J. Johnson) and Sidney (Tisha Campbell). Attempting to maneuver intimacy with one or the other of the girls, Kid crosses the path of a group of roving tough guys (played by the hip-hop performers and producers, Full Force). The plot points revolve around Kid's efforts to get a girl, avoid the thugs, and have a good time without his father finding out. Despite the black cast of characters and "[e]ven with all of accoutrements of the hip-hop/rap culture...this is basically visual candy for not particularly conscious middle-class youth. The fads, the music, the clothes, the idiomatic speech do not guarantee a raised consciousness."[7] To its credit, though, the film contains some significant messages aimed at the young viewers, as it makes "a point of dealing with issues of sexual responsibility, teen-age drinking, male-female relationships and family values. Drugs are nowhere to be seen."[8]

House Party affirms that hip hop poses no threat to the psyche of young people, and that it brings teenagers together in a positive manner. The only violence and excessive aggression is exhibited by the three tough guys who don't connect to any of the major characters and their friends. The rappers Kid and Play remain the nucleus to the circle of hip hoppers who remain committed to raising the roof in revelry. In one feel-good sequence at the party, Kid and Play take on a dancing challenge from Sharane and Sidney, reminiscent of the dance-off battles in the 1980s movies. Taking the center of a dance circle, Kid and Play initiate a number of moves, as the two women replicate the steps, forcing Kid and Play to deliver different moves punctuated by their high kicks and interlocking insoles in their energetic hops. The synchronicity of their choreography; the quick body drops and even quicker springing up; and the dynamic thrusting of arms, shoulders, legs, and head reference the earlier break dancing and popping.

The one area that blemishes the film connects to an ongoing criticism of hip hop in the 1990s—namely, the frequent degrading language associated with women and the homophobic jokes that emanate from rigid notions of masculinity. For black male hip hoppers, women become synonymous with slang and terminology for female body parts, and the sacred paradigm of manhood eliminates any inclusion of homosexuality. To this latter point, rap lyrics have referenced disdain for gays since the first hip-hop hit, "Rapper's Delight" (1979), by the Sugar Hill Gang.[9] In the film, Kid emphasizes this hyper-heterosexuality when he lands in jail with the three tough guys. Kid's innocent appearance soon attracts an assemblage of physically large and muscular black thugs who draw straws to determine who claims Kid, the "sweetest meat around." In an old-fashioned, Hollywood musical mode, Kid breaks into a rap, accompanied by music, which indicates that he is no "A.I.D.S. candidate" nor inclined to join the "rump ranglers." He firmly raps to his cellmates: "Me a homo, that's a no-no." Fortunately, Play and others arrive with bail money to release Kid from the possible sexual plight.

Moving the major characters forward in time, *House Party 2* follows Kid to college, as Play hustles his way through the music business. At college, Kid's new challenges include demanding professors; a strained relationship with Sidney, now his girlfriend attending the same college; and financial pressures. Added to the three main recurring characters are two who emphasize hip hop in distinct ways. First of all, Kid rooms with a self-proclaimed white hip hopper named Jamal (Kamron), who firmly asserts his authenticity as an MC.

Second, rapper Queen Latifah takes on a fictional role as Zora, a feminist who mentors Sidney in the ways of independent thinking and behavior in her relationship with Kid. By having Jamal and Zora included in the story, the former serves as evidence of hip hop's popularity with white kids, while the latter links the most popular female rapper to a feminist posture, suggesting the strength and resilience of the female rapper.

Supplementing the appearances of Kid, Play, and Queen Latifah, rap performers Tony!Toni!Tone!, Full Force, and Ralph Tresvant also appear in the film. In the sequence that mirrors the feel-good party atmosphere of the first film, Kid and Play organize a pajama jam as a fund-raiser for Kid's college costs. With the partygoers dressed in sleeping attire and dancing to hip hop, the stage is set for a humorous, dance-laden finish to the film. Once more, Kid and Play take center stage in their dance steps that display the high energy and athleticism of hip hop.

Worthy of mention would be another 1991 film, *Hangin' with the Homeboys*, which follows "[f]our friends—two black, two Puerto Rican—take a prosaically tumultuous Friday-night trek from the Bronx into Manhattan and back again. They argue, they dance, they meet girls and police."[10] The very fact that the Bronx setting takes a formidable place in the story line proclaims the birthplace of early hip hop where interracial friendship reflected the attitudes of early b-boys and graffiti writers. Similar to *House Party*, the focus on male bonding and youthful chillin' functions as the basis for the plot.

Willie (Doug E. Doug), an unemployed black male, wears his ethnicity into most situations, quick to articulate his suspicion that the world is targeting him due to race. Johnny (John Leguizamo), Puerto Rican, struggles with his fear of leaving the neighborhood for college and carries an unrequited affection for a local girl. Tom (Mario Joyner), an aspiring black actor suffers a job as a telemarketer and carries an edge of arrogance to those around him. Vinny (Nestor Serrano), a self-proclaimed Romeo, avoids his Puerto Rican identity by asserting what he believes is a superior Italian identity.

As these four travel the Bronx environment, the music at the Overground Club, the beats from automobiles, the graffiti on surfaces, and the clothing worn by their peers consistently reference hip-hop culture. The Bronx streets, though resonating with poverty and possible danger, have not transformed the four friends into thugs. Comfortable with the hip-hop expressions around them, the four friends display in their own manner that hip hop serves as a generational affirmation. Neither destructive nor demonic, hip hop simply accentuates the lifestyles of these late-teen males. Then, analogous to the journey that hip hop made from the Bronx to Manhattan, the four make their way to a dance club on the island, where Johnny sees the girl of his affections and confronts the truth of her porn film career.

One impetus to making the trek into Manhattan comes through the brief appearance of Louie-Louie (Victor L. Cook). Seeing Louie-Louie driving the Bronx streets in his open-top, red jeep, the four protagonists flock to him, revering him as a neighborhood legend. Although his drug dealing profession is only implied, Louie-Louie's wealth glistens conspicuously: gold rings, gold chains, and gold teeth, as well as a diamond-studded watch. Like a philosopher of hip hop's journey from the Bronx to Manhattan, Louie-Louie tells the friends: "Bronx is dead. Y'all should check out Manhattan…Manhattan is the life!" The bling that Louie-Louie displays reflects the materialistic excesses that would contribute to the pejorative assessment of commercial rap.

In a stark contrast to the innocence and feel-good aspects of hip hop in the *House Party* series and *Hangin' with the Homeboys*, the film *Fly by Night* (1993) situates itself in the competitive world of rappers and DJs, where hip hop becomes the focus rather than the background of the film. This was the objective of the filmmakers as the director Steve Gomer asserts: "Because there are so many movies about gangs that came out that had rap soundtracks, people think that a lot of rap movies came out. But virtually none have. This [film] is actually about people who are rapping… and about the process."[11]   When the film maintains its focus on that process, it delivers an engrossing story, but as one review aptly concludes: "'Fly By Night' …is an often compelling film marked by intelligence and an undeniable urgency. But [the film] is too ambitious for its own good, trying to encompass too many of the issues faced by its characters, is inconsistent in mood and ends patly."[12]

The movie focuses on three characters—I (Ron Brice), an obsessive, angry rapper; Kayam (Daryl "Chill" Mitchell), a hustling manager who worships making money; and Rich (Jeffrey Sams), a college-educated rapper who seeks fame. The last character takes the most screen time as he leaves his wife, Akusa (MC Lyte), and son to seek success. Rich's middle-class background impedes his goal, so with Kayam's help, he joins forces with I to create a rap duo, called "The King and I." Rich assumes a hardcore image to sell himself to audiences in hopes of a record deal, and I promotes his vitriolic lyrics by using Rich's naivete and stage presence. Along the way to success, Rich becomes involved with a rich white girl, Denise (Maura Tierney), who enjoys living on the edgy side, i.e., the black world. Additionally, Denise has a Latino transvestite roommate, and lurking around the club scene is a white couple who are junkies.

The crucial point of the story, however, remains Rich's decision to sell out for popular success or emerge as a man of integrity by being himself and taking care of his family. As he wrestles with these choices, the film shows his creative process and love for hip hop. One of the several people who urge him to be himself is a rival rap artist, Rock (Sollfood), who instructs him to look critically at society and to rap what he feels. Rock condemns Rich's gangsta rapper image, believing that rap artists carry a great responsibility to young listeners. Rock says: "We're the new superheroes...write one rap that's not about that negative bullshit." This sense of duty surfaces for Rich following a riot at a club when "The King and I" perform; I purposely inflames the crowd with his lyrics and ad-libbed comments, leading to a woman being stabbed and several audience members trampled in the chaos.

Ironically, the club's riot leads to three record labels calling the group for a record deal. One of the film's most provocative dialogues occurs when Rich, I, and Kayam meet a white executive to discuss a deal. Rich and the executive argue about black culture, racism, and class struggle, as Rich defends rap for voicing black pride and the concerns of the black community. The executive candidly responds that "rap politics are hilariously misinformed...if you really give a shit about your heritage, why don't you do something to save it—all the Africans that are starving every single day...if you sell two million records...what's going to happen to your politics then?"

That sequence and two others reflect on the artistic and cultural viability of rap versus the commercialism occurring during the early 1990s. The film, particularly with Rich returning to his family at the end, takes the position that personal integrity and community responsibility have to be a rapper's priority over fame and success. This message, which contradicts the greed-is-good messages in other films of the early 1990s, might be expected from a film where rapper KRS-One worked as a writer on the movie's set.[13] Then, for those audience members who know their hip-hop history, in one shot, as Rich and Kayam leave a club at night, a streetlight shines over the wall with a mural portrait bearing the name Scott La Rock. La Rock, a co-founder with KRS-One of the hip-hop group Boogie Down Productions, was murdered "by an unknown assassin in August 1987," leading to the group's emphasis on politically conscious rap.[14]

Fly by Night questions whether gangsta rap can maintain its cultural and political potency once it becomes a record industry staple. Upon crossing the line from a political concept into a business product, the whole aspect of the gangsta image becomes problematic. Consequently, the film underscores the tensions between art and commerce and the ensuing messages found in gangsta rap.

The emergence of gangsta rap in the early 1990s was a milestone in popular culture. At the risk of oversimplifying the assessments by numerous journalists and hip-hop historians, gangsta rap was and is one of the most complex and paradoxical music forms of the late twentieth century. Rife with both reality and hyperbolic fictions, gangsta rap fit effectively into American cinema as commercial and exotic territory.

The complexity of gangsta rap rests within its origins. Hip-hop authority Bakari Kitwana notes that the hardcore "style" of rap—with its graphic lyrics, aggressive delivery, and confrontational attitudes—is not synonymous with gangsta rap, which is a type of rap.[15] Certainly, some of the late 1980s lyrical content of Public Enemy, KRS-One and Boogie Down Productions, The Boo-Yaa T.R.I.B.E., and Cypress Hill exemplified the hardcore veneer when compared to what Kitwana calls "recreational rap"[16] as exemplified in performers such as The Fresh Prince (Will Smith), Salt-N-Pepa, PM Dawn, and MC Hammer.

Decidedly, scholar Eithne Quinn argues that the "genre term 'gangsta rap'…was coined in 1989 when 'Gangsta Gangsta' by NWA [including rappers Ice Cube, Dr. Dre, and Easy E] was featured in *Billboard*'s newly launched Hot Rap Singles Chart. Its first broadsheet appearance was in the *Los Angeles Times* when Ice Cube, playing on the song's title, used the term 'gangsta rap' in an interview."[17] Consequently, with the collective of the group N.W.A. and the solo albums by its members; MC Eiht and Compton's Most Wanted; Ice-T; The Geto Boys; the group 213, with members Warren G. and Snoop Dogg; the Notorious BIG; and Tupac Shakur, gangsta rap grabbed a loyal and ever-growing fan base and public attention.

Still, amid the hostile criticism of the subgenre from some sources, other positive critics praised the creativity and collaborations among rappers, most notably from 1992 to 1994, when Dr. Dre, Snoop Dogg, and Warren G developed a musical style known as G-Funk, or gangsta funk. According to journalist Robert Marriott, songs such as "Let Me Ride" and "Nuthin' but a 'G' Thang" possess "undeniable hooks punctuated with the angst and menace of atmospheric whines," giving "body to the laid-back tension that characterizes life in Los Angeles ghettos...pure street, but with enough musicality...."[18]

For some listeners, gangsta rap served a necessary purpose, as numerous scholars have analyzed the cultural, political, and social significance of the form. For example, Professor Imani Perry theorizes that "[b]lack male rappers personify, or witness-personify, the narrative of the black male engaged in criminal activity who increasingly populates North American prisons, and that narrative is one of social marginalization and its concomitant psychological and emotional issues....numerous hip hop artists instead exploit the white fear of the black assailant as the source of power."[19] Adding a professional viewpoint, music mogul Russell Simmons, concludes: "At the time gangsta rap became popular, no other medium was giving voice to the struggles of poor urban young people in the age of crack."[20] The link between the infestation of crack into urban black communities and the ensuing deterioration of individual and collective achievement inspired the belligerent tone in many gangsta lyrics and rhymes. Author Nelson George underscores that issue when he writes: "Gangsta rap...is a direct by-product of the crack explosion. Unless you grasp that connection nothing else that happened in hip hop's journey to national scapegoat will make sense....first came crack rocks, then gangsta rap."[21] Following that crack epidemic, inner-city neighborhoods slipped into a deepening quagmire of "poverty, chronic unemployment, political disaffection...police repression...[and] gang activity."[22]

Beyond the intellectual and cultural criticism that acknowledged the value in gangsta rap, the music form also gained approbation in the profit-driven business world. Initially seen as a west coast, urban, black male-centered expression, the gangsta rap image connected quite effectively to the popular mythology of the young rebel and the outlaw, which in turn could be sold to midwest, rural, white males as well. Incorporating violence, sexism, homophobia, and materialism, gangsta rap was an ideal for the controversy and sensationalism that could be exploited for the marketplace, despite the mounting negative criticism.

The negative criticism against gangster rap, though often from an older generation, usually crossed racial lines, and it developed as part of an ongoing organized movement to monitor the lyrical content of heavy metal, pop rock, and rap that began simmering in the mid-1980s. Gangsta rap emerged as an even more evil target because the lines often blurred between gangsta rappers and their personal lives that became public headlines. With the media's exaggeration, on the one hand, and the questionable behavior by the rappers themselves, on the other, a cloud of negativity hung over rap between 1990 and 1996 in many forms: the tensions of east coast–west coast rivalry; rap's link to gangbanging; Snoop Dogg's murder charge; Suge Knight's thuggish leadership of Death Row Records; a gun death at producer Jermaine Dupri's party; Tupac Shakur's rape conviction, gun battles, and later murder; and the murder of the Notorious BIG, to mention some.[23]

Of the many public debates about the value of gangsta rap, two of the most salient dominated attention in mainstream media and political offices. The first revolved around the 1990 obscenity charges brought in the Florida courts against album, *As Nasty As They Wanna Be*, by black hip hoppers, 2-Live Crew. Released on the group leader Luther Campbell's independent label, the album's songs were "intensely graphic, scatological, and brutal locker-room fantasies set to the booming, bottom-heavy sound," and the lyrical content made the rounds to the Governor's office, state sheriffs, and "a federal court judge in Fort Lauderdale, who promptly pronounced it obscene."[24] Although 2-Live Crew was not viewed by fans and journalists as a gangsta rap group, during the time of debating lyrics, there was guilt by perception. Eventually, the group was acquitted, but the discussions about morality, censorship, and misogyny in conjunction with rap intensified: Known as a black cultural spokesperson, "Harvard professor Henry Louis Gates Jr.'s letter appeared [in the *New York Times*]…to decode for white America the 'objectionable' lyrics of 2-Live Crew within the context of African American culture. He called for those who would censor creative expression to use the same criteria when judging hip-hop as they would for white rock and comedy acts."[25]

The second debate swirled around the 1992 Time-Warner release of Ice-T's album, *Body Count*, which carried a song titled "Cop Killer." Articulating a vehement dismissal of the song, "the Combined Law Enforcement Associations of Texas…demand[ed] a boycott of all Time Warner products" while "[o]ther police associations called for divestiture of stock from Time Warner."[26] In addition to the law enforcement officers, "60 congressmen signed a proclamation denouncing the song" while "Vice

President [Dan] Quayle deemed it 'obscene' [and President George] Bush called it 'sick.'"[27]

Conflicting voices of criticism and support for gangsta rap continued to echo throughout the 1990s with the issues of violence, sexism, and profanity serving as the major areas of contention. Cultural critic bell hooks attacks the mass media as one culprit in the validation of the gangsta lifestyle: "Gangsta culture is the essence of patriarchal masculinity. Popular culture tells young black males that only the predator will survive....This is the ethic lots of boys in our society learn from mass media, but black boys, way too many of them fatherless, take it to heart."[28] For hooks, one must correlate the "link between gangsta culture and early childhood consumption of unchecked television and movies that glamorize brute patriarchal maleness." [29] hooks imbues media with an overwhelming power that infiltrates the psychological development of males that can't be divorced from their teenage attitudes and behavior. In a similar manner, scholar-critic Michael Eric Dyson acknowledges the negativity in gangsta rap, but insists that the larger society shares the blame as well. He writes: "Attacking figures like Snoop Doggy Dog or Tupac Shakur...is an easy out....While these young black males become whipping boys for sexism and misogyny, the places in our culture where these ancient traditions are nurtured and rationalized—including religious and educational institutions and the nuclear family—remain immune to forceful and just criticism."[30]

The complexity and paradoxical nature of gangsta rap in the 1990s was further reinforced by the manner in which American cinema utilized it for the big screen. On the one hand, similar to the blaxploitation films of the 1970s, the Hollywood journeyed into the urban scape to visually reveal a world etched out in rap lyrics. The poverty, bullet-sprinkled buildings, vacant lots, and violence of those neighborhoods, or 'hoods, functioned well for stories of struggling outlaws, who displayed their own brand of dress, codes of conduct, and vernacular. These elements proved to be economically viable and capable of crossing over into the mainstream viewership, particularly young males.

An additional factor that appealed to that target audience was the updating of the gangster and action genres through the 'hood films. Fitting into the successful gangster genre—which maintained its appeal through Cuban and Italian American characters effectively rendered by directors Brian DePalma (*Scarface*, 1983), Francis Ford Coppola (*The Godfather* series, 1972, 1974, 1990), and Martin Scorcese (*Goodfellas*, 1990)—black urban male characters carried a cinematic appeal. The symbiosis among existing urban gangs, prison culture, and gangsta genre films created a winning business formula, as many of those 'hood films were less expensive to produce in comparison to other studio projects. At the same time, the hood films incorporated the elements of the male-oriented action genre—physical confrontations, chases, gun battles, stylized violence, masculinity themes, and revenge themes. Sandwiched between the gangster and action genres, the 'hood films held financial potential in a proven marketplace.

However, another key commercial factor was the rap music itself. This factor led to two important possibilities: rappers as actors and the movie's music soundtrack. Perhaps, the screen presence of many rappers in music videos encouraged a casting of those rappers in fictional roles; at the very least, the familiarity of hip-hop fans with those rappers guaranteed a substantial viewing audience. As journalist Gabriel Alvarez concludes: "Thanks to Hollywood's open-door policy to gangsta rappers...gangsta rap went mainstream. Rappers invaded Tinseltown via lucrative movies and soundtracks....Regardless of the growing number of rap movie stars, Hollywood's depiction of nonwhites remains less than flattering....To a certain extent, these images actually assist gangsta rap's success, which is based partly on the fulfillment of certain stereotypes about poor kids of color."[31] Rappers, particularly male, brought a discernible attitude to their roles, which were not far removed from either their actual backgrounds and/or their publicized gangsta images. Consequently, the music soundtrack for various films took advantage of rappers who appeared in the films by having them perform selections for the marketed CDs. The cross-pollination between rapper-actors, 'hood films, and movie soundtracks blossomed into a successful formula for maximizing the merchandizing of those 'hood films.

The 'hood film cycle included numerous movies appearing in the 1990s, specifically *New Jack City* (1991), *Boyz N The Hood* (1991), *Straight Out of Brooklyn* (1991), *Juice* (1992), *Menace II Society* (1993), *Belly* (1998), and *Slam* (1999). These films did not explore gangsta rap or the music industry as the primary subject, but those reality factors associated with gangsta rap were essential to the urban focus of the films. As indicated before, for many films in this cycle, the music soundtrack served as the most direct connection to the themes and stylings of rap music. Consequently, for many viewers, 'hood films and gangsta rap were seen as interchangeable works, though a closer scrutiny reveals where there was both an intersection and digression.

New Jack City exemplifies most of the attributes identified above—an urban setting, gangsta and action genre elements, a rapper-actor in a major role, and a hip-hop soundtrack. The title also suggests another example of the cross-fertilization occurring between music and movies, which in this case can be traced back to journalist-screenwriter Barry Michael Cooper. While in

New York in the late 1980s, Cooper wrote an article on songwriter-producer Teddy Riley, praising Riley as a music visionary, observing: "The orchestration slams you, the drums tear out your heart. Riley's music is *RoboCop* funk, in full effect; go-go music gunned down by rap and electronics, then rebuilt with more vicious beats, an in-charge, *large* attitude." [32]   Labeling Riley's sound as "new jack swing," Cooper was attempting to provide a musical movement with its own specialized language. According to writer Elysa Gardner, new jack swing was a blending of "gospel-based vocal stylings of traditional soul music to the aggressively funky grooves and state-of-the-street cult-cha that defined hip hop," as seen in performers produced by Riley, including Al B. Sure; Bobby Brown; Keith Sweat; Levert; Tony! Toni! Tone!; and Guy. [33]

Following the assessment of Teddy Riley's contribution to hip hop, Barry Michael Cooper went on to co-write the screenplay for *New Jack City*. Consequently, when Detective Stone (Mario Van Peebles) strategizes to take down Nino Brown (Wesley Snipes), the kingpin behind an inner-city drug zone, Stone organizes his "new jack" undercover officers, who blend street experience, hip-hop knowledge, and a respect for the law. The key officer is Scotty Appleton (Ice-T) who must embed himself into the den of thugs who exploit the black neighborhood with their drugs and dispassionately kills any enemies. However, similar to the interracial face of hip hop, the new jack squad includes a white Detective Peretti (Judd Nelson) and the Asian Detective Park (Russell Wong).

Appleton plants Pookie (Chris Rock), a recovering crack addict, as an informer into the drug producing area of Nino Brown's operations. Pookie represents the manner in which crack destroyed black males in the 'hood, reducing them to hustlers, thieves, and indifferent losers. Although he tries to raise himself from quicksand of crack, his weakness leads him to use again and eventually to be killed when his informant identity is revealed. At the same time, Appleton has also been touched by the crack epidemic, as his mother was killed by a crack head during an armed robbery. With her death as a motivation, Appleton uses his badge to avenge her memory and to help the 'hood.

New Jack City delivers a message at the end that reads: "although this is a fictional story, there are Nino Browns in every major city in America. If we don't confront the problem realistically…drugs will continue to destroy our country." With that caveat, the film definitely carries the traditional good guy-vs-bad guy element, but ironically, the same cop leading the undercover is portrayed by Ice-T, the performer of the controversial "Cop Killer." Despite the film's message, the market appeal of a rapper in a featured role takes priority. The hip-hop merchandising prevails in the soundtrack as well, with Queen Latifah rapping in the cover version of "For the Love of Money" during the opening and end credits. Additionally the soundtrack contains selections by hip-hop and new jack performers, including Levert, Guy, Troop, Ice-T, Color Me Badd, 2-Live Crew, Doug E. Fresh, and N.W.A.

When turning to *Boyz N the Hood*, the film also positions itself as a cautionary tale of the South Los Angeles ghetto, informing in its opening captions that "one out of every twenty-one Black American males will be murdered in their lifetime." From there, the film weaves its story about the friendship of three black males who must negotiate the violent and oppressive inner-city jungle. Tre (Cuba Gooding, Jr.) functions as a centerpiece for the story because his development remains connected to one of the important themes of the film: the ongoing and positive relationship between a black father and son provides a foundation for survival for the latter. As Tre's father, Furious (Laurence Fishburne) provides his son the self-esteem, ambition, and independent thinking that the film insists are key ingredients to attaining manhood. In juxtaposition, Tre's close friends and neighbors, Doughboy (Ice Cube) and Ricky (Morris Chestnut), succumb to the destructive environment, being raised by their mother and the codes of the street.

Other themes complement the major father–son relationship, but all aspects of the story have a shaping by hip hop. The codes of masculinity, language, clothing, and use of guns emanates from gangsta rap. In a conspicuous casting of rapper Ice Cube, the connection between his gangsta rap image and the volatile Doughboy promises the film's box-office success and hip hop's visibility. In responding to his character and the use of guns, Ice Cube states: "Everybody I know has a gun, and I have one too....I don't feel scared with guns around because I know how I've got to live....I feel safe with a weapon."[34] Sounding like an NRA spokesperson, Ice Cube's articulation of his right and need to bear arms situates him squarely within the gangsta ethos while serving as an affirmation of violence for impressionable audience members. The opening night of the film brought along violence that in the media's headlines, further stained the reputation of gangsta rap. A *New York Times* article indicated that "[g]unfire and pandemonium broke out at movie theaters around the nation....[and] much of the violence appeared to have been started by rival gangs....In all, there were incidents at about 20 of the 900 theaters showing the film...."[35] The film's director, John Singleton, and Columbia Pictures defended the film's intent to explain and discourage violence, indicating that earlier films from the gangster genre, such as *The Godfather*, also were accompanied by shooting incidents.

Although the filmmakers wanted to avoid the realism of violent behavior at theater screenings, the producers sought to acquire street realism by hiring three Los Angeles gang members as consultants on "fashions and dialogue."[36] The film's music supervisor, Roaul Roach, wanted to capture the director's "heart and soul" of the story by having music that would "capture that same kind of authenticity…to represent the sound of the streets [of]…South Central Los Angeles"; consequently new and established performers were brought onto the soundtrack, including Monie Love, YoYo, 2-Live Crew, Compton's Most wanted, and KAM.[37]

The box office and critical success of *Boyz N the Hood* celebrated gangsta rap, as the diegetic music score resonated within the world of the characters. In that South Los Angeles world, the thumping of bass lines of rap and the MC's urgent voice emanated from passing cars, at backyard cookouts, from parked cars at fast food stands, and along the boulevard beneath the consistent rhythm of helicopter engines and blades. The film demonstrated the inextricable connection between the characters, their environment, and their steady diet of gangsta rap.

A by-product of that diet revolves around perspectives on gender, as the characterization of women in the film received critical fire. Tre's mother, portrayed by Angela Bassett, is a working woman seeking her master's degree, but her presence in the film is brief. In general, the black women in the hood shape the dysfunctional behavior of the black males, and as in gangsta rap, the relegation of black women to "bitches" and "hos" becomes the norm. In one front porch scene as Doughboy and his homies, a chorus of masculinity, discuss the black woman with a "big country booty" and "big country titties," the former dismisses one opinion that college is a place to go "just for the hos." Doughboy reprimands his crew, declaring: "you don't go to college to be talking to no bitches…you can't learn shit talking to no stupid ass bitch." Doughboy reflects in this scene the perspective he has demonstrated throughout the film, and somewhere as the line blurs between character and real-life gangsta rapper, the pejorative messages about women becomes solidified.

The priority in *Boyz N the Hood*, as indicated from the opening captions, is the black male, and to that point, the film succeeds in presenting an alarming west coast story. When Ricky is gunned down on the streets by a rival neighborhood crew, Tre and Doughboy seek revenge, continuing the urban drama of black-on-black crime. Tre changes his mind before committing violence, while Doughboy completes his objective, but in the aftermath, both friends still feel the emptiness of having lost Ricky. Ricky's death simply adds to the statistics, without his life being humanized and valued. At its best, gangsta lyrics sought to convey this catastrophe to its listeners. At this juncture of political purpose, gangsta rap and the end of the film intersect, as Doughboy tells Tre: "Turned on the teevee this morning...had this shit on about living in a violent world. Showed all these foreign places...started thinking man—either they don't know, don't show, or don't care what's going on in the 'hood." Here, "they" refers to the media, to the larger society, and to those forces of power that have helped to create the very life-destroying urban environment that remains neglected and dismissed.

The third film in the 'hood cycle, *Straight Out of Brooklyn* (1991), was certainly influenced in its title by the 1988 *Straight Outta Compton* album by N.W.A. In this film, the setting is not the Los Angeles area of the album, but the cold, snow-bordered street of Brooklyn's Red Hooks housing projects. Consequently, this film follows the dismal limitations in the lives of three African American friends—Dennis (Lawrence Gilliard), Larry (Matty Rich), and Kevin (Mark Malone).

Of the three, Dennis serves as the central figure who, representing the perspectives of many in his teen culture, perceives a college education as a massive waste of time. The primary concern is to make quick money as a way of traveling to the Manhattan promised land across the river. Adding to Dennis's anger is the abusive marriage endured by his parents, as he observes his mother suffering verbal and physical pain from his father. For Dennis, the world around him constantly displays futility, and the quickest access to money, i.e., success and power, is to rob a local drug dealer. As one popular film critic remarks: "For most of the movie, the characters stand poised between two possible choices—between crime and trying to do the right thing....It all adds up to a convincing portrait of a big-city black teenager who feels that if he does not take some sort of conclusive action, life will clamp him into poverty and discouragement."[38]

With the film *Juice*, the setting shifts to Harlem, where once more four young black male friends unite to confront the streets and to overcome their sense of futility. The Harlem streets are no less threatening than those in the Red Hooks Projects or Los Angeles, as the high school friends seek to etch out their young manhood in a world that seeks to deny them their futures. The twist here, however, finds the four turning upon one another as the streets distort and dissolve their close bond. As scholar Ed Guerrero reflects: "*Juice*'s overriding insight does not concern redemption. Instead...the film confronts the audience with the alarming situation facing a large segment of black urban youth today."[39]

With a more direct connection to hip hop, the character Q (Omar Epps) dreams of being a hip-hop DJ. For Q, his personal love for hip hop serves as his survival tool and his inspiration to dream a future beyond the streets. In comparison, his confused and angry friend, Bishop (Tupac Shakur), searches for ways of gaining "juice" (power and street reputation). Similar to Ice-T in *New Jack City* and Ice Cube in *Boyz N The Hood*, Shakur's appearance in a major role takes advantage of the audience recognition of the rap performer turned screen performer. The added value of imbuing a sense of realism with the gangsta rap star and the promotion of a soundtrack become inextricable marketing tools. As for the film's content, the flaw in Bishop's characterization, according to Professor Guerrero, surfaces in "concessions to dominant narrative theme...attributing Bishop's violent rage to individual pathology, rather than connecting it to the collective determinants of discrimination and social injustice inflicted on an oppressed community."[40] This rather safe approach to the film's most lethal character avoids heavy social commentary, while providing a good guy (Q)-versus-bad guy (Bishop) showdown at the film's conclusion.

Appearing a year after *Juice*, *Menace II Society* surfaces as a bold interpretation of the South Los Angeles environment and its devastating effect on the lives of young black males. The movie's press kit attempted to emphasize that fact, providing the U.S. Department of Justice statistics that "Black youth make up 42 percent of the number of juveniles held in custody—while they represent only 16 percent of the U.S. population under 18."[41] The filmmakers shaping this interpretation were Albert and Allen Hughes, two black filmmakers who had gained attention from their directing "of music videos for top rap and hip-hop artists, including Tone-Loc, Tupac Shakur, KRS-One, Too Short, and Yo-Yo."[42]

Unlike the other 'hood films that implied the link between felonious behavior and the social and economic facets of the 'hood, *Menace II Society* incarnated criminality through the character of O-Dog (Larenz Tate), a live-for-today, indifferent urban predator. O-Dog, a volatile personality, remains what the protagonist Caine (Tyrin Turner) calls "the craziest nigga alive. America's nightmare. Young, black, and didn't give a fuck." Early in the film, O-Dog robs and murders two Korean grocers in their corner market for a small amount of money and personal satisfaction, as he takes the surveillance videotape to display the killing to others.

O-Dog has already been lost, his personal dreams and humanity long destroyed by his environment. With Caine, latent hope exists, as he vacillates between O-Dog's madness and the caring mentoring of Pernell (Glenn Plummer), an older, incarcerated gangbanger. Pernell endows Caine with the responsibility of protecting Pernell's son and former lover, Ronnie (Jada Pinkett). However, for "Caine, the realities of his situation are poverty, life in the projects, the temptations of drugs and drug dealing, the economic and social lure of crime, the threat of death, and police oppression."[43] This police oppression, which connects back to the early lyrics of gangsta rap, is emphasized in the film when Caine and his friend, Sharif (Vonte Sweet), suffer racial profiling and a physical beating by police officers who then drop them off in a rival gang neighborhood. The film visualizes the calculated brutality of the officers, explaining the black male characters' lack of respect for authority and the legal system. Importantly, by the film's end, Caine accepts the responsibility passed on to him from Pernell, but the mistakes made during his earlier street actions with O-Dog leads to Caine's regretful death at the climax. The audience realizes through Caine's voiceover that the entire film has been narrated by the protagonist from the grave.

Hip hop argot pervades the film, and in supporting roles, real-life rappers get sufficient screen time. "Rappers Too Short…Pooh Man, and MC Eiht of Compton's Most Wanted, all make their acting debuts in the film as Caine's homeboys."[44] Again, the visibility of the popular rappers adds a bit of authenticity to the film, while further opening the Hollywood's door to hip-hop performers.

The anthology film, *Tales From the Hood*, might appear an odd film to include in the 'hood film cycle since it appropriately belongs in the horror genre. Similar to its cable television namesake, *Tales from the Crypt*, the feature continued the elements of graphic violence and gore to tell its four stories weaved into one film connected by three characters who are gangbangers—Bulldog (Samuel Monroe, Jr.), Ball (De'Aundre Bonds), and Stack (Joe Torry). Of particular interest, the last story, titled "Hard Core Convert," focuses upon the bloody killings between rival gangs, the lack of remorse, and an appointment with Satan and hellfire.

In the story, a gangbanger named Crazy K (Lamont Bentley) murders a rival thug, only to be shot down in the streets by three of the thug's fellow gang members. Stranded between life and death in a scientific lab, Crazy K endures an aggressive program to force him to see the human effects of his violent gangbanging life. Refusing to be remorseful for his actions, Crazy K dies as he returns to his body in the original street shooting. At the same time, Bulldog, Ball, and Stack realize they are the three thugs who killed Crazy K, sealing their fate in the hellfire that abruptly surrounds them.

The saga of Bulldog, Ball, and Stack relates to the cautionary themes emphasized by all the dramatic films in the hood cycle. The features acknowledge the deleterious urban causes of gangbanging, but the need to choose a different lifestyle. In other words, the oppressive environment is beyond the control of the young black males, but the individual always possesses the capacity to select an alternative path.

Toward the end of the decade, the film *Belly* (1998), by veteran music video director Hype Williams, attempts to offer some possible ways out of the urban malaise. The film utilizes the talents of two popular rappers as the central characters—Sincere (rapper Nas) and Buns (rapper DMX), both leaders of the same crew of thieves. After years of crime, Sincere wants to leave the street life behind to have a family with his girlfriend, Tionne (Tionne "T-Boz" Watkins), and their child. Sincere struggles to change his life, finding solace in religion. Moving from theft to drug dealing, Buns descends toward an inevitable stint in prison, eventually becoming an undercover informant within a Black Muslim organization. Unable to murder the religious leader, Buns converts, while Sincere and Tionne leave the country to live in Africa.

The digression of life choices between Buns and Sincere echoes the observations that cultural critic Todd Boyd makes about contemporary rap: Buns finds motivation in money and materialism ("entrepreneurial ideas"), while Sincere articulates both conscientious and political thinking ("life of enlightenment").[45] Boyd writes: "There are generally two opposing camps when it comes to hip hop music. The gangsta camp, for instance, could be represented by figures like Jay-Z, Nas, Snoop, DMX, and Mob Deep. These artists are often contrasted with a more overtly conscious political camp identified with artists like Common, Mos Def, the Roots, and Talib Kweli."[46] The inclination of *Belly* to make this distinction between the two visions and to further insert a spiritual component as a strategy for survival provide a marked distinction when compared with earlier works in the 'hood cycle.

With its stylized visualizations and rapid shifting among the settings of Queens, New York; Manhattan; Omaha, Nebraska; Jamaica; and Atlanta, *Belly* designs a captivating story, as it alternates between the first-person narrations by Sincere and Buns. Their thug lives abound with mercurial violence and treachery from all sides, leaving little space for virtue or optimism. When Buns argues to Sincere that there "ain't no money like dope money," he announces his personal desire for a life of drug dealing, a decision that changes their closeness and inevitably destroys Buns' world.

Punctuating scenes with the heavy bass thumping of rap music, *Belly* deserves credit for telling a story of the black underworld where the protagonists have choices to ponder. Perhaps, due to its late appearance in the 1990s, the filmmaker's hindsight framed a story that aspires to move beyond a mere recapitulating of socioeconomic ills. However, mixing an inspiring message while using the conventional visualizations risks the former being lost in the latter. As one critic writes, "'Belly' is a film that begs for a pat on the head for its virtues while catering to cinematic tastes more interested in crotch shots, topless dancers, wall-sized television screens, ganja galore and, whenever possible, crime without punishment, all to the accompaniment of a high octane soundtrack."[47]

In a salient manner, the independent'hood film, *Slam*, avoids treading into the mixed waters of tone, visual, and thematic intention. The film's political and cultural messages are continually pressed at the audience, but done so in an alluring fashion. Beyond the messages, the film remains one of the best films during the decade to connect rap, rhyme creations, and performance poetry to the protagonist's *raison d'etre*.

With its documentary feel, *Slam* follows Ray Joshua (Saul Williams), a well-known, well-liked drug dealer in Washington, D.C.'s Dodge City area. Part of Ray's charisma stems from his pleasant personality and his talent at free-styling rhymes—often to amuse neighborhood kids. Picking up a bag of marijuana from his homeboy Big Mike (Lawrence Wilson) in exchange for an original love poem written for Big Mike's girlfriend, Ray scurries from the gunshot that downs Big Mike, only to get caught by the police. Advised by his public defender to take a plea and receive "eighteen months" or go to court and possible face ten years, Ray refuses to believe that simple possession of marijuana would leave no other options. His black lawyer calls Ray a "casualty of war," reminding him that "you're black, you're young, you come from the inner city, you don't have a chance."

Ray, held over in jail for the weekend, finds himself forced to choose between two rival black gangs, but when pushed to a point of violence, Ray breaks into free styling a poem that both confuses and impresses one gang leader, Hopha (Bonz Malone). However, Ray's meeting and subsequent affections to Lauren (Sonja Sohn), a creative writing teacher and poet, eventually save Ray once he returns to the streets. With Lauren's belief in him and the freedom his poetry brings, Ray seems prepared to face his court date and the legal decision, rather than running away.

In Ray's 'hood, the squalor and hopelessness are obvious as he walks the trashy, decayed streets. For him, selling drugs becomes the normal means of employment, a part of the milieu that frames his life. Through his creativity and his MC skills, Ray finds a method to root himself, a way to survive the madness of his inner-city environment. However, in an emotional confrontation, Lauren confesses her past as a junkie, selling her body for drugs, forcing Ray to recognize that selling any drugs places people like herself in that prison of addiction. She insists that her prison was as real and as much a soul-destroying slavery as the prison sentence that Ray fears.

Similar to *Belly*, *Slam* exposes the urban blight while insisting that the victims can gain power over their lives by refusing to follow the stereotypical expectations of the system that oppresses them. In contrast to its predecessor, *Slam* avoids graphically visualizing the very aspects of victimization that it criticizes. Instead, the film chooses to spend more time showing the enriching and invigorating results of imagination and creativity. In that vein, the audience observes those shots of Ray crafting his verse, scribbling his poetic lines through reflection. Ray's rapping avoids the easy doggerel about sex, money, and cars, as it explores deeper, more thoughtful motivations about individual purpose, community, and the political system.

The strength of Ray's character comes from the performance of Saul Williams, who in 1996 "won the grand Slam Championship, a competition among spoken-word artists who bring a hip-hop aesthetic to poetry."[48] The authenticity here derives from Williams's skills as a writer-poet, rather than from any notoriety of being a gangsta rapper. The content, rhythms, and delivery that Williams gives to Ray's verses are dynamic, relevant, and provocative.

With the films examined above that made up the 'hood cycle—with numerous straight-to-video movies not mentioned—the stark issues that existed in society and that peppered gangsta rap lyrics merged in popular culture in an unavoidable manner. Hip hop and American cinema functioned together as a popular forum where audiences could find social and political commentary kept within the custodianship of the entertainment business. In measuring the benefits and malignity of the 'hood cycle, the oppositional perspectives all contain valid claims and contentions. The cinematic depiction of gangsta rap that assails the established power structure and that emerges as one by-product of that power structure remains as paradoxical as the music form itself.

Before leaving the decade's treatment of hip hop, two nondramatic films deserve discussion in their common approach to gangsta rap and popular culture. *CB4* (1993) and *Fear of a Black Hat* (1995) provided whimsical, yet penetrating, assessments of the shifting currents in hip hop.

The first film, *CB4*, employs satire to investigate gangsta rap's appeal and its fan base. Co-written by journalist-critic Nelson George and comedian Chris Rock, the film is presented as a "half-parody, half-tribute to the ever-expanding rap and hip-hop genres," delivering "biting comments about the nature of the music business, as well as the impact rap is having on our society."[49]

The film smartly begins with a documentary filmmaker, named A. White (Chris Elliot), showing the rough cut of his footage to the established gangsta rap group CB4–MC Gusto (Chris Rock), Dead Mike (Allen Payne), and Stab Master Arson (Deezer D). In that documentary that fills the screen, testimonies are articulated about CB4 by real-life rappers and celebrities, including Ice-T, Halle Berry, Ice Cube, Flavor Flav, Shaquille O'Neal, and Easy E. From there, as the documentary filmmaker tags along with the group and while under the threat of wild gunfire from a neighborhood gangster, MC Gusto confesses the truth about the group's background, which is shown in a series of flashbacks. In short, all three alleged gangsta rappers come from a middle-class background, and they perpetrated the gangsta image of CB4—which stands for Cell Block 4—as a way to get fame, money, and women.

In its strongest satirical scenes, the film captures the potency of image making in popular culture. Displaying the appropriate scorching lyrics, profanity, groin clutching, unruly attitudes, and the 40-ounce malt liquor drinking in public, the three aspiring middle-class kids assume a gangsta mask that corresponds to the expectations of the media and concert audiences. When the trio approach well-known rap mogul, Trustus Jones (William E. Pugh), for a record deal and promotion, he asks them a series of questions: "Do you cuss on your records? Do you defile women with your lyrics? Do you fondle your genitalia on stage? Do you glorify violence and advocate the use of guns?" Receiving an affirmative to these questions, the trio signs a deal and a shot at stardom. The group's popularity increases when targeted for censorship by a conservative white politician and when the trio does jail time for their offensive stage performance of their hit song, "The Sweat From My Balls."

The movie works effectively at juxtaposing the early passion that the three friends have for rap with the later manufactured lyrics for commercial consumption. Before their transformation to CB4, Albert (Rock), Euripides (Payne), and Otis (Deezer D) cherish the roots of Kurtis Blow, Grandmaster Flash, and Run-D.M.C. In one scene from the early years, as they drive together towards a club, the three lip-sync a Run-D.M.C. tape with memorized precision. In another sequence, Albert bemoans the televised performance of the frivolous and clownish rapper, Wackee D (Stony Jackson), a character spoofing MC Hammer. As serious rappers before becoming CB4, Albert, Euripides, and Otis valued the personal expressions and their close friendship that was inextricably tied to a pure love for hip hop. Once they plunge into the CB4 image, however, the meanings of and passion for rap and hip hop become lost behind the gangsta façade.

Developed less effectively in the satire is the character of Sissy (Khandi Alexander), the experienced rap groupie who becomes a lover to the members of CB4. Sissy insists that her attention to and seduction of successful rap performers is simply business, devoid from any questionable morality on her part. In one scene between Sissy enlightens two music video dancers: "it's fine and dandy to go out with these guys…to drive around in their cars and have them take you to an expensive restaurant. But if all you get out of it is [sex], then you're a ho.…But you get your self a fabulous… vehicle…fine house…and pay for your own meals, then you're a business woman." Framed within a presumed feminist tone, Sissy explains that she gains financial power by dating rich rappers and that her camera captures the "right picture of the right man doing the wrong thing." Displaying a diamond-studded watch, Sissy shows the tangible results of her blackmailing strategy, but she remains blind to her materialism and flaws.

As the major female character, Sissy's prominence in the film undermines the derision aimed at that kind of rap groupie. Two other black women characters remain minor and underdeveloped—Deliha (Rachel True), Albert's wholesome girlfriend from the old neighborhood, and Eve (Theresa Randle), a journalist for *Source* magazine. When the character MC Gusto calls Eve a "ho," she calls him a "sexist slime," stating: "I am not a girlie, a video, a skeezer, a prop, a hoochie…or most certainly not a ho…I am not a groupie, but a journalist." Her defiance and self-assured identity creates a much stronger image than the one emanating from Sissy.

By the last part of the film, the astute satire unravels completely, as the movie rushes towards an upbeat ending, with Albert/MC Gusto cross-dressing to ensnare the gangster who has been terrorizing the trio. Despite the movie's final message to "be yourself " by the closing credits, the film has been reduced to a teen comedy rather than an insightful journey through the hip-hop world. At its best, the film serves as a celebration of hip hop as "many of the musicians associated with the film are well known to rap fans.…[Chris] Rock's voice is provided by Los Angeles rapper Hi-C, Allen Payne's by New York-based Daddy-O, and Stony Jackson…is voiced by longtime rap favorite Kool Moe Dee."[50]

In another satirical vehicle, the mockumentary *Fear of a Black Hat* succeeds in achieving a clever examination of the rap world and the often contradictory aspects of gangsta genre. Written and directed by black filmmaker Rusty Cundieff, the film's title was based upon "the title of the Public Enemy album 'Fear of a Black Planet.'"[51] In an interview, Cundieff argues that "[p]eople who are anti-rap and people who buy into rap both need to realize that it's really just, at its basest level, show business…. Perhaps there was one point where the music and the voices coming out of it were perfectly pure. But at the point where it starts making millions of dollars a year, that ceases to happen."[52] From Cundieff's position, gangsta rap quickly loses its factuality when transformed into a consumer product, and his film explores the potential benefits and disasters resulting from that commodification.

At the beginning of *Fear of a Black Hat*, a fictional black professor, Nina Blackburn (Kasi Lemmons), tells the audience that the documentary to be viewed serves as part of her research for a Ph.D. in sociology. Following that opening, the film traces one year in the creative and public life of the rap group, N.W.H., which stands for Niggaz With Hats. In one of many interviews, the group members—Ice Cold (Rusty Cundieff), Tasty Taste (Larry B. Scott), and Deejay Tone Def (Mark Christopher Lawrence)—explain that the group's "name connects back to slavery when blacks were compelled to work in the hot sun all day—hatless. Consequently, the sun-soaked blacks were too tired to rebel; but now as black men in the 1990s, they wear hats of all shapes and colors to show their intentions to rebel."[53]

Rising to the top of rap popularity with such songs as "Booty Juice," "Grab Your Shit," "Guerillas in the Midst," and "Kill Whitey," the members of N.W.H. embody the hardcore style of the day. However, along the way to fame, the group endures the shootings of several managers, threats of censorship from conservatives, and police harassment. Eventually, the tight-knit trio separates following jealousies over a divisive groupie who calls herself Cheryl C (Rosemarie Jackson). Forced into solo careers, the individual rappers find an audience, but they eventually come back together, realizing their strength as a group.

The movie marries documentary-style visuals with music video techniques to achieve the verisimilitude of both forms. The pacing and humorous tone accentuate the inventiveness of the piece, as it maintains its quality throughout the development of the story. Although unkind at places to the creativity and integrity of commercially successful rappers, the film maintains a respect for hip hop's foundation as a youth movement. By shaping the documentarian as an academic who eventually moves from an ivory tower elitism to becoming a hip hopper, the movie also affirms the cultural significance of hip hop to black culture. The value of hip hop to young people and the black community never surfaces as a question; instead, the ridicule remains focused of the exploitation of hip hop by performers and business people.

Both *CB4* and *Fear of a Black Planet* owe much to the mock documentary stylings of heavy-metal focused *This Is Spinal Tap* (1984), but both approached the rap as a more complicated, misunderstood musical form than rock.   Both films achieve a common goal of dissecting the contradictions within and the real issues surrounding gangsta rap. Offering another approach to the much-debated subgenre augments the methods of investigating and judging the hip-hop musical form.

By the end of the 1990s, the feel-good innocence of hip hop had been decimated by the omnipresent gangsta rap. At the same time, the spate and repetition of the 'hood films had overfed even the most gluttonous fan of gangsta rap. American cinema moved toward ways of maintaining the hip-hop audience while providing some fresh screen images for those viewers. One response that developed was to explore middle-class black and white characters who, loyal to hip hop, were more inclined to be intellectually and romantically chillin', rather than indiscriminately and aggressively killin'.

3

Skimmin' the Phat: Players, Poets, and Professionals, 1996–2005

In the dramatic film *8 Mile* (2002), the troubled life of the character, Rabbit (Eminem), right, finds validation through rhymes and rhythm when facing one of his enemies. Courtesy of the Academy of Motion Picture Arts and Sciences.

As the "hood films" began to ebb in the late 1990s, Hollywood expanded its presentation of hip-hop culture on the screen. The sobering, nihilistic gangsta images of black men running lawlessly through the inner city had reached its saturation point for theatrically released films, though they still found life in the straight-to-video market. Hollywood wanted to maintain the youth market, but there was a preference for fresh depictions to provide for that audience.

To a great extent, this move toward fresh cinematic images corresponded to the changes occurring in hip-hop culture in general. At the end of the twentieth century, the operative word with hip-hop culture was "commercial," as the youth movement seemed inseparable from the mainstream marketplace. Although an ongoing target for attack for its messages about hyper masculinity, women, and bling, hip-hop culture, nevertheless, dominated popular culture, particularly in regard to music, dance, and films.

Before focusing upon the hip hop in American cinema between 1996 and 2005, an appreciation of the status of hip-hop music and dance provides an essential background for evaluating the films of the era. The numerous shifts and trends is music and dance at times appear overwhelming, but transitory nature indicates the norm in a hip-hop culture known for its temporary tastes.

In the previous chapter, the significance of new jack swing was mentioned which situated itself in the larger realm of hip-hop soul, where artists like Mary J. Blige, Jodeci, Faith Evans, TLC, and R. Kelly found a faithful audience. Hip Hop Soul became the territory where hip-hop beats, gospel, r&b all merged together, with an emphasis on melodic vocals. Then, by the middle of the 1990s, the term "neo-soul" labeled a trend in music where black artists, such as Erykah Badu, D'Angelo, Jill Scott, Maxwell, Angie Stone, Alicia Keys, and India Arie blended soul, r&b, hip hop, and alternative modes into music. Author Jeff Chang suggests that neo-soul "put the groove back into the music and the love back into lyrics."[1] However, Chang emphasizes the commercial and politics of neo-soul, concluding it was "a clever marketing strategy…to package r&b artists," as it "also created space for voices to dissect the masculinist attitudes and ideals projected in the hip-hop mainstream."[2] With neo-soul spotlighting artists who were women in the majority, those artists and their material underscored the discrepancies existing in regards to hip hop's images and messages about gender.

Hip-hop soul and neo-soul augmented the musical dimensions of hip hop, insisting that rap, and certainly gangsta rap, was not the primary musical expression for the youth movement. More than anything else, though, by the end of the decade and into the new millennium, the variety within rap was evident. As scholar William L. Van Deburg concludes: "Like bebop, rap deconstructs its sources and then reconfigures familiar elements—song samples, sound bites, TV jingles—into a new commodified whole. Both the resulting songs and the public personas adopted by individual acts are remarkably diverse….The result is a smorgasbord of styles."[3] By 2005, hip hop splintered into various flavors, including commercial gansta rap (50

Cent, Mobb Deep), party hip hop or pop hop (Nelly, Ludacris), reggae hip hop (Sean Paul), southern hip hop (TI, Mike Jones), reggaeton (Daddy Yankee, Tego Calderon), politically conscious hip hop (Common, Talib Kweli), Christian hip hop (T-Bone, BB-Jay), and fusion hip hop (Kanye West). With the fusion hip hop, Kanye West was taking the lead in not only merging rap, gospel, soul, and r&b, but he was fusing images as well. On the one hand, his music and music videos carried established rap language ("nigga," profanity, and sexual terms) and established images (women as bitches and golddiggers). On the other hand, his upscale dress code, lack of tattoos, and lack of a grill, proclaimed a middle-class image, hinging on a metrosexual nattiness. In a similar fashion gangsta rapper Jay-Z, turned record mogul by 2005, and rapper-producer Diddy, turned stage actor and voting activist by 2004, also displayed the more "GQ" look. These three, and others, framed the debate about street authenticity and the flexibility of hip hop to a wider array of looks for black masculinity.

Adding to the musical styles, between 2003 and 2005, several trends in hip hop also caught attention of both music labels and the popular audience. The first trend was called "intimate club" music that showcases "recordings arranged over minimalist beats and reliant upon 'homemade' sound effects such as whispering, snapping, whistling and slamming doors"; this form include tunes such as Snoop Dogg and Pharrell Williams's "Drop It Like It's Hot": Juelz Santana's "There It Go (the Whistle Song)"; the Ying Yang Twins' "Wait (the Whisper Song)"; and David Banner's "Play."[4] At the same time, in regard to music production, one critic writes: "According to a number of top selling producers and industry observers, the beat has largely superseded the rapper performing over it as the driving force of the industry"; specifically producers "build beats with mass appeal" and then sell them to rappers or labels as the creative foundation for hit tunes.[5] With this trend, the rapper develops words to accompany someone else's rhythmic structure, with profit stimulating the creative process rather than inspiration.

The third trend flows from hip-hop dancing, gaining national attention through television news shows and the feature-length documentary *Rize* (2005), screened at the Sundance Film Festival before its theatrical release. "Krumping" or "Krump Dancing" evolved from "clowning," which was a birthday party entertainment form originated in inner-city Los Angeles by Thomas Johnson, known as Tommy the Hip Hop Clown; dressed in clown costumes, make up, and colorful wigs, the routines of Tommy the Clown and his co-dancers evolved from parties to The Battle Zone competitions to vie for the most outstanding dance movements.[6] From that origin, krumping, without clown attire and make up, developed as an accelerated "breakdancing, gymnastics and spasm-like movements," an alternative to gangbanging for some and boredom for other teens.[7] With a semblance of physical combat, stripper gyrations, and West African tribal dance, krumping allows dancers to "pop their limbs, gyrate their torsos and stomp their feet to hip hop music."[8]

Given all of these various styles and trends, how did American cinema reflect and mainstream hip hop for theatrical audiences? In some movies, such as *Phat Beach* (1996), *B.A.P.S* (1997), *Fakin da Funk* (1997), *Finding Forrester* (2000), *How High* (2001), *Fast and the Furious* (2001), *Glitter* (2001), *2 Fast and 2 Furious* (2003), *The LadyKillers* (2004), hip hop assumed a visibility through minor and/or supporting characterizations of American youth, who, due to their age, were the embodiment of hip-hop nuances strictly as members of a younger generation. The omnipresence of hip hop was indicated as characters in these movies were often from various racial, cultural, and class backgrounds. In other movies, such as *Caught Up* (1998), *He Got Game* (1998), *Training Day* (2001), *Drumline* (2002), *Barbershop* (2002), *Biker Boyz* (2003), *Barbershop 2: Back in Business* (2004), *Beauty Shop* (2005), *Coach Carter* (2005), hip hop was referenced through dialogue-language, diegetic background music, and clothing of significant and/or major black characters living in or residing close to an urban area.

Importantly, Hollywood began to tell stories of hip hoppers who were more than thugs, criminals, and prison-bound losers. These were the counterparts to the 'hood rats who led lives of violent desperation; instead, American cinema revealed a hip-hop generation that could survive society's challenges and could negotiate mainstream standards. In its own particular fashion, between 1996 and 2005, Hollywood offered three cycles of films where hip hop served as the topic, theme, and/or focus in the story's plot. Often within the genre of romantic comedy, these collective films contained a pronounced ethnic flair and multidimensional characters. Sometimes the flair and characterizations were broad, over-the-top presentations, but in a number of cases, these films were distinctive due to casting, script quality, and production values. The first distinctive cycle included films that presented "hip-hop relationships," as 20-and-30-something characters dealt with the choices of being a "player" or committing to a monogamous relationship. The second cycle presented films that examined "hop hop and white awareness," as white protagonists and supporting characters traveled physically and psychologically through an identity crisis clarified or resolved via hip hop. The third cycle contained films that depicted "hip hop ambitions," as characters sought to move into a profession of rapping, music producing, and/or dancing.

Using Bakari Kitwana's time line to define "the birth years 1965–1984 as the age group for the hip-hop generation," by the late 1990s there was an older cohort of hip hoppers of the "three distinctive subgroups within this generation."[9] This older group, in their 20s to late 30s, grew up on hip hop, and consequently their ethos was influenced by, if not shaped by, the decades of hip hop's evolution from the counterculture movement to a mainstream element. Author Gary Dauphin argues that "an entire generation of fans came into a cultural adulthood where hip hop was a day-to-day given, and so hip-hop relationship movies appeared—direly limited flicks from *How to Be a Player* to *Booty Call* to *A Thin Line between Love and Hate* in which the often woeful gender politics of hip hop were translated into screen images of black sexuality."[10]

It was this very gender politics that made these "hip-hop relationships" movies appealing to Hollywood, which conventionally presented romantic comedies as primarily the battle of the sexes. In addition to the easy genre fit, a number of young black actors, including rappers, held a crossover box-office appeal across racial lines: Morris Chestnut, Gabrielle Union, Ice Cube, Queen Latifah, Taye Diggs, and Sanaa Lathan, to mention some. Mainstream audiences were willing to view these young characters, usually professional, in the urban enclave utilizing the language and attitudes of hip hop, without the guns and graphic violence. In terms of quantity, this cycle was the largest of the three, including films such as *Sprung* (1997), *The Best Man* (1999), *Love and Basketball* (2000), *The Brothers* (2001), *Two Can Play That Game* (2001), *Deliver Us From Eva* (2003), *Love Don't Cost a Thing* (2003), and *Breakin' All the Rules* (2004). With humor shaping most of these movies, collectively they displayed a positivity in regards to black male friendships and the potential for black male–female romantic unions; furthermore, these movies often depicted urban black professionals with earned credentials and ambitious dreams. In comparison to the representation in the decade of 'hood films, these romantic comedies elevated the images and messages about African Americans. Exemplifying the best and worse of this cycle, five films draw attention in their treatment of players, poets, and professionals: *A Thin Line Between Love and Hate* (1996), *Love Jones* (1997), *Def Jam's How to Be a Player* (1997), *Booty Call* (1997), and *Brown Sugar* (2002).

Turning an eye on the dilemma of a player, *A Thin Line Between Love and Hate* frames itself as a cautionary tale about contemporary male, Darnell Right (Martin Lawrence), and his sexist attitudes toward women. With a nod toward the dramatic *Fatal Attraction* (1987), *A Thin Line*'s humorous tone still allows for its moral message to emerge. As such, the filmmakers express a conspicuous warning to hip-hop males like Darnell who, on the one hand, express love and protection to mother and sister but, on the other hand, pursue single women merely as trophies and the source for bragging rights to other men.

Under Darnell's voiceover, the film opens with three bodies tumbling from a home's second floor into the swimming pool below. With only Darnell's face discernible, the story moves into a flashback story that brought him to that end. Darnell, a Los Angeles entrepreneur, brags openly of his skills with women and his ability to fulfill female desires. During an early montage, while visiting three of his regular women, Darnell reflects, "if God wanted all women to be happy, he would have made all men like me." Intrinsic in that thought is the belief that Darnell's womanizing adds something of value to his many lovers, and that beyond his control, women must bear the burden of being unhappy when it comes to relationships. Darnell's world view finds support through the equally self-proclaimed player, Tee (Bobby Brown), Darnell's homey and co-manager of the night club called Chocolate City. In the quest to grab the newest phone number and the hottest female body, the two articulate their code: "Never tell her you love her." For Darnell and Tee, to assert "love" undermines a player's code of conduct, and it encourages the woman to assume an emotional bond, or even worse, commitment. For these hip hoppers, relationships with women remain merely a social endeavor, just "kicking it," that is enjoying the casual sexual union without further obligations.

For Darnell and other players, one significant skill becomes the male's romantic rap, a part of his "game" or strategy to meet, manipulate and sexually conquer the object of desire. Darnell's skills face a formidable challenge when he approaches Brandy (Lynn Whitfield), a classy, confident real estate agent who owns a Malibu home. Unlike other women from the 'hood, Brandy's assertive nature and financial independence provide no entrée for Darnell's usual "game," so his usual offers of flowers, dinner, and VIP passes to his nightclub fail to bring the desired results. But having made a bet with Tee to "hit that," Darnell rolls up in a limo and approaches Brandy as a potential buyer to an estate; goes to art galleries with her; and endures a galloping horseback ride along wooded trails. As a final way to have sex with Brandy and win his bet, Darnell states that he "loves" her, breaking his own code.

The primary character who inspires a transformation in Darnell is the even-tempered Mia (Regina King). A childhood friend to Darnell and a recent Army enlistee, Mia and Darnell share a genuine affection for one another, and both can be open and at ease with one another; with Mia, Darnell can be himself and not the player image. Unfortunately, Darnell recognizes his actual feelings for Mia after proclaiming "love" to Brandy and being physically intimate. Furious at being dismissed as a sexual conquest, Brandy mounts her campaign of vengeance: running Darnell down with her car; bruising herself to have Darnell jailed for physical abuse; vandalizing his car; stalking his home; and threatening Mia. The trail of revenge ends in a life-and-death battle at Brandy's home, as Darnell, Brandy, and Mia wind up crashing through the window and into the pool as seen in the opening images.

The intent of the film is evident as it spends its final act showing the repercussions of Darnell's mistreatment of Brandy. The film, therefore, criticizes Darnell's selfish role as a player, as other characters warn him about the pitfalls of exploitation of women. In an early scene, his Mother (Della Reese) tells him: "Your ways are going to catch up with you. A night time of passion can give you a lifetime of pain." Augmenting that concern, Smitty (Roger Mosley), the owner of Chocolate City, confesses: "Ain't a day go by, I don't see some booty I wouldn't mind taking a peek at. But when I think about what me and Shirley [his wife] got going, there ain't nothing worth ruining that. Life is about choices, son. The older your mind gets, the better choices your dick makes." Darnell fails to grasp Smitty's wisdom until his near-death experience.

One of the best of the offerings in this cycle of films was *Love Jones*, which won the Audience Award at the Sundance Film Festival before making it to the theaters.[11] In this film, first-time black director Theodore Witcher "plunges [the audience] into a world of coffee houses, bookstores and Coltrane-cool characters riffing Sonia Sanchez-sharp dialogue….The main action is black folks talking about hopes, dreams, fears and—most revolutionary of all—their need not just for love, but tenderness."[12] In a salient departure from *A Thin Line*, *Love Jones* showed images of young black men and women aspiring toward dreams of their own choosing and efforts, lives that were not decimated by the urban environment.

Living in Chicago, Darius (Larenz Tate), an aspiring novelist, meets Nina (Nia Long), a photographer, in his favorite jazz-and-poetry club called "The Sanctuary." Hanging with friends, both male and female, Darius recites a poem at the open microphone to capture Nina's attention. From that initial meeting, Darius and Nina begin a journey that's filled with the excitement, insecurities, mistakes, and fears of contemporary dating and commitment. The story highlights the gender tensions, lust, and pain of modern romance among twenty-something heterosexuals, but in particular, it accentuates—through its language, music, foods, and casting—the concerns of the young black community.

At places, the language merges hip-hop argot and literate banter. On their first date, Darius and Nina discuss literary passages and authors. As for the music, hip hop exists as a mainstay, but so too are the references and appreciation of jazz and r&b. In the casting, the filmmakers trust the engaging qualities of their characters who are undeniably "black" in their cultural roots, but not preoccupied with discussing and criticizing white society. To the story's credit, there is no obligatory white friend who pops into the story to legitimize the characters for non-black viewers. Instead, *Love Jones* is "one of those rare all-African American films that is set outside the 'hood, possesses no neo-Stepin Fetchit shuck-and-jive, and doesn't bury its story under a political agenda....[it] revels in its culture–in the sounds, the slang, and yes, the soul."[13]

Although the film is unashamedly middle class in its professional emphasis, the characters are not materialistic and designer-label addicts. Displaying more depth than typically seen in romance stories, these characters propel themselves through their daily grinds with the passions of their interest, their friendships, and their love and intimacy. As one review notes: "beyond the commercial tsunami of gangsta rap, hip-hop has always harbored a more reflective, alternative edge. Now, as the rap scene reels from the murders of Tupac Shakur and the Notorious B.I.G., the bohemian fringes are starting to bloom....the romantic comedy 'love jones' showcased the Chicago poetry scene, turning hip-hop generation lovers loose in a boho playground of John Coltrane's LP's, Gordon Parks photos and sexy raindrops."

Within that poetry and love of the spoken word, the characters in the film connect most conspicuously to hip hop. Their verses avoid the easy rhymes, and similar to the movie *Slam*, the use of the open microphone allows for the expression of thoughtful, provocative lines. Although not as political as the poetry in *Slam*, it remains just as powerful.

As expected in romantic comedies, the lovers find a way to sabotaging the possibilities of their union, and Darius and Nina are no exceptions. Despite their intelligence, they allow their jealousies and insecurities to impede the natural evolution of their affections for one another. Frightened by actually finding what each is looking for in a lover and friend, they distrust their emotions and the looming commitments. They both attempt to rationalize feelings that merely have to be accepted and cherished. As Darius's friend, Eddie (Leonard Roberts), tells him: "love...passion doesn't make sense. It is what it is." Darius and Nina eventually reach that understanding by the last scene in the film.

As working model for all that's wrong about hip-hop male attitudes and feature filmmaking, *Def Jam's How to Be a Player* (1997) serves up the details. A product of HBO's Def Comedy Jam and Def Jam records, along with Island Pictures, this alleged comedy follows "Drayton 'Dray' Jackson (Bill Bellamy)...a bona fide 'player'—a male who is intimate with numerous women without commitment—and without being caught."[14] Dray appears to be quite accomplished at maintaining his reputation, as he is accompanied on one holiday by three friends who wait in the car while he stops off to service his various lovers. However, Dray's skills become challenged when his sister Jenny (Natale Desselle) and her friend Katrina (Mari Morrow) team up to teach Dray a lesson and reform him of his womanizing ways. The women fail at first, when trying to trap Dray at a party where they have invited his many lovers, but later Katrina seduces Dray, knowing that his steady girlfriend, Lisa (Lark Voorhies), will arrive to catch him with another woman.

With Def Jam's name in the movie title and its association with the hip-hop world, the movie announces itself as a statement about the dating scene of the younger generation. Due to that position, as one reviewer observes, "you have to wonder about its impact on young males. What [the film's] writers...are essentially saying is that it's in the nature of men to score with as many women as possible, and the trick is merely for them not to get caught doing it by their girlfriends."[15] Despite the movie's ending which shows Dray's eventual defeat, the plurality of the story displays Dray's skillful techniques as seduction and deceit. After providing ninety minutes of effective methods of being a "player," the last minute of being caught seems disingenuous. In fact, the movie fails to criticize the value system to which Dray adheres, but it merely suggests that "getting caught" remains the major problem. Additionally, the movie "exposes a great deal of naked flesh...but doesn't address some of the contemporary issues of safe sex, pregnancy, and AIDS."[16]

The movie includes music selections performed by such notable hip hoppers as Slick Rick, Master P, Foxy Brown, and Dru Hill, and the movie's director, Lionel Martin, had helmed the music videos of "international multi-platinum recording artists Boyz II Men, Whitney Houston, Toni Braxton, TLC, 2 Pac, Bobby Brown, BellBivDeVoe, Public Enemy, R. Kelly, Jodeci, Jazzy Jeff and the Fresh Prince, and Keith Sweat."[17] Contrary to the potential fun, energy, and positive messages in such a movie, the result was a comedy that was flat on style, imagination, and respect for its audience, particularly the women viewers.

In that same year, *Booty Call* sought urban African American audiences by presenting a "mixed bag of street humor, broad, bawdy jokes and hip-hop music."[18] From its title, the focus of the film is set, as two home boys, Bunz (Jamie Foxx) and Rushon (Tommy Davidson), are determined to have sex with their dates, Lysterine (Vivica A. Fox) and Nikki (Tamala Jones). Rushon believes the sexual intimacy is long overdue after seven weeks of dating Nikki, and Bunz, a self-proclaimed player, merely believes that any woman is a potential sex partner, though he prefers the 3 a.m. "booty call" that ensures sex without commitment. With a "gentlemen's bet" that Rushon will fail to "hit that ass" before the following morning, the two head out on their dates with lustful intent. Early on, as the two escort their dates into a Chinese restaurant, Bunz is confident that he will win the bet, telling Rushon: "College got you too sensitive....You ain't got no player left in you." Here, Bunz's dismissal of college, and by inference education, demeans the value of higher learning as injurious to the street-preferred masculinity.

Although true affection exists between Rushon and Nikki, they both have something to prove: confirming a manly image for the former and avoiding the "ho"-ish image for the latter. Bunz and Lysterine, though combative at first, eventually succumb to their mutual body heat and the potential for "freaky" sex with each other. Eventually, the women agree to the intimacy, and the last half of the film follows the tribulations of the men in their efforts to secure condoms and dental dam in order to consummate the much anticipated coition.

While *Def Jam's How to Be a Player* flirted with a condemnation of the "player" mentality, *Booty Call* tries to expose insensitive male attitudes and, at the same time, to present them as entertaining and harmless. Specifically, by connecting Bunz's player's personality with Lysterine's kinky nature, any criticism of the player's game loses its sting. Once Lysterine agrees to the intimacy, her sexual agressiveness eclipses Bunz's sleazy innuendos. Lysterine pressures Bunz to do impersonations of black men of authority as foreplay; she mounts Bunz in wild banshee yells; and she straps Bunz to the bedposts while wearing an S&M outfit with matching whip. Far removed from a feminist characterization, Lysterine embodies the very type that justifies the "player" posing maintained by Bunz.

Rushon and Nikki emerge as the couple whose inner feelings dictate more than their sexual urges, but in this exaggerated comedy, their occasional statements of affection seem thin at best. In their own way, they demand game playing in a more subtle fashion, as their intimacy develops as the result of bartering and control.

In their world of booty calls, sexual insults, and sexual manipulation, the four main characters share viewpoints about sexuality that appear to be understood by minor characters as well. In the restaurant, a Chinese mobster complies to Bunz's request to stop smoking in order to assist his efforts to "get some ass" from his date. In a corner market, a Chinese grocer offers an aphrodisiac and lambskin condoms to enhance sexual stamina and enjoyment. In another corner market, the Punjabi clerks consult on a variety of condom choices, once they know Bunz and Rushon are not gay but prepared to "lick it, before you stick it." The notions of black sexuality, as raw, unrestrained, and depraved, assume recognition and understanding across ethnic and cultural lines. *Booty Call* mocks civility, intelligence, romantic love, and homosexuality under a "mix of hip hop and r&b, including performances by Slick Rick, SWV, Missy Elliot, R. Kelly, and Ginuwine."[19]

With *Brown Sugar* (2002), the filmmakers explored a love for hip hop which paralleled a romantic love between childhood friends Dre (Taye Diggs) and Sidney (Sanaa Lathan). The movie focuses upon their adulthood, as each attempts to make a professional life in hip hop: Dre struggles to begin his own record label and Sidney works as a music critic for *XXL* magazine.

Similar to *Love Jones*, *Brown Sugar* brings the audience into the world of black urban professionals, and in this story, New York City functions as the setting for the two lovers, and their friends, to lead lives of contemporary desperation, attempting to balance personal desires with professional aspirations.

The film opens with several real-life hip-hop artists—Doug E. Fresh, Slick Rick, Dana Dane, Big Daddy Kane, Kool G Rap, DeLa Soul, Talib Kweli, and Common—all responding to the question: When did you first fall in love with hip hop? Their responses demonstrate the reverence and significance that hip hop music holds and continues to bring to them. From there, the younger versions of Dre and Sidney discover hip hop together as they play on a street corner. The film's director Rick Famuyima asserted: "You don't think of hip-hop when you think of a romantic comedy. There's a certain connotation that comes with the music….I feel that there's always been romance in the music. It's always been a music that's true, so whether the truth is violent, whether the truth is love or friendship—hip-hop has always been multilayered. I wanted to do something that showed a different side of the music I love."[20]

Having remained friends since childhood, Dre and Sidney's platonic relationship faces a major test when Dre marries Reese (Nicole Ari Parker), a beautiful lawyer, who craves attention but has little understanding for Dre's passion for music. Dre believes that Reese represents the ideal woman, explaining to Sidney: "We all looking for wifing material. A woman that's fine, smart, classy, but not a snob...sexy, but not a 'ho'. That's brown sugar." Reality strikes them both, however, when Dre and Sidney share an amorous kiss before the wedding. Denying their true feelings, when Sidney eventually accepts the proposal from Kelby (Boris Kodjoe), a professional basketball player, the two protagonists seem doomed to a future with the wrong people. Eventually, after some honest confessions when Dre catches Reese at a romantic lunch with another man, and after some painful decisions when Sidney returns the engagement ring to Kelby, the two childhood lovers follow their true emotions. Dre and Sidney finally answer the question posed at the film's beginning, realizing that their love for hip hop and their love for one another began at the same time and has endured over the years with the same intensity. In one place in the film, Dre tells Sidney: "You remember that feeling. Just how hip hop made you feel. It was so real, it was like air." In the same manner that hip hop is essential to living, so too is the mutual love between Dre and Sidney.

Even though the reflections about hip hop by Dre and Sidney seem almost spiritual at places, and despite the moments when the two protagonists behave in ways deliberately tailored for the romantic-comedy genre, *Brown Sugar* remains a notable film. As one critic writes, "'Brown Sugar' is a sly and sophisticated romantic comedy with a depth of characterization matched by its appreciation of the world of hip hop. It's a mainstream movie in the best sense: an all-too-infrequent big screen depiction of successful, affluent African Americans facing complex personal and professional choices."[21]

One of the favorable aspects of the movie is the effective use of real-life rappers Mos Def and Queen Latifah in supporting roles worthy of more screen time. Mos Def portrays Chris, the rapper who aspires to his art rather than money. Dre signs him as the first and only act on his independent label, and the two become friends in their struggle to get their demo critiqued and played on the radio. Queen Latifah portrays Francine, Sidney's close friend whose confident attitude and insight enables her to advise honestly about the love game played between the protagonists. The presence of these two popular rappers in the film complements the opening segment where other real-life rappers talk about their love for hip hop.

Because hip hop functions as a character within the film, the integration of hip-hop music becomes a primary objective. From the title track through the various scenes of the film, selections are performed by a variety of talents, such as Mos Def, Faith Evans, Erykah Badu, Common, Angie Stone, Jill Scott, Eric B and Rakim, and Mary J. Blige. The movie's co-Music Supervisor, Barry Cole, explains: "The music is a love letter to hip-hop as defined by the characters....It is a reflection of what it was like for the first generation of hip-hop, growing up as the music began, and maturing as the music continues to evolve."[22]

Unlike the "hip hop relationships" cluster of films, the second cycle that emerged in the late 1990s contained a smaller number of big-screen stories. Exploring the topic of white characters affected by hip hop and black culture, these "hip hop and white awareness" films ranged from comedy to drama, connected by "the notion that blacks exist largely to put white people in touch with their deeper, earthier selves."[23] To varying degrees of success the films *Bulworth* (1998), *Black and White* (1999), *Save the Last Dance* (2001), *8 Mile* (2002), *Bringing Down the House* (2003), and *Malibu's Most Wanted* (2003) depicted white protagonists whose lives are shaped dramatically by hip-hop culture.

A film such as *Bulworth* possesses such a self-conscious attempt at political and social satire that it resonates an engaging charm. With auteurish zeal, Warren Beatty—as central actor, co-writer, co-producer, and director of *Bulworth*—relishes the characterization of a jaded, suicidal white politician who discovers a vein of integrity by publicly adapting a hip-hop persona.

Set during the final phase of the 1996 Democratic primary campaign, the story opens with Senator Jay Billington Bulworth drowning in tears of depression, flipping a television remote that connects the shallow images of popular culture programming to the campaign ad of his own shallow image. As the camera pans his office walls, the photos of Martin Luther King, Jr., Malcolm X, Rosa Parks, Huey Newton, Thurgood Marshall, and Bobby Kennedy become the markers of his former liberalism. However, his current campaign platform, displayed through television sound bites, announces a conservative position against affirmative action and unemployment benefits. An obvious man of contradictions, hypocrisy, and expediency, Bulworth emerges as the conventional white politician who plays it safe in the mainstream. Despairing over his lost idealism and down in the polls, Bulworth has arranged his own public assassination during the weekend that frames the film's setting and time. Unsure when the hit man will strike, Bulworth absolves his political mistakes by communicating his honest feelings about issues and his fellow white colleagues who run the government.

Significantly, his transformation begins in a black church, symbolic of the grassroots people who have been consistently disenfranchised and exploited. Facing their tough questions and the spiritual atmosphere, he is born again as the voice of truth. When asked by one parishioner if he plans to help improve the neighborhood, Bulworth responds: "You haven't contributed any money to my campaign, have you?"

After duplicating his gospel of truth at a Beverly Hills event where he insults Jewish filmmakers and businesspeople and after dancing at an after-hours hip-hop club, Bulworth becomes mesmerized by hip-hop rhymes, which he adapts, along with trendy hip-hop attire. His political exorcism, honesty, and hip-hop argot quickly catches on with the public, and Bulworth assumes an invigorated attitude and a purpose to live.

On the level of political ridicule, the film works effectively, resulting in both provocative and humorous elements via Bulworth's erratic hip-hop eruptions. As one critic observes, "*Bulworth* goes well beyond the usual late-night political attack on political correctness: It says that our politics are now so completely devoted to propitiatory lies that anyone who speaks candidly would have to be—by definition—half-crazy....Beatty obviously means for us to believe that rap is the language of protest, of social truth."[24] The writing is clever and insightful, serving up the inextricable connection between convenient political party dogma and the callous opportunistic manipulation of the American public. At the same time, the film identifies hip hop as more than just a youth movement, but the method for claiming clarity about and the articulation of social oppression. In a 1998 *New Yorker* interview Warren Beatty stated his views on rap: "the same people who are objecting to rap music now would in the sixties have been objecting to Huey Newton or Bobby Seale or Eldridge or Stokely Carmichael....Anybody who doesn't deal with rap, including gangsta rap, with the utmost respect and attention ought to wake up and smell the coffee."[25] Beatty's praise of hip hop, and particularly the framing of rap in a historical connection to black power activism, provides a salient contrast to the vilification conducted in much of mainstream media throughout the decade.

In the film, Bulworth's transformation supercedes the verbal and physical humor of the character, as he assumes a more spiritual, symbolic significance of a leadership "for the people and by the people." The filmmaker punctuates this significance through a recurring character, identified in the credits as the Rastaman, who appears frequently to deliver his mantra: "you got to be a spirit...can't be no ghost." This homeless-looking character, portrayed by activist-author Amiri Baraka, delivers the belief that someone must embody the authentic meaning of the nation's codes, rather than simply shouting empty slogans and aphorisms.

In one scene, Bulworth, wearing his hip-hop attire of a knit cap, baggy shirt and pants, sunglasses, and gold chains, appears as a guest on the television show. When asked about his new campaign and appearance, he delivers a long, free-style response: "We got babies in south central dying as young as they do in Peru/ we got public schools that are nightmares, we got a Congress that ain't got a clue/ we got kids with sub-machine guns, we got militia throwing bombs/ we got Bill getting all weepy, we got Newt blaming teenage moms/ we got factories closing down, where the hell did all the good jobs go/ well, I tell you where they went...Mexico/ oh, a brother can work in fast foods, if he can't invent computer games/ but what we use to call America, that's going down the drain."

The film's undeniable reverence of hip hop as a political tool draws attention to race in still an additional manner. Simply, when a white man uses rap in the movie, he receives serious media attention and platforms for his views. When blacks use rap, they are merely perceived as entertainers, with rap serving as a marker of a lower class status. For a Hollywood venture, *Bulworth* makes a significant, insightful assessment of American mores and institutions.

However, as important as the film is, it unfortunately falters in two respects. First of all, the character Nina (Halle Berry) becomes a slippery slope into a racist, sexist fantasy. When Bulworth first sees Nina at the aforementioned black church rally, he is immediately "sprung" by Nina's hip-hop exoticism. Nina, along with her two 'hood-rat girlfriends, exude the hip-hop attitudes that shape their speech, hairstyles, clothing, and hoodish behavior, conspicuously clashing with the white world into which Bulworth takes them as his "flygirls" entourage. Bulworth's sexual desire for Nina becomes obsession, and though Bulworth is married with a daughter who is perhaps Nina's age, Nina operates as both Bulworth's fetish and his conduit into the black world. "According to [feminist critic Laura] Mulvey, the...method that Hollywood uses to contain women's onscreen sexual power is fetishization. Fetishization in general involves excess emotional or sexual investment in a particular object....Tied to the way women are figured under the male gaze, fetishization works further to objectifying women in order to make them less of a threat."[26] Bulworth's immediate lust for Nina transfigures her into a mysterious object to be explored and, ultimately, to be possessed.

Later in the film, the audience learns that Nina's availability results from her function as the set up for Bulworth's assassination, a job she takes in order to settle family debts. Eventually though, as she conducts Bulworth into her hip-hop social life, neighborhood, and then home, Nina's affection for the older white male develops into a surprising passion. Nina chooses to protect Bulworth from the assassin, the neighborhood, and the paparazzi. In essence, Nina becomes the exotic black woman desired by the white hero and, simultaneously, a young mammy who nurtures the white hero. As if presaging her later Academy Award–winning character of Leticia in *Monster's Ball* (2001), here Ms. Berry's Nina emanates as a black woman rooted within a black community, but devoid of any fulfilling and intimate life until the white male hero appears.

The second disappointing aspect of the film emerges from Senator Bulworth's fluid immersion into hip-hop culture, the inner-city environment, and his subsequent integrity. He easily embodies the notion of "The White Negro," a condition when "white people, desperate to rebel, will throw themselves headlong into black culture—specifically black outlaw culture—to find redemption."[27] In one weekend, Bulworth finds his "soul" and purpose due to his contact with black people. In the film's finale, Nina bestows the ultimate racial approval on Bulworth for the entire black community. As Bulworth prepares to return to the campaign trail by getting into his limo, he publicly tells Nina he needs her with him. In the silence, as the gathered media and the black members of the community await her response, Nina tells Bulworth: "you know you my nigga." Then, she kisses him. Nina's nigga-rization decree and her kiss reconcile Bulworth's whiteness into black acceptability. In short, Bulworth's willingness to be honest and to shed his privileged white lifestyle, if only for one weekend, has earned him hip hop's highest honor for a white man—to be identified as a "nigga" and one with the black community. As cultural definition, critic Ernest Hardy points out that "'your nigga' is someone who's got your back, someone who's been through the fire with you or for you, and it's very much rooted in shared trials, shared blackness—it's an affirmation of blackness. When Nina calls the senator that, it's just the ultimate white-boy fantasy."[28] In that one phrase and moment, Bulworth becomes an authentic man of the people of all races, and all of Bulworth's previous transgressions as a white man, as a mainstream politician, and as a philandering husband have been forgiven.

One year after *Bulworth, Black and White* pulls the audience into multiple stories that intersect and parallel one another; stories comprised of black and white characters searching for quick answers to resolve their individual insecurities and relational problems. Following over sixteen characters around the Manhattan and Staten Island boroughs of New York, white director James Toback explores how the characters "are playing identity games. The blacks are trying to leave the ghetto without losing the anger that makes them appealing as pop-cult outlaws. The whites are slumming without giving up their option to return home to daddy when they get into trouble."[29]

In one story line, Charlie (Bijou Phillips), a white adolescent girl, engages in a three-way sexual tryst in a public park with another white girl and Rich (Oli "Power" Grant), an aspiring black rapper and a gang leader. Following her fun in the park, she goes to her affluent home for a quail dinner and an emotional argument with her father, before retiring to her room to smoke a joint and talk on the phone. Charlie represents a number of white teen characters in the film who, in their love of hip hop, affect a black vernacular and pursue a physical proximity to black characters. In a telling classroom discussion, Charlie voices the desire of her white peers, stating: "I wanna be black. I wanna get into the hip hop thing. I wanna go there." For Charlie, "there" is some mysterious and transforming state of "being" that awaits a white person who submerges into black culture. For Charlie and her friends, the essence of "cool" and personal fulfillment rests in rejecting their white identity and assuming the surface expressions of blackness. In their quest to become black, Charlie and her peers fail to perceive the actuality of white privilege that gives them that choice to pursue blackness. With her comfortable home and her parents' financial support, Charlie submerges herself into sexual experimentation, music, language, and attitudes that she assumes is the composite meaning of being black in America. Addicted to hip hop, Charlie disregards the comments from one student of color during the class discussion who states that many black youths search for ways, including rapping, to allow them to get out of the 'hood.

Through another connected character, Will King (William Lee Scott), an early-20-something white man, has physically left his family—his father being Bill King (Joe Pantoliano), the District Attorney—to live in the black neighborhood. In his search for significance, Will functions as a homey-gopher for Rich's various business interests. Working for the black gangster-aspiring rapper, Will cherishes his acceptance within the inner circle of Rich and his crew. When a group of young white businessmen opens a night club within Rich's territory, Will informs the latter of the infringement, happy with the attention and praise anointed on him. Will is "down" to do anything for Rich, including murdering Rich's old friend Dean (Alan Houston), a basketball player who throws a game for quick money, offered by undercover detective Mark Clear (Ben Stiller).

Will attains the inclusion into the black world in a way that Charlie desires but cannot achieve. Being male, Will earns a trust that is purchased with a life-and-death currency, allowing him to enjoy the spoils of gangsterism, including money, protection, and access to black women. Charlie, being female, must always negotiate her access into Rich's world with her body, as Rich perceives her through the gangsta rapper label of "bitch." However, after murdering Dean and being photographed leaving the scene by Detective Clear, Will has only one resource for protection—his father. Similar to Charlie, Will has the choice to leave behind his preferred black identity by reconciling with his father and avoiding prosecution for killing a black man.

In another connected character, Greta (Claudia Schiffer), a late-20-something white graduate student in Anthropology, lives with Dean, her black lover with whom she shares her philosophies about culture and race. When Dean shows weakness by taking the bribe to throw a game, Greta rejects him, and informs Rich about Dean's discussions with Detective Clear. Moving from informant to lover, Greta has sex with Rich, coldly placing Dean's future in the hands of a man she knows will kill him.

Greta, a manipulative character, seems obsessed with blackness as well. However, unlike the simple identity motivations of Charlie and Will, Greta gains power by intellectualizing blackness through anthropological theories and experiencing blackness through black male lovers. She resents weakness in males, and in her thinking, she equates black masculinity with strength and power. For Greta, the more brutish the male, the more enthralled she becomes, as illustrated in the film's closing scenes when Greta holds hands at dinner with Mike Tyson (as himself).

These three characters and their intersecting story lines illustrate the structuring of this tale of dysfunctionalism, as several other characters surface as well. For example, a white documentary filmmaker, Sam (Brooke Shields), follows Charlie and her friends around the city, capturing the behavior and comments of white kids who love hip hop. In tow, her gay husband, Terry (Robert Downey Jr.), joins Sam's entourage, continually eyeing possible male lovers. Casey (Jared Leto), the white school teacher at Charlie's school, challenges his students during the day, but eventually meets Terry, leading to their hand-in-hand strolling along a Manhattan street. In the center of this storm of searching characters, Rich and his homey, Cigar (rapper Raekwon), struggle to get into a recording studio and turn their street lives into raps, encouraged when they meet white Hollywood film director Brett Ratner (as himself).

As the white characters constantly look toward black culture for meaning, Rich and his crew consistently take advantage of those characters. As one critic observes: "In this film white people and black people exploit each other for thrills, for profit, in order to scandalize, and for the amoral purpose of maintaining brutal power. There are no simple demons or victims."[30] Due to such characterizations, the movie becomes both realistic and unsettling at the same time. Any possible insights into these personalities get lost, or perhaps smothered, beneath a blanket of selfish and unlikable people.

Notably, a major weakness in the film surfaces in a shifting of focus in the initial story. As critic Elvis Mitchell writes, "[b]y the end, the movie departs from the hip-hop world and settles into drama right out of the Yiddish theater: a son's need to make a connection with his dad....The story turns into one about the curative power of family."[31] At the high point in the climax, District Attorney Bill King's decision and reconnection with Will receives the spotlight. By the middle of the film, Charlie's engaging story that leads directly into the crucial failures of contemporary families and the allure of hip hop for the younger generation recedes into the background. In discontinuing the exploration of Charlie's world, the film misses the opportunity to also weigh the manner in which hip hop had become synonymous with black culture in the mainstream discourse; once again, black culture was perceived as a monolithic world where authenticity only existed within the borders of inner-city working class and poor blacks.

In another film in the cycle, *Save the Last Dance*, the white teenage protagonist, Sara (Julia Stiles), serves as a counterpoint to Charlie's obsession with hip hop. Sara's cultural awareness originates in a suburban world of white friends and classical dance, and hip hop functions as the expression that enlarges her viewpoints of the world. In an interview, the film's director Thomas Carter, asserts: "There is no question that hip-hop is the dominant pop culture in the world today....The culture comes from the poor, the disfranchised....It's certainly urban and very true to the language of the streets. It's the poetry of people who are not necessarily sophisticated with language, but there is a raw elegance about it."[32]

Set in Chicago, *Save the Last Dance* follows on Sara as she's forced to live with her jazz musician-father after her mother's death. Attending a predominantly black high school, Sara undergoes a radical emotional and psychological change, leaning on the friendship of fellow student Chenille

(Kerry Washington), a black teenaged mom, and the romantic love of Derek (Sean Patrick Thomas), a black teenager who dreams of being a pediatrician.

Still dealing with guilt following her mother's car accident, Sara faces hostility in her new environment due to her race and her cultural disconnection. Chenille intercedes instructing Sara on the current slang, the proper clothes, and the correct social circle with which to associate. Appreciative of the extended friendship, Sara sticks close and learns the way to daily navigate the school and the neighborhood.

Sara's initial friction with Derek eventually develops into an admiration, as Derek's intelligence, popularity, and love of dance distinguishes him from other schoolmates. Through the love of dance, both Sara and Derek find a common language and access into one another's personal lives and dreams. Sara, an aspiring ballerina, dreams of going to the Julliard School of Dance. On his part, Derek functions as the "crown prince of a local hip-hop club hangout called the Stepps Club," and he "guides Sara in the culture of hip-hop," resulting in their romance.[33] Consequently, Derek's coaching of Sara in hip hop and his insistence on her auditioning again for Julliard, emboldens her to blend hip hop, ballet, and modern dance into her routine and symbolically her lifestyle. The confidence that Sara gains through dance extends to her ability to deal with her new urban world.

Derek assumes the role of boyfriend, lover, and cultural interpreter, as he tells Sara: "Hip hop is more than just dance. It's like an attitude." With that pronouncement, through ensuing sequences, the lessons continue, as Derek instructs her on body language, grunts, and attitudes, walking in public, and how to move her "butt" on the dance floor. The interracial union that develops emerges from a friendship rather than a curious "jungle fever," and Derek and Sara symbolically demonstrate how racial lines can be transcended and by implication how hip hop and mainstream converge seamlessly.

Although hip hop has served as the bridge between the two lovers, the issue of race surfaces in realistic ways. First, the effect of a black male–white female romance ignites a critical response from black women. Derek's former girlfriend, Nikki (Bianca Lawson), strikes out at Sara verbally and physically when the romance becomes evident. Nikki tells Sara: "white girls like you, creeping up, taking our men. The whole world ain't enough. You got to conquer ours, too." Racial ownership trumps hip-hop tolerance, particularly in an urban black community where various social and economic pressures undermine possible relationships. Even the supportive Chenille berates Sara about the precarious state of available black men, concluding: "Derek's about something...he's for real...going to make something of himself. Here you come white and got-to-be-right, and you take one of the decent men we have left after jail, drugs, and drive-bys. That is what Nikki meant about you up in our world." Although Sara has learned hip-hop dance, she still remains naïve to the messages of hip hop with regard to endangered black males and gender tensions within the black community.

A second realistic tension evolves between Derek and his childhood friend, Malachi (Fredro Starr). Malachi perceives Derek's ambition to be a doctor and his dating of Sara as indicators of the latter's dismissal of his true identity. Having run the streets together, including a botched liquor store robbery, Malachi needs Derek to "have his back" when facing the challenges of the 'hood, but increasingly Derek rejects the thug behavior by opting for higher education. In one of the film's best sequences, the two long-time friends disagree on planning a retaliation drive-by into a rival neighborhood. Malachi insists that when it comes to the thug life, "that's a black man's life—madness and mayhem....I'm still from the neighborhood. But you? I guess that's what happens when a white girl goes to your head." Refusing to concede, Derek states: "Man, you just got out of juvie [juvenile hall], and now you talking about going out trying to start some more shit....I know what's out there, and it ain't like you can't get past it. But you're too busy getting in your own way to see that."

At the heart of their disagreement, Derek and Malachi debate the issue of determining authenticity. From N.W.A.'s *Straight Outta Compton* (1988) to Kanye West's *The College Dropout* (2004), this issue surfaces in hip hop, both in lyrics and in interviews with performers. To what extent is "keeping it real" defined only by the street life and thug behavior? Why must only one type of behavior receive glorification as "authentic" black masculinity, rejecting any other possible configuration? Specifically, why must Derek and Malachi become polar opposites in their adolescent efforts to claim manhood and success? Although the film avoids tackling these important questions, they do receive detailed discussions in reflective books, such as Kevin Powell's *Who's Gonna Take the Weight? Manhood, Race, and Power in America* (2003) and Mark Anthony Neal's *New Black Man* (2005). Mark Anthony Neal observes: "The idea of the *New Black Man* may be predicated on seeing black masculinity as something that is fluid, but it's also a dance with contradictions."[34] Consequently, a Hollywood feature film can't be expected to resolve those contradictions, but raising the issues in their significance to the characters and the hip-hop generation becomes crucial. Taking the easy way out, the film confirms Derek as the hero, as Malachai is shown handcuffed into a police cruiser following the drive-by shootout.

However, Sara remains the focus in the film, and her journey into hip hop provides her with a transformation that opens the access to her dreams, as she gets accepted into Julliard at the story's end. Returning to the Stepps Club after the audition, she and Derek move to the floor with their hip-hop movements and their relationship affirmed. Under the closing credits and music, other characters take their turn at the center of the floor, as the hip-hop environment provides the happy ending.

Following the marketing strategy of the times, *Save the Last Dance* compiles a soundtrack to target its expected audience. The film weaves its story under the soundtrack which "contains R&B, hip hop and pop artists including K-CI and JoJo, Faith Evans, Sean 'Puffy' Combs...Pink...Fredro Starr...[the group] Lucy Pearl including the rap...of Snoop Dogg and Q-Tip."[35]

Another example from this film cycle presents rapper Eminem in the lead role in *8 Mile*, a movie that dramatizes the performer's true-life experiences and showcases his MC-ing skills. In *8 Mile*, racial authenticity and hip-hop sensibilities serve as primary topics for the film's plot, as two Academy Award–winning white filmmakers—director Curtis Hanson (screenwriting winner, *L.A. Confidential*, 1997) and producer Brian Grazer (*A Beautiful Mind*, 2001)—develop the project. Consequently, the film and its subject matter earn validation as a studio-backed endeavor, as opposed to the low-budget, straight-to-video movies that often featured hip-hop sensibilities.

In *8 Mile*, Eminem portrays Rabbit, a white teen who dreams of finding fulfillment via his rhyming lyrics that capture his crumbling personal life. Set in Detroit, a city symbolic of working-class Americans, Rabbit's story parallels the familiar Horatio Alger paradigm, as a economically challenged young man seeks and wins fame—and by implication future riches—on his own terms. Even so, set also within the hip-hop world, Rabbit's story carries additional notions about masculinity and racial blending.

Rabbit inhabits a world of confrontation—at his factory job, with his desperate mother at her trailer park home, and with his ex-girlfriend. Serving as an alternative family is his crew of three friends, two black and one white. In particular, one of his black friends named Future (Mekhi Phifer) personifies Rabbit's cultural passport into the world of the black audiences at the nightclub, called The Shelter, where the open-mike rap battles occur. Through the rap battles, Rabbit believes that he, though white, can confirm his skills as a rapper, his connection to the demanding black audiences, and his ascendancy into the recording marketplace. In an important way, Future sanctions Rabbit's expertise as a rapper; Future, having judged dozens of black talents coming upon stage, handpicks Rabbit as the best. However, in the plot, to have Rabbit triumph as the best in a cultural form developed by blacks might prompt dubiosity, or at worst, a resentment as another example of the white co-opting of black culture. Consequently, Rabbit has to be transformed into a hip-hop "nigga" where his racial lines will be erased or, at the very least, carefully blurred.

The solution materializes from one of the issues often explored in rap lyrics—namely "class." Rabbit's mobile home—shared with his mother, Stephanie (Kim Basinger), and younger sister, Lily (Chloe Greenfield)—signifies his poverty, a condition he shares with the other blacks in the film. As such, his economic struggles mirror those situations within the black community. Unlike Bulworth's affluence and privilege, Rabbit, similar to his black contemporaries, fights the daily battles and indignities heaped upon the lower class. When Future refers to Rabbit as a "Negro," he underscores that sameness that prevails; their common affection for and knowledge of hip-hop history and performers valorizes their brotherhood. To illustrate that kinship, Future and Rabbit share a scene where the two berate "white" music and performers, as they improvise rhymes over Leonard Skynyrd's anthem, "Sweet Home Alabama," which blasts over the car radio. By eschewing the lyrics and forcing the melody to carry their spontaneous rhymed resentments of their living conditions, they reduce the southern celebratory song to nonsense, while they affirm their unity of hip-hop-philia.

Furthermore, in allegorical fashion, Future's name underscores the meaningful designation of what will eventually transpire for Rabbit. In the middle of the film, Rabbit deliberately confronts Future at one point, as a ruse for Rabbit to hide his fear of choking at the microphone as in the first scene and as a ruse for hiding his fear of success. However, Future, who displays more ambition for Rabbit than for himself, forgives his apologetic brother, and like a dark-skinned "Adrian," Future cheers his "Rocky" out to battle in the ring one more time. Future and Rabbit's symbiotic connection guarantees that the latter will become one white Rabbit who will leap into a future life of fulfilled dreams that will take him far beyond the environmental trappings of the "8 mile" neighborhood.

This reconfiguration of class identity as black identity undertakes an additional emphasis when Rabbit must face his rapping nemesis—Papa Doc, the defending rap champion and the leader of a crew of rappers who refer to themselves as "The Free World." Before meeting Papa Doc in that championship round, Rabbit must battle two other Free World rappers, and as expected, the black rappers attack Rabbit with white racial epithets such as "hillbilly," "Vanilla Ice," "Willie Nelson," "Elvis," and "Leave It to Beaver."

Continuing to play the race card, these black rappers extol Rabbit to "take your white ass across 8 mile back to the trailer park." This barrage of racial comments serves to gain the viewing audience's sympathy for Rabbit, who in a previous scene was physically beaten by these same rappers.

Rabbit—a smart survivor, similar to the character Brer Rabbit in numerous black folk tales—wins the support of the black audience in the club by attacking the male rappers at their weakest point: their masculinity. Rather than trying to defend himself from their racial slurs, Rabbit suggests that the Free World rappers are effeminate and soft. By attacking their exaggerated masculine behavior, Rabbit reduces them to gender ineffectuality in the public arena.

Subsequently, in the final championship round, Rabbit plays his trump card against Papa Doc. Having learned about his enemy's true background in an earlier scene, Rabbit's rhymes reveal Papa Doc's bourgeois name, "Clarence"; his private school education; and his middle-class home outside of the 'hood. Having demoted Papa Doc to a perpetrator of blackness, Rabbit triumphs because he represents the authentic "'hood." Due to his class identity, Rabbit acquires a black identity as Papa Doc embarrassingly exits from the stage.

Rabbit's victory of winning over the black audience in the club during the battle, reflects the movie's success in winning over the black audience in the movie theater. The character of Rabbit effectively connects across racial and generation lines to secure both popular and critical audiences. One critic suggests: "Eminem's rabbit is a real throwback to the classic teen anti-hero. Rebellious, surly, irate, sensitive....He is aggressive because he's so obviously been hurt....His lyrics are full of muddled rants, designed to shock, as well as heartfelt pleas for intimacy. All of which helps him connect so intensely with teenagers. It's the music of emotional confusion....It's the howl of the dispossessed."[36]

At its best, *8 Mile* showcases the appeal and rapping skills of its star, Eminem. The major rap tune from the film, "Lose Yourself," won an Academy Award for best song, and the song's title echoes the thematic suggestion of hip hop's power to annihilate racial lines. At its worst, the film delivers questionable images of women characters as Rabbit's mother, ex-girlfriend, and new girlfriend are selfishly flawed, obstructing Rabbit's pathway to fame. Significantly, only Rabbit's sister, Lily, reciprocates his love, and due to her innocence and young age, she has to be protected by his masculine strengths. In depicting the adult women as barriers to Rabbit's success, the movie reinforces gender hostility and tensions. By keeping the child-woman as vulnerable, the film maintains the conventional notions of the male protector, oversimplifying the aspects of manhood.

Despite its weaknesses, *8 Mile* remains an accomplished film that mainstreams hip hop through a white hero whose sincerity and passion for hip hop clearly surfaces in the story. Rabbit finds purpose in hip hop, not as an exploited avenue leading to a convenient "black" identity, but as a method for expression and self-realization. In doing that, the film actually demonstrates the crucial meaning of hip hop for a younger generation seeking answers to the questions in their lives.

In a contrasting manner, *Bringing Down the House* avoids a white teenage focus for hip hop's shaping of a personal ethos. Instead, in this film hip hop functions as an alien culture to the protagonist, a white upper-class lawyer. In this "black-collides-with-white culture comedy,"[37] the filmmakers borrow aspects of *Bulworth* and spin them into a tale that confirms family and friendship at the end.

Excited about meeting a beautiful, intelligent lawyer from an online chat relationship, Peter Sanderson (Steve Martin), a tax attorney, discovers that his romantic ideal is actually Charlene (Queen Latifah), a prison escapee who requests that he help her prove her innocence. Peter rejects the idea, until Charlene uses her saved e-mails to pressure him into opening her case. As she resides at Peter's home in an upscale white neighborhood, next to bigoted neighbor Mrs. Klein (Betty White), Charlene helps Peter to be a better father to his two kids and to win back his ex-wife.

Being a member of the middle-aged, white elite, Peter finds hip-hop music and language a foreign world, though Charlene translates hip-hop expressions when necessary to update him. Much of the humor in the early portion of the film springs from the clashing of attitudes and ideas between the young-black-hip-hop world and the affluent-white-conservative lifestyle. However, Charlene functions more as a conduit through which Peter discovers some important lessons about himself and interacting with the family he loves. In one scene, when Peter's fifteen-year-old daughter, Sarah (Kimberly J. Brown), gets drunk at a party, she phones Charlene to rescue her from an aggressive teenage boy. Charlene does so, dramatically hanging the offender over a balcony until he apologizes; then, at home she coaches Peter on how he should father the emotional Sarah.

More importantly, however, Charlene tutors Peter on the way to approach his ex-wife. Charlene tells him: "You got to be a beast. In the bedroom, a woman wants a man who knows how to ride her when she bucks." Extending her coaching into still another scene, she forces Peter to grab her breasts and to "talk nasty," all culminating in a physical romping on the couch as the neighbor, Mrs. Klein, enters calling Charlene "Mandingo." Charlene's lessons indicate her sexual experience and her proficiency at marriage counseling, but in particular, she becomes a devoted caretaker of Peter's family. Although she invites a crowd of black friends to a pool party at Peter's home, she never really interacts with them once she commits herself to taking care of the white family. In a quid pro quo situation, Charlene even pretends to be the family nanny, cook, and maid to help Peter win the account of the wealthy Mrs. Arness (Joan Plowright), an elderly white racist with southern roots.

One element that keeps Charlene from becoming a mere reference for jokes and servitude emerges through Peter's friend and work colleague, Howie (Eugene Levy). When Howie first sees Charlene, he's smitten by the "Cocoa Goddess," confessing suggestively to her: "I'd like to dip you in Cheese Whiz and spread you over a Ritz cracker." Enjoying the attention, Charlene pegs Howie as being "some kind of freaky." Unashamedly, he responds: "Oh, you have no idea. You got me straight tripping, boo." Howie's excitement about full-figured women in general, and Charlene in particular, places her on a level of distinction as she embodies femininity and sexiness. Howie's preference for Charlene praises black women and notes their desirability in a cinematic world often indifferent or hostile to the allure and beauty of black women. Furthermore, critic Elvis Mitchell notes, Howie's "wolfish smoothiness...doesn't condescend," and he speaks his hip hop affection directly, without "fak[ing] a street accent as if he's straight out of the 'hood."[38]

Eventually, Peter values his friendship with Charlene, and in an effort to gather evidence to prove her innocence, he travels to a black nightclub to confront Widow (Steve Harris), the actual culprit in Charlene's alleged crime. Buying clothes from two homeboys walking by his car, Peter dons his hip-hop outfit, a la *Bulworth*; adapts a "cool," street walk; affects an accent and speaks in rhymes; and enters the club of black patrons. Played for laughs, Peter's physical awkwardness, simplistic dance moves, and feigned aggressiveness prove the depth of his friendship, as he places himself in a life-and-death situation with Widow and his thugs. Although Peter's donning of a hip-hop identity isn't as extensive as Jay Bulworth's, the hip-hop disguise endows Peter the courage and attitude needed to save Charlene. Even so, when the movie ends, the audience realizes that hip hop has been merely played for laughs, so, consequently, the presence of Queen Latifah legitimizes the film's light-hearted approach to hip-hop culture.

In the next film, *Malibu's Most Wanted* (2003), the story offers a humorous look at Brad, a white 20-something protagonist, who calls himself

B-Rad. Having grown up listening to rap music from the age of three, B-Rad's orientation to the world is through hip hop. On the one hand, his hip-hop socialization turns him into a sincere and lovable guy, but in another vein, his transformation from a white identity to a hip-hop head connects back to the "White Negro" type.

Sent to a psychiatrist for his hip-hop condition, B-Rad (Jamie Kennedy) asserts that he wants to be the biggest rapper ever, which brings consternation to his parents, particularly his father Bill Gluckman (Ryan O'Neal), a California gubernatorial candidate. Diagnosed with an advanced case of "gangsterphrenia," B-Rad acts "ghetto," so in order to protect Bill Gluckman's campaign, his black campaign manager, Tom Gibbsons (Blair Underwood), organizes a plan. Hiring two black actors, Sean (Taye Diggs) and PJ (Anthony Anderson), to pretend to be 'hood gangstas who kidnap and verbally abuse B-Rad, the strategy is to frighten B-Rad into his innate "whiteness," in order to save him and to protect Bill Gluckman's bid for governor. However, plans go awry as Sean and PJ's masquerade as hoodrats fail, and as B-Rad's "ghetto" behavior maintains itself.

The intentions of the film are admirable, as director, John Whitesell, states that the movie "shows how infectious hip-hop music is, and how much it has transcended the community in which it was created....Kids are attracted to the culture of hip hop in large because the music derives from a very exciting, physical, gut-wrenching, down-and-dirty emotional beat, and the lyrics come from the heart."[39] In demonstrating that infectious quality of hip hop, B-Rad uses rap to inform the world about the hardships and difficulties of his Malibu 'hood. His rhymes state: "Traffic, traffic/ Lookin' for my Chapstick/ Feelin' kinda car sick/ There's a Ford Maverick." At the same time, he captures the angst of beachfront living with these reflective lines: "Mansions, movie stars, and cars/ It looks beautiful, it do/But things go on here, I'd never wish on you/ Like, life's a beach and then you die/ I could tell you stories, make your caterer cry."[40]

The farcical lyrics poke fun at privileged living, but the intent is also to comment on the accessibility that rap allows. Anyone, even white youths in an affluent environment, can find personal expression through hip hop. Simultaneously, the movie uses the characters of Tom Gibbsons, Sean, and PJ to assert that black skin color does not automatically bestow all black males with a 'hood sensibility. Specifically, the movie questions notions of racial identity in America, and the problematic manner in which society assigns substance and personality based upon skin color. Lead actor and co-writer Jamie Kennedy stated: "We were making fun of stereotypes and showing how stupid they are. I sort of felt that we were equal-opportunity offenders."[41]

However, when the film appeared, some critics bemoaned the movie's replication of the "White Negro," or as it became known at the time, a "wigger," which is "a young white who wants desperately to be down with hip-hop, who identifies more strongly with black culture than white."[42] At the time of the film's appearance, critic Kevin Powell concluded: "Let's be honest...all this fascination with hip-hop is just a cultural safari for white people," adding, "these movies would be harmless if we weren't living in a racist society."[43] Two years later, however, Bakari Kitwana appraised the movie for what it accomplishes. He writes: "On the surface, this parody is offensive, as is B-Rad's exaggerated Black ghetto accent....Most often, however, the jokes aren't at the expense of Black American culture but, rather, those aspects of hip-hop that have become parodies of themselves— from Black kids use of the n-word to rap music videos' mindless and endless parade of booty shaking, scantily clad women and misogynistic behavior. Complete with references to bitches and hos, all are targets in this film."[44]

Similar to the very rap culture that the movie parodies, however, the film displays contradictions which run the risk of confirming the very types it seeks to ridicule. For example, B-Rad eventually meets black gang member Tech-9 (Damien Dante Wayans) who's "strapped" with his guns throughout the film; in one sequence, Tech-9's black gang engages in a shootout with Latino gang members. B-Rad wins authenticity with the black gang when he grabs a weapon and in a mad rampage of gunfire scares the Latino gang away, later sharing forty-ounce beers to celebrate. Gangs, guns, and violent masculinity once again receive visual affirmation for their authenticating value.

Another example of the contradictions between intent and achievement emerges from the romance that develops between B-Rad and Shondra (Regina Hall). On the one hand, B-Rad's attraction to Shondra is presented as genuine affection, not an exotic fantasy. Similar to Howie's fascination with Charlene in *Bringing Down the House*, B-Rad finds his ideal woman in Shondra. As Bakari Kitwana accurately notes, in this film "Shondra and women who look like her are the new standard....In the multicultural hip-hop world, Black women are beautiful too."[45] On the other hand, the movie doesn't completely sell Shondra's decision to choose B-Rad as her man, considering her insightful observations about his bumbling ineptness in taking care of himself and in his questionable skills as a rapper. Unlike Howie and Charlene, B-Rad and Shondra developed a relationship based upon deception, and Howie possesses some qualities of professionalism and maturity that are absent from B-Rad. Consequently, the ending, which has Shondra securing her beauty salon and B-Rad's love, appears to acquiesce to what other contemporary films suggest: the white male privilege to have access to women of color and to win their affections. Even if unintentional, the film paints a picture of interracial romantic bliss without remaining true to the characterizations of B-Rad and Shondra.

In all of the five films mentioned in this cycle, hip hop ushers white characters into a realization about their personalities that remain dormant when living within their white world. As such, hip hop serves as a transforming expression to release the white characters from a spiritual, emotional, and psychological incarceration. In these "hip hop and white awareness films," white characters achieve a new level of fulfillment, and racial and cultural clashes find reconciliation.

In considering the third cycle of movies that began in the late 1990s, the thematic focus was on "hip hop ambitions," as these movies followed the challenges and difficulties faced by aspiring rappers, music producers, and dancers. Although smaller in number, the films in this cycle—*Ride* (1998), *You Got Served* (2004), *Hustle and Flow* (2005), and *Get Rich or Die Tryin'* (2005)—underscore the inextricable relationship between hip hop, lifestyles, and professional dreams.

Significantly, the film *Ride* differs from other movies in this cycle in that it follows the professional pursuits of a black woman protagonist. Leta Evans (Melissa De Sousa) provides a voiceover than chronicles her journey to make a giant step toward reaching her goal of directing music videos. A graduate of New York University Film School, Leta uses her position as an assistant to the famous video director, Bleau Kelly (Downtown Julie Brown), to maneuver herself behind the camera. However, Leta is forced to supervise a bus load of inner-city hip hoppers, from New York to Miami, who have been cast as extras in the upcoming video by popular performer Freddy B (Luther Campbell).

Leta's job becomes overwhelming under the strains of a low budget, a broken-down bus, and at-risk youths who only respond to the imposing presence of a community leader named Poppa (Malik Yoba). Poppa travels with the bus to meet with Freddy B who has promised to fund a new community center in New York. Eventually, Leta and the youngsters strike a harmonious chord, and once in Miami, the youngsters rally to save Leta from being fired.

Presaging the homage to hip hop that occurs later in *Brown Sugar*, *Ride* begins with some hip-hop images via photographs of performers in studio sessions and concerts. The images and Leta's voiceover provide the background for the opening credits which promise a story that explores hip-hop legacy. With a soundtrack that features "songs performed by Wu-Tang Clan, Onyx, Mia, Nas, Mack 10, Naughty By Nature, and the Notorious B.I.G.,"[46] the potential for this hip-hop film appears enormous. However, as aptly observed by one critic, this "rap-meets-road movie, sort of blows its chance at making any serious comment about the big business of black culture….a lot of the humor is either scatological, sophomoric or sexist."[47]

The film was written and directed by Millicent Shelton, a woman whose personal journey through New York University Film School and direction of music videos—for Mary J. Blige, Salt-N-Pepa, MC Lyte, R. Kelly, Aaliyah, and Heavy D—promised a story with insights about the music business and the creative process. Instead, the movie strains under the weight of wooden dialogue, peculiar plot twists, and a forced love story. The protagonist, Leta, exudes intelligence early in the film, which slowly dissipates into clumsiness as the story rambles forward. In the music, video, and film world that thrives so heavily on the male point of view, Leta could have been a possible revelation about the professional pathways into hip hop for women. Instead, *Ride* distorts itself into a convoluted excursion into hip hop's music scene.

When considering the movie *You Got Served*, a sense of déjà vu emanates from the film, as the audience watches "dance battles" reminiscent of *Breakin'* and *Fast Forward* from the 1980s. In that connection, the film possesses a disarming innocence, when compared to contemporary films about inner city youths. In *You Got Served*, young men don't use profanity, don't strap on weapons, and don't disrespect women. Subsequently, the film presents contemporary hip hop through an old-school framework.

In Los Angeles, two friends, Elgin (Marques Houston) and David (Omari Grandberry), have a hip-hop dance crew of about eight members. A group of about six boys, at first, the crew easily accept two girls who press them for inclusion. Coming from various racial backgrounds—African American, Latino, White, Asian—this crew consistently wins the organized dance battles at an indoor facility run by Mr. Rad (Steve Harvey), a local black business man and father figure. When a $5,000 challenge comes from a white crew, Elgin and David raise funds to match the challenge by running deliveries for Emerald (Michael Taliferro), a local black hoodlum. However, when an embittered crew member turns traitor and secretly joins the challenging white crew, Elgin and David's group lose the dance battle, the money, and their confidence.

Things continue to decline: David secretly romances Elgin's sister, Liyah (Jennifer Freeman); Elgin is beaten and robbed while delivering a package for Emerald; Elgin and David's friendship collapses and two crews are formed; Emerald threatens Elgin to repay him for the lost package; and a pre-teen friend called Li'l Saint (Malcolm David Kelley) is killed, off-screen, in a drive-by shooting. An answer to many of the problems surfaces in the form of a $50,000 "Big Bounce" dance contest and a featured appearance as dancers in the next music video for hip hop's Lil' Kim (as herself). However, with Elgin and David still feuding, can they reconcile in time to beat the favored white crew who demolished them earlier for $5,000?

In a predictable script, the two main characters restore their friendship and David and Liyah's romance survive. Along the way, in a story where adults are scarce, Elgin's hardworking mother and grandmother advise and support. Mr. Rad protects Elgin and David by having a friend on the police force visit Emerald at his place of business. In short, other than the menacing presence of Emerald, Elgin and David live in a hip-hop world where caring, patience, and goodwill prevail; they live in a *neighborhood*, as opposed to a *'hood*.

Despite the script problems and the thinly drawn supporting characters, this film showcases hip hop dancing, and in that regard it accomplishes some impressive results. From the opening credits and through various sequences until the finale, the dance moves reign supreme, as MC-ing and DJ-ing seem nonexistent. The choreography displays a hip-hop fusion of styles—breaking (floor spins, head spins, body torquing), krumping, popping—as routines combine individual free styles with synchronized moved between two or more members of the crew. With a meshing of styles, the dancers intersect acrobatics (back flips, front flips, hand stands), miming, and pretzeling in dynamic moves delivered with attitudes and sexual intimations. The dance moves serve as the source for creativity, an expression for emotions, and a statement of defiance to one's opponent. The film's title captures this latter point when the winning crew announces triumphantly to the losers: "you got served," meaning you were delivered a humbling defeat by better dancers.

Although a clear explanation fails to surface, it appears that Elgin and David see themselves as future choreographers and dancers. Without steady jobs and spending their days on the basketball court, these post-high school friends practice and compete for money. Their choreography does not stem from the formal training of a dance school, but from their closeness to the streets and the shared financial hardships alluded to in the opening scenes and in their reluctant employment with Emerald. Their dance techniques are raw and unrefined, which provides the edginess and dynamism that makes their hip-hop style. Winning the Big Bounce Contest at the end promises the opportunity to slip into a world where their hip-hop street style can be appreciated on a professional level.

Despite its faults in the script, *You Got Served* offers three aspects that confront some of the pejorative comments about the hip-hop world. First of all, the inclusion of women in the dance crews signals an effort to diminish the negative criticism of demeaning women. Certainly, Kiki (Amana Rodriguez) and Toya (Tanee McCall) who join Elgin and David's crew, remain in the background of the script, but the males in the crew see them as dance partners, not "bitches" or "hos." Second, the interracial aspect of the crews connects to the ethnic diversity comprising hip hop since its earliest days. Although Wade's rival crew is predominantly white, the film doesn't position whites as the enemy by their race, as white hip hoppers are seen in various crews, including Elgin and David's group. Third, one theme emphasized measured masculinity through forgiveness rather than violence. Elgin and David's friendship runs the gamut of emotions and conflict, but each finds that manhood translates as overcoming selfishness for the good of the crew.

From the innocence of *You Got Served*, the film *Hustle and Flow* takes the audience into the world of vice and moral ambiguity. One of the more controversial movies of the year, black producer John Singleton and white writer-director Craig Brewer use the suffocating, humid street life of Memphis to set the story of DJay (Terrence Howard), a pimp who dreams of becoming a professional rapper. The critics and scholars lined up on both sides of a debate about the messages and images emanating from a film whose protagonist embodies the male exploitation of women and represents the antithesis of progressive masculinity. How can a pimp be presented as a decent character who deserves the audience's support? As one critic notes: "'Hustle and Flow' tackles a seedy world the way movies often do, simultaneously sensationalizing it and de-sensationalizing it. Our hero can't just rap about pimping; he has to be a pimp....a pimp with a heart of gold."[48]

In the film's opening, DJay shares a philosophical monologue with Nola (Taryn Manning), a young white woman in his stable of three prostitutes, and he bemoans his disappointing life of running "twenty-dollar hos out the back of [his] Chevy." Indeed, as DJay later confesses to Shug (Taraji P. Henson), a pregnant black woman in his trio, he believes that he is going through a "mid life crisis." This set-up of the character seeks to evoke sympathy, or at least understanding, of a man who simply makes a living the best way he can. Consequently, his profession as a pimp emanates from economic pressures and a lack of alternative opportunities, not from a motivation to exploit women.

That very depiction of DJay, however, incited critics who placed the protagonist in a larger social context. Journalist Erin Aubry Kaplan condemns "the widespread embrace of black pathology, especially black urban pathology, as the standard for representative black images. Instead of nonthreatening maids and minstrels, we now have whores and murderous gangstas being marketed as cool, hip and, above all, *real*....A pimp isn't a bad reflection on black folk—he's our Everyman, our salt of the big-city earth." [49] Augmenting that assessment, black feminist scholar Melina Abdullah argues: "The film is part of a continuing effort to mainstream hip hop. We must remember that *Hustle and Flow* is a hip hop/pimp story told through the eyes of a white male. The film successfully removes hip hop from its political origins, making it a means through which a pimp can take his pimping to the next level rather than challenge his conditions....In this sense, the film works to mainstream hip hop culture as well as pimp culture."[50]

In the story, DJay's accidental meeting of a former high school classmate, Key (Anthony Anderson), begins the quest for hip-hop fame. Key, now married and working as a court reporter, also dreams of being a record producer, and recruiting a white musician from church named Shelby (DJ Qualls), Key and DJay begin the difficult and demanding work of developing a demo tape. The objective is to get the demo to another former classmate, Skinny Black (Ludacris), who has already obtained fame in the music business and has plans to visit home.

Because writers usually pen the familiar, DJay's scrolls rap lyrics, expressing, "it's hard out here for a pimp...a lot of bitches jumping ship." Such lines from a verse lead DJay to write a chorus with the lyrics, "beat that bitch." However, with Key's knowledge of radio requirements and Shelby's catchy musical tracks, DJay's lyrics and angst become reworked into a hip-hop joint with commercial potential. Unfortunately, after arranging a meeting with Skinny Black, DJay discovers the insincerity of the rap star, leading to a fight and shootout. Incarcerated, DJay learns that his tune makes it on the radio due to Key and Nola's efforts.

In praise of the film, *Hustle and Flow* provides an effective look at the process of making a hip-hop song on a budgetless, independent effort. The film shows the sacrifice of time and energy, as well as the inventiveness in fashioning a home studio and reworking tracks until a polished product is achieved. The sequences showing the inventiveness of the characters are invigorating, submerging the audience into the creative process. Certainly, those sequences were contributing factors in the film winning an audience award and a distribution deal at the Sundance Film Festival.

Unfortunately, with the film's characterization of women, merely appreciating the musical experience would be difficult to do. In spite of the "attempt to fuse hip-hop street credibility, art-house cachet and follow-your-dream, triumph-of-the-underdog Hollywood uplift,"[51] at some point the depiction of the women has to be addressed. Since Nola and Shug share DJay's most sincere and vulnerable moments, they represent the gold-hearted prostitutes who sacrifice to help DJay achieve his dream. The third member of DJay's trio, Lexus (Paula Jai Parker), an assertive black woman, emerges as "an uncouth loudmouth who won't give the man a moment's peace."[52] When the audience first sees her on screen, she dances at a strip club, allowing for the male gaze at the women strippers on stage, followed by the lingering camera on the naked strippers when DJay enters the dressing room. From that initial scene throughout, Lexus's insufferable yelling at DJay seems to justify a physical response, but DJay, choosing not to hit her, throws Lexus, her young child, and her belongings out of the shared house and onto the streets. With her abrasive and annoying harangues, DJay appears justified in forcing her out of his otherwise harmonic living environment.

On the opposite end from Lexus, in terms of personality, is Yvette (Elise Neal), Key's middle-class, churchgoing wife. Although refined, she appears to be insensitive to her man's dreams, concerned more with appearances and their material life. Ironically, Key cannot receive the support from the woman who loves him, while DJay is given support from the women who work for him. Assessing the film's depiction of women, Professor Melina Abdullah states: "While there are some gradations, women in the film are universally presented only as appendages to a male identity…a tool and commodity rather than a human being. She is presented as a bad whore as with Lexus, almost justifying her oppression and degradation…Nola and Shug win audiences over when they are willing to sacrifice themselves…and Yvette is presented as a gossiping nag who is overly emotional, illogical, and disloyal for refusing to support her husband as he smokes weed, partners with a pimp, and has all-night recording sessions in a whore house."[53]

The sum total of the representation of women, across racial and class lines, detract from the inspiring aspects that surface in the film. It would be difficult to argue otherwise, though the writer-director approaches the film from a different perspective. According to Craig Brewer, the initial idea for the story came from being solicited by "a black guy in a black Cadillac with a white girl in the back" while scouting locations in "a scruffy Memphis neighborhood."[54] From the director's perspective, the responses of studio executives to the proposed film reveal racism in the movie business as the more crucial problem. In an interview, Brewer recounts: "They [studio executives] had questions about a white boy from the South doing this movie….No one would've cared what color I was if I'd been doing a dumb urban crime movie where everyone's toting a 9-millimeter. But when you're doing a movie with real heart and soul, then they'd ask, 'How can you make a personal story with an African American in the lead?'"[55]

Hustle and Flow contains some memorable acting, especially by Terence Howard in the lead role, but at the same time, it remains a problematic piece with regard to its presentation of women and the black community. Its best achievement might be the effective rendering of hip-hop music, as the "raw music that resounds [in the film] is the sound of what the hip-hop world calls the Dirty South, home to rappers like Ludacris, Lil Jon, Three 6 Mafia and David Banner."[56] Ultimately, the film's theme of seeking a dream to become a professional rapper is difficult to sever from the gender and cultural messages visualized on the screen. The weight of racism and sexism burdens the film without a detailed treatment in the story, as it opts to emphasize hip hop as a redeeming force for its disgruntled protagonist.

In contrast to the southern setting and hip hop in that film, the urban streets of Queens, New York, provide the backdrop for *Get Rich or Die Tryin'*. By the time the film made the big screen at the end of 2005, 50 Cent, nee Curtis Jackson, had maneuvered himself a front-row position on the shelves of commercial rap. Having sold drugs from childhood, Jackson grew up as a thug, and sought rapping as a way out of hustling cocaine and crack. When Jackson began recording, he took the name "50 Cent" because it was "catchy" and because the "*real* 50 Cent was a stickup kid from Brooklyn who used to rob rappers. He had passed, but he was respected on the streets, so [Jackson] wanted to keep his name alive."[57] In his early music career, having signed with Jam Master Jay of Run-D.M.C., 50 Cent's efforts at fame were minimal until he later signed with Eminem and Dr. Dre.[58] The film seemed an inevitable step in the process of superstardom, and the movie's promotional and advertising campaigns caused the type of controversy that was sought. *The Wall Street Journal* charged that the movie's "marketing campaign… played up the violent nature of the movie," as the "official Web site employ[ed] smoking guns as design motifs."[59] In Los Angeles, community activists and local politicians pressured Paramount Pictures to remove from the black communities the billboards that showed a shirtless 50 Cent from the back, his arms stretched out in crucifix fashion, with a gun in his left hand and a microphone in his right. One activist condemned the image, stating, "these gangster rappers…are very poor role models and have a negative influence on children….This is the promotion of violence and, after Columbine and other incidents where young people use handguns to kill, it sends a very disturbing message that guns are very acceptable to be carried by young people."[60] Despite defending the marketing strategy, the studio took down "about a half-dozen billboard ads...near Los Angeles area schools."[61]

The film, "inspired" by the rapper's actual experiences, presents his "chaotic life from drug dealer to music superstar," assessed by one critic as "a motion picture with one foot in artistic expression and one in pulp fiction and commercialized violence. It wants the respect that goes with a quality production, but it can't resist providing the brutality and exploitation the film's core audience expects."[62] With his thug background, 50 Cent became an ideal subject for merging a hip-hop gangsta image with the urban action genre. The film certainly plays up that volatile mix, despite the rapper's proclamation that "there's no such thing as a 'gangsta rapper', because no one can be a *gangsta* and a *rapper* at the same time. A rapper can have gangsta ties, he can know gangstas, but he can't be a gangsta. He has to be an artist if he's going to be an artist."[63]

Get Rich or Die Tryin' is a contemporary gangster-crime story in the tradition of many Hollywood underworld action movies. After the film's opening with a robbery shootout and the attempted murder of Marcus (50 Cent), the bullet-riddled protagonist lies in the street, his voiceover reflecting that living in the streets was about looking for his unknown father. With an extended flashback, the young Marcus (Marc John Jeffries) eventually lives with his maternal grandparents, following the murder of his drug-selling mother. Creating rhymes to impress a neighborhood girl, the young Charlene (Rhyon Nicole Brown), Marcus grows into adolescence as a cocaine dealer himself. Under the tutelage of Majestic (Adewale Akinnuoye-Agbaje), an older gangsta, and Levar (Bill Duke), the black crime godfather, Marcus rises in street reputation and easy cash, until a prison stint encourages him to make rapping his main pursuit. Connecting romantically with the adult Charlene (Joy Bryant) and supported by a prison buddy, Bama (Terrence Howard), Marcus survives the thug life and finds his spotlight as a rapper.

Marcus gathers numerous lessons from the streets, from Majestic, and from the violent business of cocaine and later crack dealing. In his world, "respect is the most important thing in life" and the primary goals are "getting paid and get laid." With his crew of three—Antwan (Ashley Walters), Keryl (Omar Benson Miller), and Justice (Tory Kittles)—Marcus forms a mini-empire, often confronting, due to territorial proximity, members of a Colombian criminal family. In his daily volatile lifestyle, Marcus follows one of the rules laid down by Majestic: "Don't show no love. Love will get you killed....You only got respect." Indeed, one of his closest confidants, Justice, turns out to be the person who shoots him nine times in the early sequence, leaving Marcus for dead in the streets. However, Marcus does find love with Charlene, as she brings him serenity and eventually a son.

Going beyond its accomplishments as an action-gangster movie, *Get Rich or Die Tryin'* misfires in two problematic ways. First, Marcus's pursuit of rapping as an artist never really materializes; instead, Marcus pursues MC-ing merely as another money-making hustle. He mentions that "after Tupac, everybody wanted to be a rapper," but that appears to be the extent of his knowledge of hip hop. Unlike other films *8 Mile* and *Hustle and Flow* that show protagonists seeking to improve their skills as rappers, Marcus spends his time being a gangsta. He speaks lines into a tape recorder in a few scenes, but the process of writing and using language become most important while doing solitary time in prison and when finally in the studio. For an aspiring rapper, the creative component for Marcus doesn't ring true amid the obsession with being a gangsta. It could be argued that Marcus merely demonstrates the "get rich" motivation of many real-life performers, but romantically the film suggests that being shot nine times directly translates into writing and performing talents. The movie omits some pivotal scenes necessary to validate Marcus's on-stage rapping skills shown under the closing credits. Ultimately, the film presents rapping as another step in Marcus's thug career, as Bama shoots Majestic who is attempting to prevent Marcus from performing in his hood. Consequently, Marcus's turn on stage appears less about being a skilled MC than being the ultimate thug who defies Majestic. Throughout his development as a rapper, Marcus avoids any political or cultural themes in his rhymes, opting for self-serving lyrics that either extol his toughness or condemn rival rappers. The rapping in Marcus's world shares none of the activism and community consciousness inherent in much of hip hip.

The second defect that surfaces in the film revolves around the character of Charlene. As pre-adolescents, young Marcus writes his salacious rhymes to impress the young Charlene, which prompts her family to send her away from the 'hood. When Marcus next sees her as an adult, she returns for a visit, claiming to be a dancer. In striking ways, Marcus and Charlene have grown up to be different people. In particular, she appears to be intelligent, articulate, and ambitious; however, unexplainably, she surrenders all of those traits to begin a romantic relationship with Marcus. Marcus confesses to her, "I'm a gangsta and a rapper," a claim confirmed by his crew. On her part, she doesn't acknowledge her credentials or reveal her ambitions. Did she have any dance auditions planned? Was she involved with someone else? If she were just visiting, didn't she have her own life elsewhere? Charlene's motivation to enter Marcus's criminal world remains enigmatic, as she becomes the conventional gangsta's girlfriend seen in other such movies. As the story presses forward, Charlene's characterization grows thinner, and she forgets her own life to merely be a support system for Marcus. Again, there seems to be some pivotal scenes missing from the story, as Charlene diminishes into a one-dimensional character.

If scenes existed to explain the two weaknesses above, there were probably deleted to add more scenes of violence, which the film consistently places before the viewer. Many of the violent images are brutal and sadistic, too often presenting black-on-black, or black-on-brown killings. In reality, such pointless killings do indeed exist, but a skilled filmmaker can underscore that reality without the excess included in this movie.

The director in this case is certainly a skilled filmmaker: Jim Sheridan, the 56-year-old director who made the IRA drama *In the Name of the Father* (1993) and the Irish immigrant drama *In America* (2002). Commenting on his star, 50 Cent, Sheridan states: "He's a Muhammad Ali kind of character....a lot of people are afraid of his persona, this tough guy. But I grew up around people like that, so it was very easy for me to be in his world."[64] Apparently, while making the film, the racial and generational differences blurred as an understanding of underclass issues connected Sheridan and 50 Cent. Perhaps, if the class issues and systemic politics had received more of a pronounced focus in the story, the film might have overcome the flaws that cripple its effectiveness.

With the three cycle of films emphasized in this chapter, the first decade of the new century suggests that hip-hop themes, music, and cultural shaping will continue to be visualized. Over several decades from the 1980s to the present, the power and the presence of hip hop has not only identified a younger generation, but has affected the manner in which America perceives itself. Although utilized to drive the engine of marketing, the cultural ramifications of hip hop are discernible upon close inspection. The commercial absorption of hip hop is evident, and the manner in which American cinema has accelerated that process is undeniable. However, in the new millennium, hip hop appears to be moving toward possible political goals, as the older hip-hop generation perceive themselves as more than consumers, but also activists. If those political hip-hop voices gain power and national visibility, it will be interesting to watch the ways in which hip-hop politics receive future depiction in American cinema.

4

Tupac Shakur: Hip-Hop Icon
and Screen Idol

Detectives Rodriguez (Tupac Shakur) and Divinci (Jim Belushi) attempt to balance their ethics and friendship in the action drama *Gang Related* (1997). Courtesy of the Academy of Motion Picture Arts and Sciences.

By the end of 2005, many hip-hop heads would debate which MC was the most outstanding in style, content, and image. Depending upon age, geographical location, and stylistic preference, hip hoppers might fall into various cohorts that extol the particular attributes possessed by their favorite rapper. However, most would agree that the one rapper who has excelled in life and death, in both the music and movie fields, was Tupac Shakur.

With more than six books and numerous articles written about him, as well as documentaries exploring his life, Tupac accomplished a singular feat of dominating gangster rap while appearing in mainstream Hollywood films.

He was a giant during his short music career, but his reputation advanced to legendary status following his movie appearances and murder. Although Tupac was not the first rapper to portray a major role in a Hollywood film, he nonetheless garnered critical attention with convincing roles that suggested his potential significance as an actor. With a perceptible screen presence and an ability to display a dramatic range, Tupac was developing a parallel career on the big screen at the time of his death.

While making the film *Poetic Justice* (1993), Tupac stated: "My main objective is to show that the young black male has an unlimited amount of talent, and if given the chance we can do anything or surpass any mark of excellence that has been set. That's what I want to show—not only through my music. I enjoy acting because it's a way to ease some of the pain that's in everyday life….as soon as I saw a way for me to get into it where it could be a career move, I began studying and applied myself 100 percent."[1]

With an acting resume that listed six films, Tupac used his hip-hop image as a transition into the Hollywood roles. Indeed, he was a performer with a complicated image that both endeared him to his younger fans and incensed the old school crowd. By the time he did his first feature, *Juice*, in 1992, he was already a gangsta rap star. As scholar Eithne Quinn notes, "Tupac's star image was a complex combination of hard and soft, street and decent. Indeed, his gripping image of toughness and tenderness… commanded an increasing amount of popular and press attention."[2] As a pop culture icon, he demonstrated the contradictions often associated with someone in the spotlight who attempts to be many things to many people at the same time. Possibly, the pressures of that very public image encouraged him to display extremes in behavior and decision making. Living out much of his young life advocating for the urban voiceless while pursuing individual goals had to impose a weighty conflict in his private moments.

Much has been written about Tupac's background beginning with his birth in New York City in June 1971, which followed closely on the acquittal of his mother, Afeni Shakur, on conspiracy charges to set explosions in New York department stores. One of the controversial "New York 21," a Black Panther political force, Afeni named her son Tupac Amaru, meaning "shining serpent," which complemented the last name Shakur, meaning "thankful to God."[3] After she endured a phase of drug dependency, an abusive boyfriend, and poor living conditions in Baltimore, Afeni moved Tupac to Marin City, California, in 1988, for his high school years.[4] The new environment encouraged Tupac to continue to write poetry and the "underground hip hop scene in Northern California rekindled Tupac's rap ambitions. He auditioned for Shock-G, the leader of Digital Underground, and was hired as a roadie and a dancer."[5] He appeared on Digital underground's 1990 album, *This Is an EP Release*, "uttering the inauspicious line, 'Now I clown around when I hang around with the underground.'"[6]

Then, in the 1991 dark comedy movie, *Nothing but Trouble*, the group appeared as themselves performing their hit, "Same Song." In the movie, the group is caught in a speed trap and forced to set up instruments and play in traffic court before Dan Akroyd's maniacal judge who accompanies the band on an organ. With his first solo album *2Pacalypse Now* (1991), he was emerging during the era of gangsta rap, finding his niche in what scholar S. Craig Watkins called the "shrewdly calculated outlaw image."[7]

Subsequently, between 1991 and 1994, Tupac's journey toward popular culture icon took some peculiar twists, and as author Kevin Powell suggests, Tupac appeared "incapable of separating art from life."[8] His personal life became successive waves of moral and legal complications. In Oakland, in 1991, Tupac was arrested on jaywalking, filing a police brutality claim. In 1992, a Texas woman filed a lawsuit blaming Tupac's lyrics for influencing the man who shot her police officer husband; a public brawl in Marin City resulted in a 6-year-old onlooker being shot; and a fight on the studio lot where he arrived to tape the television show *In Living Color* led to his arrest. In 1993, he engaged in a fight with the filmmakers Albert and Allen Hughes, which resulted in a civil suit; in Atlanta he was arrested for shooting two off-duty white policemen; and in New York, he was accused of rape.[9] With these incidents, and others, Tupac personified the beastly black male associated by many with gangsta rap. In particular, with the rape charges, even Tupac recognized the manner in which reality and fiction had become inextricably bound to many who questioned the social, moral, and cultural value of gangsta rap. When interviewed after the closing arguments of that trial, which ended in 1994, Tupac stated: "It's not about my trial no more. It's just about loud rap music, tattoo-having thugs. It's about, you know, some nightmare that these people [are] having...there's no evidence...no nothing."[10]

During the early 1990s, Tupac, for many, embodied the thug image of the nihilistic, felonious male who sought life only through selfish excesses. Complicating that public image was Tupac's self-proclamation of being a thug, though for him, he defined the term in his own manner. As hip-hop scholar Dan Hodge emphasizes: "Tupac's image of a THUG had nothing to do with the traditional definition: a criminal, hoodlum, and thief. Tupac's definition dealt with the marginalized and downtrodden—the person who doesn't have anything and still rises and moves forward."[11]

Ironically, it was the popular perception of a thug that not only promoted Tupac's music and stage performances, but provided access to his first important movie role as Bishop in *Juice* (1992). The transition to the big screen was not incubated in a void; instead Tupac had prepared for such a possibility earlier in his life. When he and his mother lived in New York, Tupac received an early introduction to acting when he was twelve by participating "in the 127th Street Ensemble, a theater group in Harlem," and later when relocated to Baltimore, he gained acceptance into the Baltimore School for the Arts, where he studied acting and dance.[12] In an interview, director Ernest Dickerson of *Juice* praised Tupac's personality and talent: "Tupac was a brilliant artist....I knew him as an extremely sensitive, gentle soul who was very nurturing....He didn't even audition for the role of Bishop, he just came in and blew everyone away."[13]

In his role as Bishop, Tupac excavated experiences and memories from years of interacting on the streets of New York, Baltimore, and Marin City. That urban street style was no small matter in the early 1990s, for Hollywood studios were cashing in on the previous urban films *Boyz N the Hood* (1991) and *New Jack City* (1991), both of which received criticism for linking screen violence and violence in theaters. When Paramount Studios began its promotion of *Juice*, the Los Angeles Police Department became a major source of attacks regarding the "irresponsible" and "exploitative" print advertisements and movie trailer campaigns.[14] In particular, a poster showing the four main characters highlighted Tupac's Bishop in the foreground "brandishing a handgun"; eventually, Paramount conceded to the pressures and airbrushed the gun out on a replacement poster.[15]

Set in Harlem, *Juice* follows four adolescent black males who, in their typical day, hoodwink their parents, ditch school, and take to the streets to hang together and pursue their brand of fun. Typical hip-hop generationers in their clothing, shoes, music, and language, the four friends discuss and argue about numerous topics, including the acquisition of "juice" or power and street respect. Although from the same streets and seeking peer acceptance, the four young men are distinctly different from one another in personality and interests. Raheem (Khalil Kain), the leader, is the thoughtful peacekeeper who is dealing with being a teenaged dad in conflict with his baby's mother. Steel (Jermaine Hopkins), the chubby follower, is a good-natured lover of food. Q (Omar Epps), the ambitious and talented one, struggles to become a famous hip-hop deejay. Bishop, the angry and volatile one, seeks "juice" as a way of forming an identity.

The prankish behavior of avoiding police officers, hanging at the pool hall, and playing at the video arcade escalates into more felonious activity.

Specifically, Bishop constantly urges the group to make their reputations on the street through criminal activity. When Raheem obtains a handgun, the group's collective conscience leads them to rob the corner grocer. Using Q's competition at a deejay battle as a cover, the four rob the store, but Bishop, without provocation, shoots the owner. Soon afterwards, Bishop shoots and kills Raheem, and then Steel who survives his wounds. Effectively framing Q for the three shootings, Bishop assumes a position of power he desires, as the last act of the film focuses upon the confrontation between Bishop and Q.

Tupac as Bishop delivers a credible and effective performance in this ensemble piece. Although Bishop's problematic home life remains vague, the character's stormy and explosive nature is tangible. As one critic observes, "Tupac depicts Bishop's coldness as a helplessness he finally submits to, even if it means embracing depravity."[16] Excited by an old gangster image in a James Cagney movie viewed on television, Bishop worships the self-destructive hoodlum who chooses a violent lifestyle and death. Bishop declares to his friends that a man should "go out in a blaze if you got to. Otherwise, you ain't shit."

This narrow code that justifies a life of crime becomes the cornerstone of Bishop's transition across moral lines. He embodies deceit at the Raheem's funeral, comforting family members and referring to the friend he murdered as "brother." He deliberately lures Steel to a locale to murder him, and thinking himself successful, begins to destroy Q's life. His allegiance and bond to his childhood friends disappear beneath his obsession with being a street hoodlum. He relishes the fear and control he evokes, receiving an instant high which commands his addictive actions.

Tupac seizes the mercurial anger of Bishop and gives it a palpable texture in his performance. Actually, Bishop emerges as such an extremely strong character that he dominates scenes with other characters, and with more detailed rendering, Bishop could have gone beyond the functional bad guy opposing Q's good-guy persona.

Surprisingly, the movie's soundtrack does not include a performance by Tupac. However, the movie gains its hip-hop flavor with sounds of Eric B. and Rakim doing the title song, "Juice," along with tunes by Naughty By Nature, Cypress Hill, Big Daddy Kane, and Too Short.

While still in a quagmire of legal conflicts, Tupac managed to complete his second film, *Poetic Justice* (1993), which was directed by John Singleton. Of choosing Tupac for the film, Singleton confessed: "When I saw *Juice*, Tupac's performance jumped out at me like a tiger....When I decided to cast him opposite Janet Jackson in Poetic Justice, it was not without some problems. During the filming…Pac both rebelled and accepted my attitude toward him as director/advisor."[17]

Poetic Justice (1993) gave Tupac the featured male role as Lucky, the postal worker who struggles to be a responsible father and who attempts to shape a romantic relationship with Janet Jackson's titular character, Justice. Living in Los Angeles, Justice (Janet Jackson) is presented as a sensitive young woman who uses her passion for poetry to survive the chaos of her inner-city life: her boyfriend's murder, loneliness, streets filled with sirens, helicopters and searchlights, and decayed landscapes. Delivering mail to the salon where Justice works as a cosmetologist, Lucky tries to "mack" a resistant and indifferent Justice. However, the two are brought together during a trip to Oakland where Justice will attend a hair and fashion show and Lucky will visit his cousin.

Lucky and Justice are the typical water-and-oil combination that often serves romantic story telling, and their situation is exacerbated by the couple joining them on the road trip: Iesha (Regina King) and Chicago (Joe Torry). The road trip explodes into a yell fest of profanity and insults as the four characters all at some point collide with one another. Early on, Lucky says to Justice: "You one of them angry bitches." In a quick breath, Justice responds: "I'm a black woman. I deserve respect. If I'm a bitch, then your mama's a bitch."

After many additional insults over as many miles, a stop at a black family reunion and then a black cultural fair begins to allow for a softening of attitudes and a sharing of life experiences. Amid leisurely walks and glimpses of the ocean, Lucky explains to Justice: "Don't really get a chance to think in the city. This is the only time I can unwind."

This observation provides a small insight into Lucky, a young man still living at home with his mother, working a job he dislikes, and attempting to provide a positive environment for his daughter. The toxicity of the pre-school daughter's environment surfaces early in the film, as Lucky comes by to see her, only to find another man who has a son by the same mother, a freebase pipe, and then the mother herself in the bedroom with another lover. Lucky's rage ignites as he and the second father beat and stomp the lover in a violent, wild moment of frustration.

Tupac gives Lucky various emotional levels in a performance that steals the movie. Although the character Justice has more screen time, Tupac's Lucky radiates as the character bearing his emotions and thoughts while trying to maintain his code of masculinity, though that code is askewed when it pertains to women. Lucky is believable, engaging both sympathy and criticism for his extreme actions and confused thinking. In taking on the role,

Tupac stated: "My main objective is to show that the young black male has an unlimited amount of talent, and if given the chance we can do anything or surpass any mark of excellence that has been set....I enjoy acting because it's a way to ease some of the pain of everyday life."[18]

Tupac's grasp of Lucky's emotional dilemma grows stronger as the film develops. Near the end, Lucky arrives to Oakland only to find his cousin shot and dead. Having worked on hip-hop tunes with his cousin over a period of time, Lucky viewed music as his avenue out of his dull existence, and when the cousin dies, the realization of his thwarted dreams reduces Lucky to tears in an effective scene where Tupac sits amid the recording equipment. Then, in a final sequence, Lucky arrives at the salon with his daughter and apologizes to Justice for verbally attacking her. Acknowledging his mistake, Lucky demonstrates his understanding of his own weaknesses and fears, and his maturity signals the possibilities of a future relationship with Justice.

The film's soundtrack included Tupac's tune, "Definition of a Thug Nigga," as well as selections by TLC, Babyface, Naughty By Nature, the Dogg Pound, Janet Jackson, Stevie Wonder, and Usher. However, the critical responses to the film were not as inspiring as the soundtrack. Voices from mainstream presses underscored the movie's acerbic dialogue between the men and women, continually comparing the film's weakness to the accomplishments of *Boyz N the Hood*. Specifically, in regards to gender representation, scholar Gwendolyn D. Pough concluded: "Singleton's script, written from a Black man's perspective, did not really place Justice's story at the center, even if she was the title character....I would add that in addition to the booty and breast shots, we get a decentering of the woman's story.... Justice is pushed back into the margins of the film, and Lucky takes over the center."[19]

By the time the film *Above the Rim* made its way to the big screen in March 1994, Tupac's real life continued its descent. He became embroiled in a public war of words with a number of rappers, but he carried on a major "beef" with two perceived nemeses: The Notorious B.I.G. or Biggy Smalls and Sean "Puffy" Combs. In November of that year, Tupac was shot five times while exiting a New York recording studio, and he later blamed Smalls and Combs for the attack, though they both denied the charges.[20] Then, by December 1994, as the rape trial ended, Tupac was "sentenced to one and a half to four and a half years in prison for two counts of sexual abuse" while being acquitted on charges of sodomy and weapons possessions.[21]

In the context of what had occurred in his life, the movie *Above the Rim* emerged as a mere distraction with its tame and simple story. However, when assessed on its own merits, the movie features some engaging dynamics: a young, talented cast; positive themes; exciting basketball sequences; and a contemporary soundtrack. Unfortunately, Tupac plays the thinly drawn supporting character of Birdie, a neighborhood gangsta, whose hunger for money and power eclipses all other concerns. Once again, to Tupac's credit, he still commands attention when he is on the screen. He is alluring because his small frame and smooth handsome features contradict his rough vocals, dynamic physical gestures, and penetrating stares. One critic concluded: "Shakur, a notorious rapper with a violent off-screen life, brings enough natural menace to the shallowly drawn Birdie to dominate the screen."[22] Birdie's threatening figure serves the purpose in the movie of contrasting to the basic goodness of two other black male characters: Kyle (Duane Martin) and Shep (Leon).

Kyle, a high school senior, possesses basketball skills that have a college scout taking notes from the stands in an opening sequence. At the same time, Kyle displays an arrogant, selfish attitude that distances his fellow team players. The only person who eradicates that attitude is Kyle's mother, Malika (Tonya Pinkins), a single parent who works as a nurse. However, Birdie manipulates Kyle's self-importance through a glimpse of Birdie's gangsta life—the respect at a local club; access to beautiful women; free-flowing cash; and gambling. Seeing Kyle's value, Birdie invites him to play on his outdoor team for money.

Birdie has the materialistic party life that young men like Kyle crave, and Birdie sees his opportunity to exploit the very talent that Kyle believes will eventually get him into the NBA. Birdie's street authority becomes undermined with the return of Shep, a former basketball legend from the hood who never recovered from the guilt over the accidental death of his friend. Shep's quiet strength remains mysterious until the movie's second act with the revelation that Birdie and Shep are brothers.

Birdie resents the return of Shep, as it brings back the earlier years of emotional and financial pain; the days of "no lights, no electricity, no food." In an early confrontation, Birdie berates his brother saying, "we believed you were coming back to save us....but I handled shit...split level duplex, big screen tv, marble floors. Mom didn't have to work. She seen more money in her life than she ever had. I bought that...." Birdie's proud profession of exploiting the streets to survive the streets demonstrates his belief that nothing and no one is more important than money. With that perspective, Birdie rejects Shep as his brother; kills a local homeless man who insulted him; publicly humiliates Bugaloo (Marlon Wayans), a wannabe player who befriends Kyle; and threatens Kyle when he refuses to join his crew. At the final outdoor competition, Birdie even orders his henchman to shoot Kyle when the defeat is imminent.

Birdie is spiritually and emotionally lost, and he maneuvers to place others beneath his power as "the man" on the streets. His only ambition is to own others, and pursue a life of crime and quick rewards. Wearing a scar on his face, Birdie, like the cinematic *Scarface*, Tony Montoya, is destined to meet a violent death. This message comes through when Bugaloo at the end of the film shoots and kills Birdie in the club, a final act of revenge for Birdie's scathing criticisms.

This morality tale is framed in a soundtrack that includes three songs by Tupac, as well as tunes performed by Warren G, Snoop Dogg, Nate Dogg, and SWV. The movie itself received mixed reactions from mainstream critics, and many journalists had difficulty separating Tupac's screen gangsta from the image he lived in his personal life.

Even as Tupac gained a wider audience of fans for his music, concert appearances, and films, he could not escape the ongoing barrage of those who viewed him as the worst kind of role model for hip hoppers. As author Kevin Powell concludes: "Tupac Shakur represented…all that is right and all that is wrong with how we define manhood in America, and specifically what is so wickedly off-kilter about Black manhood….when the behaviors…are reduced to guns and violence, drugs and alcohol, the objectification and hatred of women, excessive materialism and extreme individualism."[23]

In the fall of 1995, Tupac's prison time ended when "Death Row Records CEO Suge Knight post[ed] $1.4 million bond to release Tupac, who immediately…sign[ed] with Death Row."[24] For many hip-hop journalists and scholars, Tupac's prison experience and the subsequent movement into the Death Row camp represented the tragic transformation in his professional and personal life. Although the sales for his first post-prison CD, *All Eyez on Me*, released in February 1996 "went straight to number one on the Billboard Chart,"[25] the thug behavior, beefs with other rappers, and confrontational attitude escalated. In the months preceding his death in September 1996, Tupac's immersion into the thug life was inescapable and racing toward a violent end.

In 1996, Tupac appeared in the movie *Bullet* that was not aggressively promoted for the big screen. In fact, most sources indicate that this producer-actor Mickey Rourke vehicle was a straight-to-video movie. Playing the character Tank in *Bullet*, Tupac was once again called upon to play the neighborhood villain, "a drug dealer decked out in black eye patch and a white ermine beret who rides around in his limo sipping on champagne and succulent fruit."[26] The film never found much of an audience on video, and few critics stepped forward to claim it as a work of interest, let alone a work of art. One Los Angeles publication gave it a dismissal that seemed to be standard: "this just-released cliché-a-thon…it's pretty much as horrible and incoherent as you'd expect any direct-to-video movie to be."[27]

The two films released theatrically after his death deserve closer attention, as they serve as examples of the progression of Tupac's acting and his ever-increasing screen presence. The first movie, *Gridlock'd* (1997), a quirky comedy with strong social commentary, offers Tupac's best screen performance, as "[h]e played his part with an appealing mix of presence, confidence, and humor."[28] Tupac, portraying the character Spoon, reached an important step in his evolution as an actor, earning a role that had complexity and displaying emotional contours that went beyond the mere physical style. As one critic noted: "Spoon is pensive, often rueful, even sweet beneath a tattooed exterior. It's acting, of course, but it also feels like revelation, a side of himself that the rapper must have hidden from fans who wanted him seething with anger and violence."[29]

Set in Detroit, Spoon lives and works with two fellow musicians, Stretch (Tim Roth) and Cookie (Thandie Newton). Sharing music, a love for performance, and drugs, Spoon and Stretch are jolted into reflection when Cookie overdoses while celebrating New Year's Eve. Making a pact, the two decide to de-tox and transition into a drug-free life. Unfortunately, their commitment to change meets up with a bureaucratic system of regulations, paperwork, and schedules, and the more they attempt to enter rehabilitation, the more they confront obstacles that impede their efforts. In their pursuit of doing the right thing, the untidiness of their lives reveals itself, as Spoon and Stretch hustle street cons during the day, socialize with drug dealers, and evade a local gangster. Although not gun-toting gangsters themselves, Spoon and Stretch become magnets to danger, bad luck, and suspicious police officers. Through their common love of music and common lifestyle, these interracial friends seal a bond of trust. The two are "[i]n some ways…mirror images of one another—talented, profane, selfish, addicted, and fearful of responsibility.…For the two, race exists, but race …doesn't matter in their daily negotiating of the volatile, oppressive environment."[30] Cookie survives, and Spoon and Stretch finally gain admission to a hospital via the emergency room, as they enter bleeding and exhausted. Stretch bleeds from an earlier gunshot wound, while Spoon orchestrates his bloody wound by having Stretch stab him several times with a pen knife.

Tupac remains captivating throughout the entire film, his presentation of Spoon moving from anxiety, to caring for a friend, to frustration at the social services system. This is one of those performances where an actor inhabits a character that possesses both lovable qualities and flaws. Spoon resonates beyond the stereotypical hoodlums portrayed in earlier movies by Tupac, allowing for a natural sensitivity that evokes sympathy. Spoon is a character a viewer cares about—a character to cheer on, to laugh at, and to learn from. In one scene in the social services office, Spoon relates the first time he tried cocaine at sixteen, reflecting on lost innocence and a future addiction. Caught in the memory of years of drug abuse, he says: "Life is funny, ain't it. Somehow I don't think this was my parents' dream for me." In that regretful moment, Tupac's Spoon both acknowledges and accepts the responsibility for the tragedy his life has become.

The film adds a hip-hop flavor to its bureaucratic criticisms through its soundtrack. Tupac contributes two tracks, including "Wanted Dead or Alive" and "Never Had a Friend Like Me," with other Death Row artists, such as Snoop Dogg and Nate Dogg, rounding out the list.

In addition to *Gridlock'd* and marketed as Tupac's final film, *Gang Related* (1997) is a cop drama containing some moments of suspense that remain underdeveloped due to the many shifts and twists in the plot. Under the opening credits, the urban night images glisten alluringly as Tupac raps the uptempo "Lost Souls." Interestingly, despite earlier movie roles as a gangsta, in this film, Tupac portrays Rodriguez, a police detective who along with his partner Frank DiVinci (James Belushi) are "posing as drug dealers" to "transact exchanges with real dealers, then mow them down on the spot in what are made to look like gang-related drive-by shootings."[31]

Rodriguez and DiVinci are crooked cops, though they rationalize that their actions help to remove criminals from the streets. Though this line of thinking eases their collective conscience, the fact of Rodriguez's gambling debts and DiVinci's supporting of his stripper-mistress, Cynthia (Lela Rochon), and future plans for retirement in Hawaii remain visible reasons that motivate both men to seize money. However, their hustle snags on the killing of an undercover DEA agent posing as a drug buyer, and when the two are assigned to investigate the case. To avoid exposure, Rodriguez and DiVinci frame a homeless man for the agent's murder, only to find out later that the homeless person has connection to one of the city's wealthiest families. As their lives unravel, DiVinci eventually kills Cynthia, and Rodriguez, to plead a deal, wears a wire to trap DiVinci. Although Rodriguez survives DiVinci's anger when he discovers the wire, the former cannot escape his fate, as the loan shark and his enforcer wait for and kill Rodriguez when he reaches home.

Tupac's performance as Rodriguez is polished and confident. As one reviewer observes, "Shakur is terrific as Rodriguez, torn by conscience, self-preservation and utter incredulity as how screwy straights become."[32] Here, playing a character in a suit and tie and with a steady middle-class job, the rapper loses his hip-hop appearance, presenting a character who is well mannered, clean cut, and articulate on the outside. On the inside, Rodriguez has reached an emotional bottom, hating his life and his desperate situation of owing over $27,000. By the time he sinks to the unforgivable act of turning on his partner, Tupac reflects the hopelessness in his voice, facial expressions, and the plodding, heavy gait that shows neither rhythm nor life.

The effort to capture hip-hop rhythms comes through the movie's soundtrack. In addition to the rap over the opening credits, Tupac contributes two additional tunes: "Life's So Hard" and "Staring Through My Rear View." The notable lists of other hip-hop performers include Ice Cube, Nate Dogg, and Kurupt.

During the 1990s, Tupac received recognition for his screen roles that he portrayed with an impressive range of skills. More so than any other hip-hop artist by the mid-1990s, he had demonstrated he possessed the talent and the popularity to please critics and fans. However, anchored in the music world, Tupac's movie achievements were consistently assessed in conjunction with his endeavors as a rapper.

After his death, critics and fans could only speculate about his future potential as an artist, entertainer, and possible cultural leader. As hip-hop scholar Dan White Hodge argues: "Tupac's legacy is his political, social, geographical, religious, and socio-economic outlook on the game, life, the 'hood, Black families, White families, Brown families, and the U.S. as a whole. Because on all these subjects, his rise from nothing, his lack of a high school diploma, but his ability to speak on issues as if he had a Ph.D., Tupac earned the title 'The Ghetto Prophet/Saint.'"[33]

Typically, when someone gains Tupac's popularity, talents, and controversiality, any consensus about his legacy and value will be difficult to gather. The best that remains is to weigh his contributions and contradictions from the broadest perspective possible. As Tupac stated himself, "some people say I was a thug and a gangsta. Other people remember me as a poet and a leader. But I'm saying to you, measure a man by his actions fully. Through his whole life. From the beginning to the end."[34]

5

Queen Latifah: From MC
to Mainstream Diva

In *Set It Off* (1996), economic desperation prompts the criminal behavior of four friends—Stony (Jada Pinkett, left), Tisean (Kimberly Elise), Cleo (Queen Latifah, 3rd from left), and Frankie (Vivica A. Fox).

When pondering which hip-hop MC has attained the most positive reception by mainstream America, Queen Latifah tops the list. Her crossover into the larger commercial arena was achieved without gimmicks or hype. Instead, she built her reputation within the hip-hop world as an influential rapper, parlaying that fame into television popularity, film roles, advertisement appearances, industry voiceovers, and a management and production company. In addition, with her autobiography, she has sought to inspire women.

Carving out a place among MCs was no easy task for a woman, as rap was male dominated by the early 1980s. Considering those early days of rap, a music journalist notes: "one reason women artists sold such measley numbers is that the core rap audience was (and is) male, and men simply weren't ready to hear women capping the tough posture that defined rap."[1] However, the presence of women in hip hop was evident at the beginning as they participated as MCs, in break dancing troupes, and as graffiti artists.[2] As scholar Gwendolyn O. Pough emphasizes: "Hip-Hop may be uniquely testosterone-filled space, but to say that women have not contributed significantly to its development is false. Women have always been a part of Hip-Hop culture and a significant part of rap music."[3] For all of its progressive efforts at fusing ethnic, cultural, and class differences, hip hop culture reflected the gender discrimination residing in the larger society.

Those existing gender biases in society sparked the rebirth of the feminist movement by the late 1960s and early 1970s in America. During that time, Dana Owens was born on March 17, 1970, placing her into that defining hip-hop age group, of "those born between 1965 and 1984."[4] It was eight years later that the "Muslim-sounding" name Latifah was chosen by Dana to keep in step with the trends in the African American community; the name, meaning "delicate, sensitive, kind," was crowned ten years later with the term, "Queen," for a professional moniker.[5] In reflecting on her professional name, the performer admitted that "[b]ecoming Queen Latifah and a rapper didn't just happen overnight. Subconsciously, I had been preparing for it most of my life. The music lessons. The talent shows. All those night clubs, the endless hours [rehearsing in a friend's] basement, the practicing, the reading, prepared me...."[6]

By her own admission, Queen Latifah enjoyed a positive and healthy childhood, with both loving parents—Lancelot and Rita Owens—spending time with her and her brother, Junior, nicknamed Winki. It was the parents' separation when she was eight that created a wrinkle in her world, as she and her brother lived with her mother, a dedicated single parent who later became an art teacher. Her mother moved the three of them to the Hyatt Court Projects in Newark, New Jersey, before eventually securing an apartment in East Orange, New Jersey, where Latifah gained popularity singing in talent contests and participating in athletics during high school.[7]

Although Queen Latifah viewed her early interest in rap as a "hobby," thinking of a future as a "newscaster" or "lawyer,"[8] she called "herself the Princess of the Posse because she was the only girl in the Flava Unit," a group of aspiring male rappers.[9] With the Flava Unit, she made consistent trips to clubs to hear and experience hip hop, eventually recording her own song which led, at age 19, to a contract with Tommy Boy Records, releasing the album *All Hail the Queen* in 1989.[10] In weighing her love of hip hop, Queen Latifah admits: "I was attracted to the sound and the content and freedom of rap....To me, it's like a free art form. It flows. It's smooth. It can be anything you want it to be."[11]

By the time Queen Latifah released her first album, women rappers had been stirring the interest in hip-hop music since the early 1980s. In a personal roll call, scholar Gwendolyn O. Pough identifies the significant women during and since that decade: "I remember seeing and hearing US Girls in the movie *Beat Street* (1984)....More female MCs, such as the Mercedes Ladies...followed them, as would female rap groups such as Finesse and Sequence, Salt-N-Pepa, BWP, JJFad, and Sweet Tee and Jazzy Joyce; solo artists such as Dimples Dee, Sparky D, Roxanne Shante, the Real Roxanne, Pebbles Poo, Sweet Tee, MC Lyte, YoYo, Boss, and Da Brat; and the Trinas, Eves, Li'l Kims, Foxy Browns, and Missy Elliots that grace the airwaves today."[12] Of note, in 1985 women rappers stirred up interest in hip hop through the "infamous dis (or response) records craze,"[13] where women MCs recorded songs that boldly blasted back at male rappers delivering negative remarks about women. Emerging as the "Mistress of the Dis" was "14-year-old Roxanne Shante" who influenced the trend,[14] and who helped to keep the spotlight on women MCs.

However, when Queen Latifah moved into the spotlight, she brought her own distinctive image and lyrical content. Shifting between hip-hop baggies and African-influenced apparel, Queen Latifah pursued a more culturally rich look that both connected to hip hop and honored her heritage. Emphasizing the sense of regality in her name and her first album's title, Queen Latifah displayed a presence that avoided overt sexuality while provoking thought about issues pertinent to women. Cultural critic Tricia Rose concludes that "Latifah's second release from her debut album is a landmark example of centralizing a strong black female public voice....without referring to or attacking black men, 'Ladies First' is a powerful rewriting of the contributions of black female political activists."[15] Scholar Cheryl Keyes believes that "Queen Latifah's maternal demeanor, posture, and full figure contribute to the perception of her as a queen mother...her stature and grounded perspective cause fans to view her as a maternal figure or as a person to revere or, at times, fear....reflected most vividly through her lyrics, which, at times, address political-economic issues facing Black women and the Black community as a whole."[16] Both Rose and Keyes acknowledge a public persona that was linked to the personal attitudes expressed by the rapper. Queen Latifah's ascendancy in rap as the political voice for women, as a cultural voice for the black community, and as a mature voice of the younger generation shaped a formidable and unique hip-hop image.

Queen Latifah's arrival in 1989 becomes more impressive when placed in context with the hardcore rap and gangsta rap styles capturing the attention of fans and critics alike. Along with the anger and socially biting messages came the elements of misogyny that further polarized those camps that supported and condemned rap's content. Queen Latifah's philosophy about such lyrics and messages remained principled: "In the 1990s, Gangsta Rap was ruling at the time–bitch this, ho that…we have the power to set men straight. If you don't feel like a bitch, no one can call you that and make it stick. I realized it was more important to start building women up and making them look inside themselves than to bash the fellas. It starts with your own self-esteem, and too many women don't have any."[17] Although she continually avoided the "feminist" label of a feminist, Queen Latifah, nonetheless, articulated the progressive approach to women's self-worth and the critical assessment of the American system often expressed by feminists. Hip-Hop feminist Joan Morgan appears to expand upon Queen Latifah's comments when she writes: "Yeah, sistas are hurt when we hear brothers calling us bitches and hos. But the real crime isn't the name-calling, it's their failure to love us….but recognize: Any man who doesn't love himself is incapable of loving us….It's extremely telling that men who can only see us as 'bitches' and 'hos' refer to themselves only as 'niggas.'"[18]

In 1991, Queen Latifah second album, *Nature of a Sista*, was released, containing the tune "Fly Girl," which "reminded men to respect women."[19] In that same year, Spike Lee's *Jungle Fever* invaded theaters, giving audiences the chance to see Queen Latifah in her first big screen role. In the film, Queen Latifah appears in one restaurant scene that serves as a metaphor for the larger black community and its response to the interracial romance between the protagonist, Flipper (Wesley Snipes) and Angie (Annabelle Sciorra). Working as the waitress, LaShawn, in a soul food establishment, she confronts the couple with attitude and resentment. Avoiding them at first, she finally steps to the table, taking their orders with deliberate comments and opinions. When Flipper angrily inquires as to whether she has a problem, she responds with the same level of agitation. "Yes, I do have a problem, to be honest…fake, tired brothers like you coming in here. That's so typical. I can't even believe you brought her stringy-hair ass up in here…why don't you parade your white meat around somewhere else." The tension intensifies, as Flipper calls for the manager, with LaShawn refusing to recount her comments.

In the movie, director Spike Lee "takes a politically charged situation and stirs it up with color, music, and irony."[20] Queen Latifah's LaShawn works effectively as a note of public prejudice in this "provocative, quintessentially Spike symphony."[21] However, the film's symphony of story lines ultimately unravels the coherence of the movie, as major and minor characters, such as LaShawn, become less important than the director's style. In her brief appearance, Queen Latifah gives a one-dimensional minor character a memorable presence. The attitude of resentment flows from her body language through the intonation in her voice, and she personifies to close-minded position of prejudice—rigid, brazen, and confrontational.

In that same year, Queen Latifah won a supporting role that allowed her to have a more prominent character in the plot and theme. Playing Zora in *House Party 2* (1991), Queen Latifah displays her potential, as she convincingly swings from assertive to empathetic, from anger to sweetness. With the film's story set on a college campus, when Zora first speaks, she emerges as a feminist barrier coming between Kid (Christopher Reid) and his love, Sidney (Tisha Campbell). Assertive and intolerant of players exploiting sisters, Zora reads Kid as just another male attempting to use a woman for his own sexual pleasure.

However, in a subsequent scene, at a student rally, Zora, in African clothing, surfaces as a student activist and leader. Giving a speech at the rally, Zora tells the crowd: "If we allow the administration to cut back on ethnic studies, we will be letting them deny the contributions of all of our cultures that made this country great. Knowledge is power!" From there, Zora breaks into a rap about education, ride, and knowledge.

Queen Latifah portrays Zora with vigor as an intelligent, independent, and aware college student whose priority is clearly on getting educated. As Sidney's roommate and friend, Zora consistently reminds her of the purpose of college and the need to avoid being a boy-toy. Zora tells Sidney: "I like men, but I don't need one to define me. And any woman who wants to define herself, by herself, and for herself, just has to free herself of all that tired, lame male bullshit." Zora has little tolerance for the male games she observes, and she remains committed to helping Sidney to find her self-esteem.

Queen Latifah is the ideal choice for Zora. Her physical appearance places her as a young, but bright university student, and she strikes a balance in delivering speeches about men and cultural speeches at rallies. Her entire demeanor is authentic, and her performance avoids being forced or over-the-top in intensity. As one critic remarks: "Among the film's more notable performers...[Queen Latifah] is fine as an actress and sensational as a singer."[22] The movie takes advantage of her MC talents and recognizable image and, therefore, "keeping it real" for the hip-hop audience, while making her hip-hop edginess palatable to mainstream viewers.

In *Juice* (1992), which is explored in chapter 2, Queen Latifah is all hip hop as Ruffhouse MC, the take-charge organizer of the deejay competition for which the main character Q (Omar Epps) auditions. She certainly fits the role as the experienced ear who listens to Q's tape, nodding her head to his creative mastery of the turntable. Later, during the segment showing the competition, Ruffhouse MC dictates the terms of the contest and controls the audience. As expected Queen Latifah knows her character and understands the hip-hop setting, as the veneer of authenticity layers the role. However, the screen time is short and fleeting in this film that commits itself to focusing upon black male protagonists.

Queen Latifah's next big screen character remains vague and remote, as *My Life* (1993) gave her the role which only had her on the screen for three short scenes. Playing Theresa, a home care nurse, she moves into the home of cancer victim Bob Jones (Michael Keaton) and his wife, Gail (Nicole Kidman). Spirited but compassionate, Theresa enters toward the end of the film to assist Bob's efforts to adjust to the inevitable. Throughout the earlier portion of the film, Bob prepares himself and his unborn child for his death by videotaping his opinions about cooking, cars, family, and shaving, among numerous things, hoping the tapes will allow his child to know him as a father. Theresa arrives as Bob's physical condition is disintegrating, as he becomes bedridden and incapable of feeding and caring for himself. Without being fully developed, Theresa is merely a perfunctory character who, having seen many such patients, tells Gail that going quickly at the end is perhaps the better way for Bob.

One critic gave the film a lukewarm review, noting the "sturdy supporting appearances by Michael Constantine as Bob's loving father and Queen Latifah as the hospice nurse who provides great comfort in the film's later scenes."[23] Of interest, this role works to take Queen Latifah a step further away from her hip-hop persona and closer to an actress identity. Her character, Theresa, is a professional who apparently knows nothing of hip hop as Queen Latifah never rhymes, nods her head, or speaks in an argot that connects her to rapping or hip hop. The hip-hop link in *Juice* fails to emerge in this film, as she steps deeper into a screen image that sheds any semblance of her MC background. In the movie's press kit, her bio notes Queen Latifah as a "popular rap artist" who "co-stars in Fox's new show 'Living Single.'"[24] Here, the word "popular" signifies much more than the words "rap artist," as the goal seems to be to establish her as a crossover talent at this juncture.

In 1993, her crossover talent resonated in her third album, *Black Reign*, which was dedicated to her late brother. The song selections on the album presaged the varied musical expressions that would widen her audience in the coming years. As one biographer notes, "in addition to rapping, Latifah did more traditional singing than on her first two albums. The range of her songs, from rap to rhythm and blues to jazz, established her as [a] singer of immense talent. *Black Reign*...became the first gold record by a solo rap artist."[25] Adding to the accolades, she also earned three Grammy Award nominations, as well as a Grammy Award for the Best Solo Rap performance.[26] With the commendations in the music world and the casting of her in a dramatic part in *My Life*, Queen Latifah was selected to be a co-star in Fox television's sit-com, *Living Single*. The show enjoyed a five-year run and created an even larger audience and fan base for the rising star.

By the middle of the decade, *Set It Off* (1996) gave Queen Latifah a role in an ensemble cast of four black actresses that allows her to demonstrate her acting abilities. The film received critical praise for remaining "aware of the economic struggles of its characters....The movie is not about overt racism, but about the buried realities of an economic system that expects these women to lead lives the system does not allow them to afford."[27] Playing Cleo, a woman struggling to survive the economic pressures of contemporary Los Angeles, Queen Latifah personifies a character who is hip hop in attitude and a committed friend to the end.

As Cleo, Stony (Jada Pinkett-Smith), Frankie (Vivica A. Fox), and Tisean (Kimberly Elise) work their low-paying cleaning service jobs, they share desires and the disappointments of their lives in the hood. After bearing the strains of the legal and social service systems, the four friends decide to rob a bank to obtain quick and necessary cash. After an initial robbery that goes without problems, the four find that their financial needs pull them into repeating subsequent and more dangerous robberies.

Of the four, Cleo is the wild, daring, and aggressive one who openly lives her life as a lesbian with her girlfriend, Ursula (Samantha MacLachlan). With her hair in tight corn rows; with her attire of pants, boots, and loose-fitting tops; and with a forty-ounce bottle in hand, Cleo's femininity disappears beneath a tough exterior and no-nonsense approach to situations. Cleo's passion for automobiles is surpassed only by her love of stealing cars, and she drives as confidently as she wields a gun doing the bank robberies.

Cleo is the "muscle" and the protector of the group of friends, and she knows and accepts who she is. When Stony muses about using the stolen money to leave and make a new life elsewhere, Cleo states: "Stony, you can go to suburbia and start a new life, but we ain't nothing but hood rats. Now, I can live with that...this is where I belong."

Queen Latifah pulls off a winning portrayal of Cleo as she embodies the complicated shapes of the character. Taking on physical movements and a street-wise attitude, she makes Cleo a believable woman. Shifting from moments of braggadocio to seconds of sensitivity when teased by her friends, Queen Latifah transforms Cleo into a character about whom viewers care.

Being pursued by police cars and helicopters following a robbery that goes awry, Cleo forces her friends from their car to escape on foot. Then, "as she's cornered with no way out, the poignant melody from the song 'Up against the Wind' comes over the visuals," Cleo is caught in a "shootout where dozens of cops return fire and she dies. In that juxtaposition of music and visuals, Cleo is raised to heroic status, forcing the viewers to connect to Cleo's final sacrifice."[28]

The role elevated Queen Latifah's dimensions as a serious actress with numerous critics, and the honors were justifiable. One reviewer notes about the film: "The great performance, however, is Latifah's. It's as if she's chewed up Ice Cube and Marlon Brando and incorporated them into her fabulously macho female body and voice....When Latifah's on screen, 'Set It Off' soars to a higher level. In a film that's about women's courage in defying the law, her performance is the most courageous act of all."[29]

The character Cleo avoids breaking into rhymes as an aspect of her personality, but Queen Latifah's tune, "Name Callin'," was included on the movie's soundtrack.[30] Writing about the part of Cleo, Queen Latifah indicates, "I am more proud of that performance than any other.[31] However, along with the praise of the acting, the insinuations about the star's sexual orientation snaked into the media once more. In her 1999 autobiography, *Ladies First*, Queen Latifah writes about her various male lovers during adolescence and into adulthood. Additionally, in 1995, her romance with NFL player Ferris Collons gained visible attention.[32]

Regardless of those referenced heterosexual relationships, the rumors of lesbianism continued. Addressing the issue, she writes: "There's still all kinds of speculation about my sexuality, and quite frankly, I'm getting a little tired of it....It seems that in this country, sexuality is never a nonissue [sic]....A woman can not be strong, outspoken, competent at running her own business, handle herself physically, play a very convincing role in a movie, know what she wants—and go for it—without being gay? Come on."[33]

For those not concerned with tabloid issues, the breakout performance in *Set It Off*, raised expectations for Queen Latifah's next big screen role. In a disappointing way, *Hoodlum* (1997) took Queen Latifah back to a minor role as she played Sulie, the friend of two of the significant black women characters in the film: Francine (Vanessa L. Williams) and Pigfoot Mary (Loretta Devine).

Francine is the Garveyite who captures the heart of black gangster Bumpy Johnson (Laurence Fishburne) in 1930s Harlem, while Pigfoot Mary has an ongoing affair with Bumpy's cousin and partner in crime, Illinois Gordon (Chi McBride). When Sulie first appears, she's walking the streets with Pigfoot Mary discussing strategies for playing the numbers. Holding her child's hand, Sulie receives canned good for Francine with the announcement that the food is "for your kids." Although Sulie's husband or partner doesn't appear, Sulie manages time away from the children in a later sequence to join Francine and Pigfoot Mary for an evening at the Bamville Club, a jazz and dance night spot. When Bumpy draws near to the table, Sulie encourages Francine to get to know, saying,"you can't judge a book with just one look." Queen Latifah has little more to do than to be the supportive and good-natured friend. The part of Sulie remains on the periphery, and no demands are made on Queen Latifah to demonstrate acting or singing skills.

Her following screen appearance is equally disappointing, as she's anchored to a character who never has a chance to be three dimensional. In *Sphere* (1998), Queen Latifah gets little to do as the movie revolves around its big name stars—Dustin Hoffman, Sharon Stone, and Samuel L. Jackson. A psychological science-fiction film, one source notes that "this low-voltage…tale falls between several different stools in the sci-fi arena: alien spaceship mystery, theological/philosophical inquiry, monster thriller, time travel adventure, close-quarters pressure cooker, and voyage into the mind."[34] The movie attempts to grab the audience via tensions among characters, emotional upheavals, and enigmatic unexplained phenomena. Unfortunately, these elements fail to be a winning combination, and the film's exploration of human primal fears becomes an exercise in tediousness.

When an alien spacecraft is found 1,000 feet beneath the sea, several scientists are brought to the sight. Exploring the alien craft, the scientists discover a giant, glowing ball-shaped structure hovering silently. As the three main characters—portrayed by Hoffman, Stone, and Jackson—enter the sphere, they are bestowed with the power to physically manifest their inner thoughts. However, in each case, they merely manifest their inner fears which, in the form of killer jellyfish, giant squids, and explosions, kill off the other crew members.

Queen Latifah plays Fletcher, a communications specialist who monitors the numerous screens and sonar images on the Habitat, the home vessel located beneath the sea. Basically, Fletcher appears in a number of head-and-shoulder shots as she busily fingers control knobs and computerized equipment. With little dialogue or scenes devoted to her character, Fletcher serves as one of those supporting characters who is likable but doomed. In fact, Fletcher receives the most screen time in the scene in which she dies.

Going outside of the Habitat to carry information to a nearby submarine, Fletcher in her diving suit tranquilly makes her way along the ocean floor. She begins to see numerous jellyfish, which she greets with, "it's beautiful down here. So tranquil." Before the words are completed, Fletcher is surrounded by a thick school of jellyfish which tear into her suit and crack her face mask, as she drowns amid dozens of lethal stings. Unable to be helped by the rest of the crew members who are inside, Fletcher's screams fill the speakers of the Habitat, as she becomes the first crew person to succumb.

Queen Latifah's appearance in *Sphere* doesn't require her to extend herself as an actress, and her hip-hop identity never emerges as an aspect within the film. It is one of those safe roles where she can gain experience and credit in a major feature with marquee actors, and the role signaled the manner in which Queen Latifah was edging toward a mainstream movie career, leaving the MC world in a salient manner.

Perhaps, the fleeting appearances in *Hoodlum* and *Sphere* connected to the busy off-screen activities: the production of her fourth album, *Order in the Court*, released in 1998; the writing of her autobiography; and the ongoing business of her Flavor Unit Entertainment company in representing musical acts. If so, the year still resulted in the release of *Living Out Loud* (1998), the movie that offered her the best role since *Set It Off*.

In *Living Out Loud*, Queen Latifah portrays Liz Bailey, a lounge singer at Jasper's Club, performing popular standards, such as "Lush Life," "Going Out of My Head," and "Darling, Be Mine." Eventually, Liz moves from the stage to become a close friend to the film's major characters.

The story follows Judith Nelson (Holly Hunter) who, enduring a divorce after sixteen years of marriage, examines her life and the mistakes made. Honestly dealing with her choice to remain with her cardiologist husband for sixteen years because it was a safe, predictable life, Judith now attempts to shape a new life where much is unknown. At the same time, working as the doorman and elevator operator, Pat (Danny DeVito) is attempting to recover from his divorce after twenty years of marriage and seeking to find a new direction in his life. Judith and Pat form a friendship where they share their personal experiences and questions about the future. For Pat, he longs for the friendship to develop into an intimate relationship, but Judith wants to avoid plunging back into the comfort zone of having a steady partner.

Prone to indulging in fantasies which are visualized for the audience, Judith often plays out life in a controlled manner in her head. However, in addition to her fantasies, another method for enduring her new single life is for Judith to frequent Jasper's, a night club where she can both lose her anxieties in Liz's performances. In Judith's fantasy, she meets Liz personally and opens up about her cheating husband. Liz understands her turmoil, revealing her own problems with an ex, stating: "One day he tells me it's my fault that he saw other women. So, I picked up a knife and told him it was his fault that I was stabbing him. I did a little jail time, but it was worth it." For Judith, her fantasy shapes Liz as tough and bold with a take-charge attitude about life. There exists a bit of a stereotyping as Judith's affluent, secluded background leads to racial generalizations.

However, later when the two women finally do meet one another, Judith discovers that Liz possesses the same questions and desires for love. In essence, the two women are similar in that respect, as Liz sings to endure and Judith fantasizes to endure the emotional upheavals in their lives. With her insight into the role, Queen Latifah comments on the two women characters: "The characters in this film wake up and begin to deal with reality. Whatever it is, they face it and learn how to live with it and become fulfilled human beings....Liz and Judith discover that they both are going through some of the same emotional highs and lows. Very quickly, there's a connection, and they become friends."[35]

Queen Latifah fleshes out the role of Liz with an ease that resonates on the screen. Her delivery of lines and physical nuances belong to the character, as she never comes off as self-conscious or stiff in her role. Although relegated to those segments when she serves as a support buddy for Judith, Liz's personality never disappears in order to enhance Judith's presence. Liz is clearly drawn, and Queen Latifah presents her as a woman who is assured yet still making mistakes when it comes to men. One critic delivered a well-deserved accolade: "Queen Latifah—big and sultry and wry—is an amazing screen presence, and her commanding way around a standard like 'lush life' will startle those who know her only as a rapper. You want more of her story than the movie gives you."[36]

At this phase in her transition to develop a screen image, Queen Latifah reaches back into her childhood and grabs the early love for jazz and r&b, as well as the talent contests and roles in school musicals. For mainstream ears, it becomes a revelation. One review of the movie took extensive time to acknowledge her: "Queen Latifah, sumptuously outfitted as Judith's favorite bosom-heaving cabaret singer and stealing every scene she's in. The sometimes rap star transforms herself sensationally to play a glamorous nightclub performer who helps to change Judith's life, delivering sultry musical numbers along the way....She becomes the film's most attention-getting figure."[37]

Portraying the lounge singer becomes noteworthy at this stage in her career, as many seeing the film only knew of her rapper label. However, as Liz, Queen Latifah demonstrates her vocal skills in performing songs which belong to an older generation. The role, therefore, serves as an announcement that she is an accomplished vocalist and that she is reaching out for an audience beyond hip hop. Dressed in colorful evening gowns from one segment to the next, there are no hip-hop accoutrements to this character. Liz is urban and streetwise, but she is not from the 'hood.

Then, leading into one of the most expressionistic scenes, Liz gives Judith a "recreational drug" and takes her to the after-hours "Club Confessional," an all-women's disco. As the two enter and separate, Judith, affected by the drug, begins dancing, and all the women surrounding her move to the same choreography. Finally, Judith is drawn to a teenage girl seen in an earlier fantasy; this teenager, who is the younger version of Judith, dances with Judith as the fantasy and reality merge. In this section, Liz has functioned as the catalyst for helping Judith to reclaim that part of herself lost long ago as she entered adulthood trying to please others, particularly men.

If the character Liz was omitted from the film, the story would lose its coherence. The character functions "as a kind of Greek Chorus to Judith's uncertainties."[38] Queen Latifah's deft handling of the character signaled the level of acting possible in the future. Although the film never found a popular audience, critics recognized its achievements.

In 1999, with her autobiography in bookstores and guest appearances on television shows, Queen Latifah stepped into the position of talk show host of her own, *The Queen Latifah Show*. The program contained "live music and celebrity guests, combined with solution-oriented discussions of social issues,"[39] but the show premiered in September and was cancelled by the following May, 2000.[40] During the same period, the movie *The Bone Collector* (1999) made it into theaters, with Queen Latifah assuming another supporting part.

Receiving screen credit behind leading lady Angelina Jolie, Queen Latifah portrays a dedicated, stalwart assistant and friend who dies before the movie's end. As the character Thelma, she is the nurse-assistant-friend to the protagonist, Lincoln Rhyme (Denzel Washington), a brilliant criminologist whose paralysis anchors him to a bed. One source summarized the movie as "a cinematic game that might be called Urban Creep Show, New York Style, and its rules are comfortably predetermined."[41] Carefully ornamented with graphic scenes of murders, moody settings, and tense moments, the film delivers thrills and shock in a plot-driven story of a serial killer.

Queen Latifah's Thelma is a live-in caretaker who must attend to the basic and emotional needs of Rhyme. She washes him; prepares meals; checks his vitals, monitors his life-sustaining equipment; and coaches him through severe seizures that could attack his respiratory system. A professional companion, Thelma appears adept in the medical area, but she also displays compassion for Rhyme and his condition. In preparing for the part, Queen Latifah met with Christopher Reeve, confessing: "I definitely felt inspired. Christopher has a lot of love for what he does. He understands the situation, has hope, a positive attitude, and he's able to share that with other people in the same situation, and that's important."[42] Taking those observations to the role, she renders another professional but personable character who wins over the film's characters and the viewers.

As an interesting angle, the plot brings Amelia Donaghy (Jolie) into Rhyme's life, when she responds as a beat cop to a homicide scene. Impressed by Amelia's handling of the evidence and encouraged by his intuition, Rhyme manipulates Amelia into being his eyes and legs at the succeeding crime scenes which contain conspicuous items placed near the dead bodies. Reluctant at first, Amelia and Rhyme find a connection and develop an emotional closeness which promises—despite his paralysis—a romantic connection after the film ends.

Thelma serves as the mediator to the growing partnership between Rhyme and Amelia. Listening to every conversation that occurs in Rhyme's loft, Thelma's facial expressions and body gestures are often shown in cutaways that isolate her on camera. Thelma also functions as an interpreter of Rhyme's health. After watching him endure a seizure, Amelia feels helpless as Thelma takes charge. Thelma explains to her: "It's the seizures. Anyone can put him into a vegetative state. That's what he fears more than anything." Later in the movie, Thelma steps in and adds her perspectives to the investigation, as Rhyme and Amelia study evidence of large monitors mounted above his bed. Helping to solve the puzzle of the planted evidence, Thelma is intelligent and articulate.

At the same time, Thelma comes off as a feisty spirit who protects Rhyme and his work. When the inept and meddling Captain Cheney (Michael Rooker) demands to enter Rhyme's apartment to search for missing evidence, Thelma confronts the cop and his threats at the door, barring his entrance. Frustrated with her defiance, Cheney warns that her "smart mouth" may get her in trouble. Thelma responds: "Yeah, and it may bite your ass if you don't stop trying to aggravate my patient."

Queen Latifah excels at this kind of character at this point in her career. Physically imposing and effectively using her facial expressions and voice, she delivers another convincing performance as Thelma. She gives the character a credible nature; she can shift from the professional to the personal without any abruptness. There's a smooth authenticity and three-dimensional aspect imbued in this thinly written character. Queen Latifah makes the character larger than how it is written in the script; she's trustworthy, loyal, and morally decent, but always human. These qualities, therefore, make her stabbing death, by the serial killer who comes for Rhyme, even more distressful. Thelma dies as she attempts to protect her patient and friend.

In her next movie, Queen Latifah's character is still another friend to the leading character, except on this occasion she is not fated to die before the end credits. In *Brown Sugar* (2002), which is discussed in chapter 3, Queen Latifah plays Francine, the close friend of the leading woman character Sidney (Sanaa Lathan). Francine is that close friend who places her friend's well-being before her own. Constantly reading Sidney's emotions, Francine attempts to tutor her friend on following her deepest desires rather than hiding them. When Sidney's love interest marries another woman, Francine is there to pick her up, pushing her to take the "opportunity" to meet a new man and a new relationship. At the same time, Francine is patient and grounded when the aspiring rapper, Chris (Mos Def), makes his romantic move on her. Rather than rushing toward a man who is obviously attracted to her, Francine keeps him at length. She tells Sidney that Chris is "kind of young," adding: "Ever notice how when a guy trying to mack to you, his voice either goes real high or real low." However, once Sidney's love life has been settled, Francine takes the charge and tells the bumbling Chris: "You want to go out with me."

As she has done in the past, Queen Latifah manages to deliver a robust performance to a thinly developed role. In a Hollywood trade paper, one critic expressed his positive evaluation for the supporting characters: "In the obligatory 'best friend' roles, Mos Def and Queen Latifah bring considerably more to the parts than what is usually the case. While Queen Latifah isn't given enough screen time, she takes full advantage of the minutes she has."[43] Francine is an endearing character, with some of the lovable qualities that Queen Latifah has given to earlier characters. However, in each scene in which she appears, the performer makes the character genuine, assuring the audience that something interesting exists beyond the limited screen time provided.

Interestingly, though Mos Def reflects his real-life MC skills through the character of Chris, performing his rhymes in a night club scene, Queen Latifah avoids any affiliation between her rapper image and the character, Francine. At this point in her screen career, she distanced her MC talent from her acting career, forcing the audience to assess her on the merit of her achievements on the screen.

She takes an even larger leap away from hip hop in the film *Chicago* (2002), the movie that reinvigorated the musical genre, receiving thirteen Academy Award nominations, including a Supporting Actress bid to Queen Latifah. Similar to her part in *Living Out Loud*, Queen Latifah's role as Matron Mama Morton in *Chicago* broke away from her foundation as a rapper. Looking more full-figured and older than in her previous films, she played a role which had been coveted by numerous established, white actresses.

With a lengthy history on screen and stage, the "tale of murder, manipulation and the hunger for adulation was born as a stage play, *The Brave Little Woman*, in 1926, and went first to screen as a silent (*Chicago* in 1927) and the Ginger Rogers swinger *Roxie Hart* (1942). It was the song and dance gurus John Kander, Fred Ebb and Bob Fosse who sexed it up as a stage musical by adding flashes of silky thigh, fishnets and high heels in 1975."[44] The story focuses upon an ambitious singer, Roxie Hart (Renee Zellweger), who murders her lying lover, and, after thrown in jail, plots with murderer-cabaret performer Velma Kelly (Catherine Zeta-Jones), opportunistic lawyer Billy Flynn (Richard Gere), and scheming jailer Matron Mama Morton (Queen Latifah) to gain both freedom and celebrity in 1920s Chicago. The film avoids the traditional musical structure of "people bursting into song," as it "cuts from plot events to a surrealistic stage setting when numbers begin. To enhance this metaphysical [technique], [the director] reworked the movie through the eyes of the lead character, Roxie Hart....It is in Roxie's glossy dreams that the songs unfurl."[45]

After protagonist Roxie enters Cook County jail, her dreamy perception envisions Mama's grand entrance with the introduction: "And now, ladies and gentlemen, the keeper of the keys, the countess of the clink, the mistress of murderers' row—Matron Mama Morton." From there, Queen Latifah sings the equivocal tune, "When You're Good to Mama." As the lyrics promise an exchange of Mama's influence for money and gifts, Queen Latifah, struts and shimmies in a flapper-style haircut and sequined gown with a thigh-high split. Her song, filled with sexual innuendoes, ensures that she can deliver results with the proper financial incentives. According to one critic, "Queen Latifah, as the prison matron, has a number dripping with the honey of the young Bessie Smith."[46]

The song translates directly into Mama's interaction with the residents of murderers' row, particularly with Roxie and Velma, the two killers who gain the greatest notoriety. Always an opportunist, Mama cajoles, manipulates, and demands payment from the two convicts for personal items obtained and contacts made with outside sources. The personification of the hard-knock life, Mama knows the game both inside and outside the jail. She rationalizes Roxie's murder of her lover by concluding: "I ain't never heard of a man getting killed when he didn't get just what was coming to him." Later, when explaining the frenzy and publicity surrounding Roxie's trial, Mama states: "In this town, murder's a form of entertainment." Mama functions as a confidante and business manager, but she always maintains her position of power, and though "race" is not written into the script, Mama's visible blackness adds an additional dynamic to the woman of power.

Queen Latifah assumes the role with the kind of bravado seen in actresses with more years and roles to their credit. Her singing was thoroughly impressive, and she doesn't shrink in the scenes shared with the marquee cast. Her rendition of Matron Mama Morton is solid and eye-catching, considering the fact that Zellweger and Zeta-Jones occupy most of the screen time. Queen Latifah explains: "As a kid, I watched all those old musicals....I played a lounge singer in 'Living Out Loud', but I'd never been in a movie musical. When I heard they were making 'Chicago' into a film and when I heard who was starring in it, I really wanted to try to earn the part. Initially, they didn't have me in mind for Matron Mama, but I kept going for it."[47] After three auditions,[48] she finally won the part and delivered an effective and memorable performance.

With the mainstream success of her turn in *Chicago*, Queen Latifah took a smart step in getting involved behind the camera as an Executive Producer on her next film. *Bringing Down the House* (2003), which is examined in chapter 3, allows her to gain the kind of power that Matron Mama Morton would have seized. As the character, Charlene Morton, in a contemporary setting, she is able to connect her screen persona with hip-hop sensibilities. Although she doesn't rap in the movie, the character's disposition, dialogue, and friends connote a connection to hip-hop culture.

With *Scary Movie 3* (2003), Queen Latifah appears to be simply putting in a pay day in one of the more lucrative and inane movie series. In her segment which parodies *The Matrix* films, she portrays Aunt Shaneequa, the oracle-like character with the power to see the future of the main character, Cindy (Anna Faris). Cindy shows Aunt Sheneequa a mysterious tape, a la the horror film *The Ring*, which contains ominous black-and-white images that promises to kill any viewer who watches. As Aunt Sheneequa advises Cindy, the former eventually engages in the hair-pulling fight with the ghostly image of woman on the tape; breaking dimensions, Aunt Sheneequa punches and battles the woman who emerges from the tape and the television.

Queen Latifah's turn in *Scary Movie 3* had little to do with acting, and perhaps little to do with humor, but the target teen audience, no doubt, connected to her as a hip-hop icon. As her appearance brought teenage chuckles, it also kept her visible among a younger audience who cheered her on in *Bringing Down the House*.

In 2004, Queen Latifah released her fifth album that celebrated her love of singing. Titled *The Dana Owens Album*, she performed a collection of songs honoring jazz and r&b stylings. Reclaiming her birth name in the title, the tunes—such as "Lush Life," "Mercy, Mercy, Me," and "California Dreamin'"—recalled her pre-MC passion for older forms of music. In that same year, she showed up in *Barbershop 2: Back in Business*, originating her role of Gina, the full-figured and fully opinionated hair stylist who surfaces again as the protagonist in *Beauty Shop* (2005).

When first seen in *Barbershop 2*, Gina works as one of the cosmetologist· at the beauty parlor adjacent to the title business. When Calvin (Ice Cube) enters with his baby, looking for the salon owner and the rent, it becomes clear that Gina and Calvin have a romantic past. Gina explains to all the women in the shop: "Somewhere along the line when Calvin and I stopped dating, he started thinking small. He opted for the happy meal instead of the super size." Calvin defends his breakup and subsequent marriage to a black woman with long hair derived from the "Cherokee in her family." Gina assures Calvin that his wife has "perm in her family," as the two enjoy the good-natured exchange.

Queen Latifah gives Gina a healthy mix of self-esteem and confidence. She always seems in control and comfortable with the person she is—her physical size, her profession, and her lifestyle. Surrounded by coterie of beautiful black women in the shop and at a later cookout, Gina never doubts her own self-worth, nor is she timid in standing her ground. This latter aspect emanates in the movie when the barbershop's resident philosopher-critic, Eddie (Cedric the Entertainer), berates Gina's niece at the shop's cookout.

When Gina defends the young girl, she and Eddie square off for verbal sparring as the revelers look on. At times biting and personal, the insults swirl around the grill with Gina refusing to yield to the cantankerous older man. After Gina insists that "the last woman [Eddie] slept with was battery-operated," she gives him a final warning: "Let me tell you something, you old Negro spiritual...the next time you snatch some food out of my niece's hand, I'm going to kick your ass, and then I'm going to burn your freedom papers." Queen Latifah's Gina enlivens the film and steals the scenes in which she appears. The character's strong personality is evident, providing little doubt that she will survive her surroundings and the people who inhabit the 'hood. Despite the inner-city Chicago environment of the film, Gina doesn't display any MC skills, nor does her manner of dress or vocabulary denote any specific hip-hop allegiance. Queen Latifah maintains her separation between her former rap image and her evolving actress status.

The next movie, *The Cookout* (2004), credits Queen Latifah as co-producer, which is a dubious accomplishment with this piece. The farcical vehicle—which includes the varied talents of Danny Glover, Megan Good, Frankie Faison, Jennifer Lewis, Farah Fawcett, and Ja Rule—is one of those ensemble movies that began with a promising idea but failed to have a script with a well-written story. The plot follows an outstanding black high school basketball player who goes as the first draft pick for the NBA. With his new wealth and fame, the player buys an expensive home in the exclusive Garden Ridge Estates, organizing a cookout for all of his family and friends from the 'hood.

Billed as a "special appearance," Queen Latifah portrays Mildred Smith, a security guard working the front gate at the elite estates. However, consistent with the other characters in the film, her part is a mere type that never resembles an effective comedic role. Surprisingly, with her experience, she plays the security guard with an over-the-top flair, complete with bugging eyes, pratfalls, loud talking, and assorted mugging. Queen Latifah's Mildred resembles an ethnic image from Hollywood's 1940s archives rather than a contemporary black woman of the twenty-first century. It is her most forgettable role in her most forgettable movie.

Without question, the best thing that the film *Taxi* (2004) has going for it is Queen Latifah. The film is "[b]ased on a French film comedy and its two sequels from writer-director Luc Besson. The original 'Taxi' became the highest-grossing film in French cinema,"[49] but the successful European film definitely lost a great deal in its translation. The filmmakers appear to be relying upon Queen Latifah to work magic when the film is in need of a miracle.

Queen Latifah plays Belle, a woman whose obsession with speed and extreme danger is visualized during the opening credits. With Beyonce and Jay-z's "Crazy" blasting over the opening credits, Belle races her bicycle along Manhattan streets, through Macy's department store, and down the subway platforms to beat a record at her Mercury Messenger Service job. The only woman amongst the gaggle of male messenger bikers, Belle explains her reason for being the fastest cyclist; sticking out her ample derriere, she says: "I just stay ahead of you because I know you enjoy the view."

Queen Latifah sells the character Belle in that opening segment and in the character's enthusiasm for earning her hack license to drive her customized new taxi. Even at the cost of missing a romantic dinner with her boyfriend, Jesse (Henry Simmons), Belle's focus stays on her love of driving. At the same time, she keeps a cultural edge on her job; picking up a white man who requests to be rushed to the airport, she confesses: "I don't usually stop for white guys. It's my way of balancing the universe."

Belle's life, and the movie, transforms when police Detective Washburn (Jimmy Fallon) commandeers her taxi to pursue bank robbers. Having lost his license and his respect due to his wreckless driving, Washburn pulls Belle into his scheme to regain his status by solving the case of the Manhattan bank robberies. As it turns out, the robbers, led by the high-cheekboned Vanessa (Victoria's Secret's model Giselle Bundchen), are actually supermodels disguised and dangerous with guns and fast cars.

Washburn's character never possesses the energy and charisma of Belle, and as Queen Latifah carries each scene, the former never really seems necessary in the film. At this juncture in her career, Queen Latifah knows how to utilize her facial expressions, her body movements, and her voice to make a scene work effectively. She's convincing as an aggressive, skillful, slightly maniacal driver, and at the same time, she can handle the tenderness of the romantic moments with the boyfriend. The film attempts to develop into a "buddy film," but Queen Latifah's Belle consistently outshines Fallon's Washburn. As one source comments: "Queen Latifah has been drafted...to represent some kind of irrepressible life force, supposedly unavailable to uptight white folks. Her bursting ethnicity somehow liberates Mr. Fallon's character, a timid young man who lives next door to his alcoholic mother."[50] The discrepancy between the two characters surfaces throughout the movie, but in a telling manner when Belle attempts to teach Washburn how to drive. Belle tells him: "If you ever going to learn how to drive, we have to play to your strengths...and thinking ain't one of them. So, just clear your mind."

With its contemporary, urban setting, the inclusion of hip-hop music would be an expected element, but oddly enough, the movie veers away from having a pronounced hip-hop flavor. The movie contains some pop music tunes such as Tone-Loc's "Wild Thing" and War's "Cisco Kid," but Queen Latifah doesn't rap or sing in the vehicle. Keeping true to the character, Belle insists: "Driving Nascar—that's my dream!" In Belle's world, there's no connection to hip hop, and the only song heard coming through the taxi's radio is Natalie Cole's "This Will Be."

The step away from performing rap on screen continued into Queen Latifah's first leading role. With *Beauty Shop* (2005) she received her most fully realized starring role as she reprised the part of Gina from *Barbershop 2: Back in Business*. Queen Latifah reads the character as a positive model, stating, "I like playing strong characters who are vulnerable at the same time….Gina reminds me a lot of my mother, a lot of myself."[51] With the story set in Atlanta, Gina, a single mother to adolescent daughter Vanessa (Paige Hurd), has moved from Chicago and struggles to build a clientele in the white salon owned and run by arrogant stylist, Jorge Christophe (Kevin Bacon). Although working with a white clientele, Gina is in demand, much to the annoyance of Jorge, and she makes friends with Lynn (Alicia Silverstone), a southern-belle hair stylist, and two affluent customers—Terri (Andy McDowell) and Joanne (Mena Suvari). Gina dispenses advice and philosophies on beauty, relationships, and dinner parties tactfully, reading the needs of her rich patrons.

After an inevitable conflict with Jorge, Gina quits and obtains a small business loan to open up her own salon in the black neighborhood. Gina's beauty salon grows in popularity, as it attracts an assortment of personalities, including the stylists who work for her: the aforementioned Lynn; Chenelle (Golden Brooks), a sharp-tongued diva; Ida (Sherri Shepherd), a pregnant, food junkie; and Ms. Josephine (Alfre Woodard), a talkative, poetry-quoting free spirit. Gina handles argumentative workers, needy clients, and annoying neighborhood regulars by balancing a firm attitude and a street-wise affection.

Full-bodied and confident, Queen Latifah plays Gina with a number of contours. The role requires both physical and verbal humor, as scenes vacillate between humor and emotional moments. Inside of the shop, the one-liners and biting comebacks flow in waves, and Gina, like a drum major, knows when to control the tempo and atmosphere. Sometimes with an ethnic affectation and at other times with a mainstream blandness, Gina participates in and steps back from the discussions. On one occasion when talking about language, she sets the rules as she joins the fun, stating: "You can be black, white, ghetto pass, no ghetto pass...ain't nobody saying the 'n' word up in this shop. And no bitches and ho's either...except for the ones who won't leave a tip."

The emotional rhythms for Gina revolve around two main relationships. First, she has a close connection to her daughter, who attends a private school specializing in music. Vanessa dreams of being a pianist place a financial strain of Gina, but, alluding to the desires of her dead husband, Gina commits her efforts to parenting. At the same time, Gina develops a romantic relationship with Joe (Djimon Hounsou), an electrician who lives in the apartment above the salon. She keeps Joe at a distance at first, slowly moving into an affectionate phase. Rather than viewing a relationship with him as the answer to her problems, Gina brings Joe into her life on her own terms.

At the beginning of the movie, Gina is shown lip-syncing to her CD player as she dresses for work. However, unlike *House Party 2* and *Chicago*, her character doesn't break into a rap or a vocal performance. In this venture, Queen Latifah seems intent upon selling herself to the audience as a leading actress. Winning over numerous critics with her performance, one source extols her performance in this manner: "For all the vivid, amusing characters that surround Gina, 'Beauty Shop' rightly belongs to Latifah, who comes into her own as a star and an actress in this film. She has an easy, earthy presence, and most important, she suggests that strength and vulnerability are not contradictory qualities in a character."[52] With the arrival of *Beauty Shop*, Queen Latifah displays the winning screen presence that was promised from her earlier roles, and she leaves little doubt about her magnetism to be a leading actress with an appeal to a mass audience.

By the end of 2005, Queen Latifah had charted an effective journey from an MC popularity to a successful box office star and film producer. As she shifted from MC stage performer, to television personality, to movie star, she brought with her a wider recognition of hip-hop culture and the talented youths who participate in its various expressions. Although some might view her transition as a rejection of hip hop, it seems that her career has served hip hop in a positive manner. First of all, she demonstrated the role of women in the creative evolution of rap music, bringing the spotlight to the intersection of gender, race, and class issues. Second, she affirmed the potential for hip hop and other musical forms to have compatibility, dispelling hip hop as an oppositional form to r&b, jazz, and mainstream tunes. Third, she made hip hop acceptable and digestible for those listeners outside of the musical form, demonstrating that hip hop was not a monolithic entity defined only by destructive aspects.

Similar to the growth and diversification displayed by Russell Simmons, Diddy, and Jay-Z, to name three, the success earned by Queen Latifah is also hip hop's success. Having contributed immensely to the rap legacy, she took her talents to different expressions and seized the opportunities coming her way. She continues to "keep it real" because she remains connected to attitudes and people who shaped her days as an MC. In her accomplishments, she still appears to embody the perspective she professed in her motivational autobiography: "I don't act the way society dictates that a woman 'should'. I am not dainty. I do not hold back my opinions. I don't stay behind a man…I'm not here to live by somebody else's standards. I'm defining what a woman is for myself."[53]

6

Beyond the Reel: Rappers, Bling, and Floss

One of the most popular and financially successful MCs to transition into acting, Will Smith takes on the title role in the biopic, *Ali* (2001). Courtesy of the Academy of Motion Picture Arts and Sciences.

As noted earlier, hip hop was not the first youth movement represented in American cinema. Consequently, the visibility of hip hop in films has not been surprising. However, unlike earlier marriages between youth culture and mainstream movies, Hollywood has seemingly absorbed hip hop as a part of a ravenous ingestion of the popular culture landscape. As one journalist remarks: "Hollywood films these days don't look fully cast without at least one rapper among the actors, and products from trainers to soft drinks are marketed by hip hop stars.[1] Like a cultural juggernaut, hip hop has conquered the visual and aural aspects on films, finding a representation even in films which are not explicitly exploring the hip-hop world. Through hip hop cultural elements and through the ascendancy of rappers in front of the camera, hip hop is pervasive and, by the end of 2005, a standard in American cinema.

The reciprocity between hip hop's mainstream acceptance and cinema's exploitation of trends has resulted in a distinctive example of "norming" a countercultural phenomenon. The co-optation of any formidable opposition to the status quo is the conventional strategy of preservation by the American system. Accordingly, when a movement contains expressions categorized as "entertainment," the absorption of that movement becomes an even easier task. Without oversimplifying hip-hop culture, two salient reasons expose the interesting suitability of hip hop's place within mainstream culture.

First, even in its most conspicuous political challenge to the American system, such as graffiti writing and politically conscious lyrics, hip hop, while generally positioning itself in opposition to the status quo, has searched for acceptance and visibility within the larger mass culture. As such, hip hop at its most radical dimensions never asserted itself as a strategy for an alternative governing system, targeting an overthrow of capitalism and American institutions. Instead, the objective was to remind America of its narrow vision and stilted mores, and to praise the manner in which hip-hop expressions revealed the weaknesses and biases of the American society. Even among the older, 30-something hip hoppers the goals are to transform America rather than replace the prevailing economic and political system. Consequently, these older, professional hip hoppers have formed coalitions among themselves through organizations such as the National Hip-Hop Political Convention or the League of Pissed Off League and have placed their activism into local and national efforts, believing the political potential of the hip-hop nation to improve the American system has yet to be reached.[2]

Second, as hip hop evolved into its second decade of existence in America, its popular and commercial forms always referenced and aspired to the "bling." A term "coined by New Orleans rap family Cash Money Millionaires back in the late 1990s," the word "describe[s] diamonds, jewelry and all forms of showy style."[3] As the term entered mainstream lexicon, it became synonymous with various forms of financial success, materialism, and conspicuous consumption. As indicated in one assessment, "hip-hop is perhaps the only art for that celebrates capitalism openly....Raps' unabashed materialism distinguishes it sharply from some of the dominant musical genres of the past century."[4] Even in its most aggressive form, such as early gangsta rap, the MCs themselves embraced commercialism as they used their rhymes to attack the same system that made them wealthy. Simply put, hip hop has never been a revolutionary movement, but one suited to effectively complement American commercial sensibilities. Hip hop's integration into Hollywood functions as an ideal match.

As indicated in earlier chapters, the visual dynamics of graffiti and break dancing added that novelty appeal for movie magic in the 1970s and early 1980s. Graffiti was the coded expression that signaled the edgy, dangerous, and decayed aspects of an environment, offering a rather paradoxical beauty of colors and lettering to a blighted city landscape. At the same time, break dancing in Hollywood films fostered another kind of awareness on the urban scene, where the primitive, spontaneous, and innovative movements were as unpredictable as the volatile poverty-stricken neighborhoods that harbored the dance forms. Both graffiti and break dancing offered movies a method for "keeping it real" to the streets, which in turned attracted a paying audience.

However, by the late 1980s, it became clear that hip hop music was an even more alluring element for movies. The hope was not in reviving the musical film, but to utilize the popular hip hop musical style to drive the pacing of the film and to send the viewer into a record store to purchase the soundtrack. As author Guthrie P. Ramsey Jr. notes, the "music in contemporary Hollywood films divide into two broad categories. The first is the composed score, which consists of music written specifically for that film. The second type is the compiled score: songs collected from the sources that often preexisted the film."[5] Hip-hop music emerged at an opportune time for Hollywood, as the soundtrack alone from film *Saturday Night Fever* (1977) gathered in millions of dollars. Hip-hop music began to be used as both the "source music" or diegetic music, which is the music having a origin "within the narrative world of the film" and as "dramatic scoring" or nondiegetic music, which is music coming from outside of the "narrative world of the film."[6]

Framing the film and the viewers' sensibilities with hip hop created two noteworthy results. First, the diegetic music "help[s] to situate [the audience] in the plot and to identify with its characters," prompting the viewer "to make external associations with the song in question and these reactions become part of the cultural transaction occurring between the film and the audience."[7] Second, the nondiegetic music "serves the narration by signaling emotional states, propelling dramatic action, depicting geographical location or time period, among other factors."[8] The compiled soundtrack from a film could contain both the diegetic and nondiegtic music, offering the consumer ownership of the songs and the reclamation of the film experience. Hip-hop soundtracks became a viable marketing tool, and as the hip hop's popularity increased, the primary strategy for producing a film project. Hollywood soon learned that a low budget hip-hop venture could be a minimal investment while making considerable box office and merchandising profits.

The musical element quickly opened the door for the MC to be attached to the film in cameo appearances or as a contributor to the soundtrack. Such visibility in either capacity enhanced the legitimacy of the movie for hip-hop fans. In *Breakin'* , Ice-T portrayed himself performing a rap tune on camera, while *Krush Groove* highlighted numerous hip-hop performers, including Run-D.M.C., The Fat Boys, and LL Cool J, to mention some. However, hip hop in American cinema wasn't an automatic hit with fans during the decade, as indicated when the "1988 feature film 'Disorderlies' bombed at the box office" and the "pointlessly violent 1988 film 'Tougher Than Leather' dealt a costly blow to the pioneering rap duo Run-DMC."[9]

However, by the 1990s, with the 'hood film cycle and the marketability of gangsta rap, MCs moved more into fictional roles rather than simply performing a tune in the movie. In his essay on the topic, British writer Allister Harry remarks: "It's easy to see why rappers have segued into film. After all what is rap but high drama….Rap music is extremely theatrical. It's about telling a story, which might be personal—but not necessarily so—and then playing out that drama….Rarely short of charisma, they're at home in the spotlight….Many rappers have developed their acting skills in increasingly cinematic rap videos….And once you get a rapper on a film set it's a lot easier to get them to record a track for the obligatory mega-selling soundtrack."[10] By 1991, Ice-T was featured in *New Jack City*, LLCool J appeared in *The Hard Way*, Queen Latifah stood out in *Jungle Fever*, and Ice Cube triumphed in *Boyz N the Hood*. These four rappers were not only famous MCs, but they all gained accolades for their acting abilities in their fictional roles. In box office measurements, two of the films gained impressive returns. *Boyz N the Hood* "grossed nearly $60 million on a production budget of between $6 and $8 million,"[11] while *New Jack City*, "[s]hot on a budget of $8.5 million…within weeks of its release, grossed…over $44 million."[12]

With the appearances of other rappers, such as Tupac Shakur, MC Lyte, Method Man, and Snoop Dogg by the late 1990s, American cinema had both mainstreamed hip hop and invited hip-hop performers to take on acting roles crucial to the movie's plot. Notably, not all critics celebrated this growing relationship of rap and cinema, as many found the movies of the 1990s to simply be promoting stereotypical images. The 'hood cycle brought out voices of dismay about the collective "thug" depiction of black males, and at the same time "[f]eminist critics such as Valerie Smith, Michele Wallace, bell hooks, Wahneema Lubiana, and Jacquie Jones…noted that the perceived 'realness' of the rapsploitation film genre is also real hostile to black women."[13] During the ongoing dialogue about the deleterious effects of hip-hop cinematic images in the 1990s, Hollywood continued to find that hip-hop cinema was the means to a lucrative end. As for the quality of images and acting of rappers, Hollywood responded by promoting the success of two of the most successful rappers turned actors: Will Smith and Mark Wahlberg.

In the case of Will Smith, Hollywood found the golden goose of MCs. Having gained a large fan base as half of the rap duo, DJ Jazzy Jeff and The Fresh Prince, Smith and his DJ partner, Jeff Townes, released their first album, *Rock the House*, in 1987, and their second platinum album, *He's the DJ and I'm the Rapper* in 1988, the latter winning the Grammy Award for Best Rap Performance.[14] Their third album, *And in This Corner* came out in 1989, and by that time the duo enjoyed a wide popularity due to their safe-and-clean image. At the same time, the two were critically targeted by the "rap purists who insisted that, unlike most rappers, the team was not addressing the legitimate problems of black youth."[15] Smith expanded his audience when he was offered the lead in the successful situation comedy, *The Fresh Prince of Bel-Air* in 1990, which aired for six years.[16] Taking advantage of his television visibility and celebrity status, Smith did several additional albums with DJ Jazzy Jeff, but by 1992, Smith had won a small role in his first film, *Where the Day Takes You*.

With the achievements in rap and the fame from television, Smith was the ideal hip-hop performer to place on the big screen. Between 1992 and 2005, Smith appeared in thirteen movies, and during the late 1990s, he became a megastar based upon the box office success of several films. In eleven weeks, *Independence Day* (1996) earned over $434 million worldwide; in twenty-five weeks, *Men in Black* (1997) pulled in over $549 million worldwide; and in twenty-one weeks, *Enemy of the State* (1998) made over $234 million.[17] With such a successful three-year box office returns, Smith was able to demand $20 million salary per movie, and by 2005, he remained a box office charm as his film *I, Robot* (2004) gained over $346 million worldwide in twenty-one weeks, and *Hitch* grossed over $356 million worldwide in thirteen weeks.[18]

To his credit, despite reigning as a box office "star," Smith delivered some strong performances in several films. His supporting role in his early film, *Six Degrees of Separation* (1993), brought him critical praise for his role as a gay con man. However, his best performance emerged in his title role as *Ali* (2001), which led to an Academy Award nomination as Best Actor in a leading role for Smith.

Portraying such an iconic and legendary figure as Muhammad Ali, Smith faced formidable challenges in assuming the role. Smith understood the career risks, changing himself physically and vocally for the one-and-a-half year commitment to a project about a well-known public figure. Reflecting on the role that covered the years 1964 to 1974, Smith stated: "I really had to go back and learn about Muhammad Ali. I knew he was a fighter, but I also knew that he stood up against the Vietnam War. Kids who are 21 today have no real sense of that era, no real sense of the Civil Rights Movement or the anti-Vietnam War Movement. Still, somehow they associate Ali with all that. But they have no idea of the depth of suffering that went into forming that association."[19] The immersion into the character resulted in a performance that captured ten years of the Ali's life when the boxer shouldered all kinds of difficult decisions, leading to both mistakes and achievements in his public and private lives. Smith went beyond mere mimicry of the Ali's professional image, as he embodied the man's complicated and often contradictory personality. In the role, Smith gives a layered portrait of a superior athlete, civil rights activist, religious believer, political spokesperson, entertainer, father, and husband. Smith's acting encompasses the "adulation, scorn, celebration, heartbreak, disgrace, defeat, and ultimate triumph" of Ali in a most convincing and memorable manner.[20]

In a parallel journey from hip hop to Hollywood, Mark Wahlberg, at age 13, joined his brother Donny as members of the 1984 pop group, New Kids on the Block, but Mark left the group after a few months, culminating his troubled adolescent years with confrontations with the law.[21] Resurrecting his music career, Mark formed his own hip-hop act as Marky Mark and the Funky Bunch,[22] completed two albums,[23] and enjoyed a "widespread popularity for a time, most notably with [the] 1992 hit single "Good Vibrations."[24] With brother Don helping with both albums, the group's appeal was more to younger teen fans, and rap critics dismissed Marky Mark's "mediocre lyrical skills, lame samples, and tired beats."[25]

In a 2003 interview, Mark Walberg commented on his transition from rap to the movies: "I was going through hard times as far as how I was being perceived in the music world, because of my association with my brother's group, and then I had had a troubled past, but [un]like most rappers…I didn't say anything about it….I was put in a position by my record company, and kind of pushed in a direction I didn't want to go….So, I said I was going to wait out my contract….Then I met [director] Penny Marshall….and she told me I could be good at [making movies]."[26] With Marshall's encouragement, his pop music fame, and his visibility as a model for "the 1992 Calvin Klein ad campaign,"[27] Wahlberg shifted into movies, completing sixteen films between 1992 and 2005.

Wahlberg moved from supporting roles, in films such as *Renaissance Man* (1994) and *The Basketball Diaries* (1995), to a leading man who attracted audiences across racial lines, in movies such as *The Corruptor* (1999) and *The Truth About Charlie* (2002). His appeal has always been steady in action films and dramas, and he hit a large pay-off as a star for 20th Century Fox when *Planet of the Apes* (2001), in twenty weeks, earned more than $357 million worldwide.[28] It would be difficult to argue that action films and heist movies require extraordinary acting skills, but Wahlberg demonstrated his scene-stealing abilities in dramatic films such as *Boogie Nights* (1997), *Three Kings* (1999), and *The Perfect Storm* (2000). Of the three vehicles, the first stands out for his portrayal of a character whose life undulates dynamically over a seven-year time span.

Boogie Nights explores the controversial business of pornography, as Wahlberg portrays the central figure of Eddie Adams who leaves his menial job to become the x-rated star, Dirk Diggler. The films "follows the extended family of filmmakers who struggle to redefine and revolutionize the adult entertainment industry," while it "also captures an authentic snapshot of Los Angeles during the late 1970s and early 1980s—an era when disco and drugs were in vogue."[29]

Among a cast of veteran and skilled actors, such as Burt Reynolds, Julianne Moore, William H. Macy, Don Cheadle, John C. Reilly, and Philip Seymour Hoffman, Wahlberg succeeds in playing an emotionally confused young man who seeks and finds purpose in a problematic world formed by dysfunctional people. Wahlberg's character finds a portion of what he seeks, but he falls victim to his addiction to self-delusion and drugs. Numerous critics hailed Wahlberg's portrayal, as one concluded that "this chunk of movie dynamite is detonated by Mark Wahlberg…who grabs a breakout role and runs with it….Moving from naïve kid to cynical burnout, Wahlberg gives a blazing performance."[30] In an ensemble cast of characters, Wahlberg creates a distinctive persona, as he "imbues Eddie with a boyish eagerness that draws the audience to his story….Eddie's rocket to stardom reads like a twisted variation on the American dream."[31] Wahlberg's performance in *Boogie Nights* confirmed his inclusion into the ranks of hip-hop talents who brought in a wide audience, and during the next ten years, he continued to deliver the roles and the audiences for big-budget Hollywood films.

Even with the undisputed crossover successes of Will Smith and Mark Wahlberg, by the first decade in the twenty-first century, the majority of rap performers making it to the screen took smaller steps to cinematic fame and fortune. With those steps came a collection of forgettable movies, lacking in both production values and quality execution. As one critic suggests, "[m]ore often, movies with rappers are garbage, like Snoop Dogg in last year's offensive 'Soul Plane' [2004], with scripts so abysmal they make the average booty-and-cars hip-hop video look like a cinematic masterpiece."[32] Due to such a quantity of hip-hop talent in films and such questionable quality, some people, both filmmakers and critics, continually decry the manner in which Hollywood appears to be transforming into hip-hop-wood.

Popular actor Samuel L. Jackson articulated his concerns in a 2002 interview, remarking: "It's not my job to lend credibility to so-and-so rapper who's just coming into the business...I know there's some young actor in New York or LA who's spent half his life learning how to act and sacrificing to learn his craft, but he isn't going to get his opportunity, because of some actor who's been created."[33] The reservations about the acting skills of rappers remain a source of discussion today and a point of criticism by many, but the Hollywood criteria for casting decisions primarily connects to perceived marketing potential. Although career actors prepare themselves for developing a craft and an art form, commercial cinema prepares itself for the next box office windfall.

The MCs have become accustomed to negative comments from various sources, but they also realize they have an access to Hollywood that offers possible riches. Rapper Ice Cube, who's been in at least twenty movies by 2005, comments, "[w]e have a built-in audience and the movies that we do don't cost a lot of money [so] there's a potential for a whole lot of return on it....[s]ince we've been successful on that, they've been looking for us to do more mainstream, big budget movies."[34] The recognition is augmented by famed record producer-actor Dr. Dre, who has appeared in nine movies: "I'm learning that the movies are a better business than records....[w]ith one bangin' movie, I could make more money than I've made in my entire career in the music business."[35] For MCs who have courted fame and fortune through the music world, movies simply serve as another pathway to success. For most, words such a "craft" and "art" contain little value when compared to the phrases "millions worldwide" and "three-picture deals." Hollywood's greed and the monetary ambitions of rappers make a compatible coupling. This merger confirms that "hip-hop movies are a perfect fit with today's synergistic studio economics. They're dirt-cheap to make, they come armed with a terrific marketing tool—a soundtrack from the star of the movie—and everything stays in the corporate family" since many studios also own record labels.[36]

This connection was underscored in another manner when the 2002 Academy Award for Best Original Song was given to Eminem for "Lose Yourself" from the film *8 Mile*, and the 2005 Oscar went to Three 6 Mafia for "It's Hard Out Here for a Pimp" from the movie *Hustle and Flow*. When interviewed about the award, Three 6 Mafia member Jordan "Juicy J" Houston stated: "This is big for hip-hop, but we're also representing for the black community, letting kids know you can do something positive and make it bigger than life."[37] The sentiments of the statement rang inspirationally, though the clashing debate about *Hustle and Flow*'s focus on a black pimp and three prostitutes swirled around the prestigious award. The movie and the award serve as a contemporary example of the ongoing, acrimonious discussions concerning hip hop's commercialism and its messages surfacing in the public arena.

In still another tributary from the hip-hop flow, by the late 1990s, a number of popular rappers and hip-hop producers had taken their market appeal into that celebrated American area labeled "entrepreneurship." Taking pride in their "floss," that is the "sheen of success,"[38] these male hip hoppers have stunned many with their conspicuous business success of forming empires of recording labels, movie contracts, clothing and accessories, restaurants, fragrances, alcohol products, and celebrity status. In a 1999 *Forbes* magazine article, three well-known hip-hop figures owned record labels whose market value alone was a small fortune: Sean "Diddy" Combs had Bad Boy Records valued at $250 million; Russell Simmons had Def Jam records valued at $240 million; and Master P had No Limit Records valued at $230 million.[39] When adding in their other business interests of these three hip-hop figures, the degree of financial success is staggering.

In a similar manner, Rapper Jay-Z single-handedly exemplifies the degree of fame and visibility desired by many hip-hop fans. By December 2005, Jay-Z retired as a rapper at age 36, with an estimated "worth more than $320 million."[40] He assumed the powerful position as President and CEO of Universal Music Group's Def Jam record label, with a salary "between $8 million and $10 million a year."[41] Additionally, he is President and part owner of Rock-A-Fella Records; a board member and part owner of the NBA's Brooklyn Nets; and the winner of four Grammy Awards.[42] In his diversification, Jay-Z was part owner of Rockawear fashions, "which ha[d] grossed more than $500 million since it was founded in 1999; a co-owner of two night clubs; a co-owner of Armdale Vodka; and the owner of "two multi-million-dollar Manhattan apartments."[43] Jay-Z's street hustler-to-riches biography personifies the myth of the American system, even as it inspires other wannabes to follow his path.

As an element of contemporary hip-hop entrepreneurship, name dropping and spotlighting particular brands function as a method of showing status and celebrating access to elite products. As one journalist noted in the late 1990s, "the hip hop nation, once so proudly self-sufficient, became obsessed with the finer things in life: designer clothing, imported champagne, Cuban cigars, luxury automobiles, and fine jewelry—all the things that prove how successful you are by American Dream standards."[44] The makers of the products, including fashion names such as "Gucci, Versace, Calvin Klein, Armani, Cerruti, [and] Louis Vuitton,"[45] benefit from the anointing of their goods by famous rappers, while the MCs enjoy the privilege of confirming the trendy acceptability of a product for the hip-hop fan base. In a 2002 article, one author delivered this observation: "Though rappers have long found inspiration in brand names like Adidas and Tanqueray, it's the prestige logos that sparkle the brightest. Stars like Busta [Rhymes], P. Diddy, Ja Rule and Jay-Z have expensive tastes and have made themselves powerful pitchmen, lifting the aspirations of youth culture for life's finer things while spiking sales of the Cadillac Escalade, Bentley, Cristal champagne, Burberry, Prada and Louis Vuitton....An artist deems a product cool, sales jump, the rapper looks like a tastemaker and brands... enjoy blinding exposure to a youthful crowd of new customers."[46] As the article goes on to insightfully point out, the risky aspect of such rapper endorsements rests in the trendy and transitory nature of pop culture that can quickly render a product passé.[47] The question of responsibility and moral codes remain outside the province of concern for rappers and corporations, as the label of "good business" condones any semblances of materialism and greed.

Rappers have learned effective ways to navigate the marketplace which for generations excluded people of color, particularly those who claimed origins in inner-city poverty. The resulting mixed messages plague hip hop as younger fans equate the street image of MCs with the inevitable acquisition of wealth and fame.

On its part, Hollywood contributes to the "bling' and "floss" by keeping the doors open for those hip-hop luminaries who can increase the box office revenues. Each studio competes for the widest mainstream audience by assembling what's perceived as the best marketable hip-hop performers and elements. To gain a better perspective on a Hollywood studio, a glimpse at a corporate structure and its business affiliations helps to clarify the intricate connections. For example, in November 2005, Paramount Studios released the action-drama, *Get Rich or Die Tryin'*, starring rapper 50 Cent. The film suffered a weak theatrical run, as it made only $35 million worldwide in eleven weeks.[48] However, Paramount Pictures Corporation survived that one disappointing movie, as it purchased Dreamworks SKG in early 2006 while owning Paramount Home Entertainment and Paramount Vantage, which produces and distributes independent films.[49] When pulling back farther and focusing on the conglomerate picture, Hoover's Incorporated, a research and business information company, offers the following profile. Paramount Pictures Corporation is owned by Viacom Incorporated which "split into two, separate publicly traded entities in late 2005."[50] One-half of the conglomerate is still named Viacom, owning Paramount Pictures, MTV, Nickelodeon, Comedy Central, Black Entertainment Television (BET), and the Famous Music publishing firm.[51] The other half, named the CBS Corporation, owns CBS Network, UPN Network, Showtime, King World Productions, CBS Radio (180 stations), the CBS Outdoor advertising business, and Simon & Schuster book publishers.[52]

Considering the aforementioned corporate profile, it becomes clear that Hollywood is not in the business of consciousness raising, building role models, or improving social conditions—unless there's a connection to profits. Consequently, a minimal effort should be expected in regards to a Hollywood studio deconstructing the worship of "bling" and "floss" for the sake of younger, impressionable viewers. Nonetheless, maintaining a profit-driven business structure should not condone any lapses in ethics or shield corporations from any criticisms regarding exploitation and greed. For instance, there are a number MCs who have been praised for their positive lyrics and public images, but curiously those talents have not received the same Hollywood embrace as those rappers intent upon delivering thuggish, misogynistic, and materialistic messages. Hollywood's penchant for the latter leads to an issue raised by one scholar, who insists that "there has been a steady wave of low budget black films which have turned a solid profit...If the films have done so well with limited production and marketing costs, might they not generate substantially larger profits with full scale support?"[53] In other words, the ingredients for making quality hip-hop films that explore a variety of experiences and that deserve widespread marketing are available. However, the preference for straight-to-video fare, low-budget theatrical releases, and the big-budget vehicles with a "safe" crossover star such as Will Smith, reveal a discernible and troubling pattern concerning the utilization of hip hop in American cinema. Is there substantially more than just "bling" and "floss" that motivate the greenlighting of a film project with rappers? Why does Hollywood deliberately dismiss positive and progressive hip hop, which could also deliver profits in the marketplace?

As for the MCs, the rags-to-riches experiences that they endure certainly deserve admiration as examples of survival skills and perseverance. With Hollywood opening the door, both logic and opportunity dictate a quick entrance into the inner sanctum of movie glory while it's available. However, all art is propaganda, and all creativity carries a message. MCs must understand that their popularity fosters an accompanying responsibility to viewers, whether the rapper chooses to accept it or not. Consequently, to be blinded by the "bling" and "floss" disables both the rapper and the community. As surely as Hollywood has mainstreamed hip hop, the reciprocal, ethical effect of hip hop upon Hollywood could be measurable. Historically, hip hop in American cinema may merely be measured as another youth movement exploited and absorbed to fill the coffers of capitalism, or significantly, hip hop could be the strategy for illuminating existing weaknesses in society and mapping out avenues to progressive changes. As it presently exists, hip hop in American cinema functions as an indicator of decades of amazing youthful creativity, while elevating the mythical superiority and desirability of the American economic and political system.

Filmography

The following films, from 1982 to 2005, explored hip hop as a theme, topic, and/or aspect of their content. Additionally, in some cases, the films featured popular hip-hop performers and/or displayed a recognizable hip-hop flavor or attributes which intentionally highlighted various expressions of hip-hop culture, such as music, language, clothing, and so on.

These fictional films were released theatrically, as opposed to straight-to-video, made for television, or cable network vehicles. This list does not include documentaries, concert films, or animated films. The titles in bold print include credits, and those films are discussed and/or analyzed in *Hip Hop in American Cinema*.

1. ***Wild Style.*** Performers, Easy A.D., A.J., and Patti Astor. Director, Charlie Ahearn. Producer, Charlie Ahearn. First Run Features, 1982.
2. *Flashdance (1983)*
3. ***Beat Street.*** Performers, Rae Dawn Chong, Guy Davis, and Jon Chardiet. Pictures Director, Stan Lathan. Producers, Harry Belafonte and David V. Picker. Orion, 1984.
4. ***Breakin'.*** Performers, Lucinda Dickey, Adolfo Quinones, and Michael Chambers. Director, Joel Silberg. Producers, Allen DeBevoise, and David Zito. Cannon Pictures, 1984.
5. ***Body Rock.*** Performers, Lorenzo Lamas and Vicki Frederick.Director,Marcelo Epstein. Producer, Jeff Schechtman. New World Pictures, 1984.
6. ***Breakin' 2: Electric Boogaloo.*** Performers, Lucinda Dickey, Adolfo Quinones, and Michael Chambers. Director, Sam Firstenberg. Producers, Yoram Globus and Menahem Golan. Cannon Pictures, 1985.
7. ***Rappin'.*** Performers, Mario Van Peebles, Kardeem Hardison, and Eriq LaSalle. Director, Joel Silberg. Producers, Yoram Globus and Menahem Golan. Cannon Pictures, 1985.
8. ***Krush Groove.*** Performers, Run-D.M.C., Blair Underwood, Sheia E., and The Fat Boys. Director, Michael Schultz. Producers, Doug McHenry and Michael Schultz. Warner Bros. Pictures, 1985.
9. ***Fast Forward.*** Performers, John Scott Clough, Don Franklin, and Michael DeLorenzo. Director, Sidney Poitier. Producer, John Veitch. Columbia Pictures, 1985.

10. ***Turk 182***. Performers, Timothy Hutton, Robert Urich, and Kim Cattrall. Director, Bob Clark. Producers, Rene Dupont and Ted Field. 20th Century Fox, 1985.
11. ***Delivery Boys***. Performers, Josh Marcano and Mario Van Peebles. Director, Ken Handler. Producers, Craig Horrall and Per Sjostedt. New World Pictures, 1986.
12. ***The Disorderlies***. Performers, The Fat Boys and Troy Beyer. Director, Michael Schultz. Producers, George Jackson and Doug McHenry. Warner Bros. Pictures, 1987.
13. ***Tougher Than Leather***. Performers, Run-D.M.C. Director, Rick Rubin. Producers, Russell Simmons and Vincent Giordano. New Line Cinema, 1988.
14. ***Do the Right Thing***. Performers, Danny Aiello, Spike Lee, and Rosie Perez. Director, Spike Lee. Producer, Spike Lee. MCA/Universal Pictures, 1989.
15. *Def by Temptation (1990)*
16. ***House Party***. Performers, Kid N Play, Martin Lawrence, and Tisha Campbell. Director, Reginald Hudlin. Producer, Warrington Hudlin. New Line Cinema, 1990.
17. ***House Party 2***. Performers, Kid N Play, Martin Lawrence, Tisha Campbell, and Queen Latifah. Director, George Jackson and Doug McHenry. Producers, George Jackson and Doug McHenry. New Line Cinema, 1991.
18. ***Hangin' With the Homeboys***. Performers, John Leguizamo and Doug E. Doug. Director, Joseph B. Vasquez. Producer, Richard Brick. New Line Cinema, 1991.
19. ***Nothing but Trouble***. Performers, Chevy Chase, Demi Moore, Dan Aykroyd, and Digital Underground. Director, Dan Aykroyd. Producers, Lester Berman and Robert K. Weiss. Warner Bros. Pictures, 1991.
20. ***Jungle Fever***. Performers, Wesley Snipes and Annabella Sciorra. Director, Spike Lee. Producer, Spike Lee. Universal Pictures, 1991
21. ***New Jack City***. Performers, Wesley Snipes, Ice-T, and Allen Payne. Director, Mario Van Peebles. Producers, George Jackson and Doug McHenry. Warner Bros. Pictures, 1991.
22. ***Boyz N the Hood***. Performers, Laurence Fishburne, Cuba Gooding Jr., and Ice Cube. Director, John Singleton. Producer, Steve Nicolaides. Columbia Pictures, 1991.

23. ***Straight Out of Brooklyn***. Performers, Larry Gilliard Jr., Matty Rich, and George T. Odom. Director, Matty Rich. Producer, Matty Rich. Samuel Goldwyn Company, 1991.
24. ***Juice***. Performers, Tupac Shakur, Omar Epps, and Khalil Kain. Director, Ernest Dickerson. Producers, Peter Frankfurt, David Heyman, and Neal H. Moritz, Paramount Pictures, 1992.
25. ***Menace II Society***. Performers, Tyrin Turner, Larenz Tate, and Jada Pinkett. Directors, Albert Hughes and Allen Hughes. Producer, Darin Scott. New Line Cinema, 1993.
26. ***Poetic Justice***. Performers, Janet Jackson and Tupac Shakur. Director, John Singleton. Producers, John Singleton and Steve Nicolaides. Columbia Pictures, 1993.
27. ***Fly by Night***. Performers Jeffrey D. Sams and Ron Brice. Director, Steve Gomer. Producers, Mark Gordon and Calvin Skaggs. Lumiere Productions, 1993.
28. ***My Life***. Performers Michael Keaton, Nicole Kidman, and Queen Latifah. Director, Bruce Joel Rubin. Producers, Hunt Lowry, Bruce Joel Rubin, and Jerry Zucker. Columbia Pictures, 1993.
29. ***CB4***. Performers Chris Rock and Allen Payne. Director, Tamra Davis. Producers, Nelson George and Chris Rock. Universal Pictures, 1993.
30. *Just Another Girl on the I.R.T. (1993)*
31. ***Above the Rim***. Performers Duane Martin, Leon, and Tupac Shakur. Director, Jeff Pollack. Producers, Benny Medina and Jeff Pollack. New Line Cinema, 1994.
32. ***Fear of a Black Hat***. Performers, Rusty Cundieff, Mark Christopher Lawrence, and Larry B. Scott. Director, Rusty Cundieff. Producer, Darin Scott. Samuel Goldwyn Company, 1994.
33. *Jason's Lyric (1994)*
34. *Friday (1995)*
35. *Higher Learning (1995)*
36. ***Tales From the Hood***. Performers Clarence Williams III, Joe Torry, and Rusty Cundieff. Director, Rusty Cundieff. Producer, Darin Scott. Savoy Pictures, 1995.
37. *Phat Beach (1996)*
38. ***Set It Off***. Performers, Jada Pinkett Smith, Queen Latifah, and Vivica A. Fox, Director, Rusty Cundieff. Producer, Darin Scott. Savoy Pictures, 1996.
39. ***Bullet***. Performers, Tupac Shakur and Mickey Rourke. Director, Julien Temple. Producer, John Flock. New Line Cinema, 1996.

40. ***Gridlock'd***. Performers, Tupac Shakur, Tim Roth, and Thandie Newton. Director, Vondie Curtis-Hall. Producers, Erica Huggins and Damian Jones. Def Pictures, 1997.
41. ***Gang Related***. Performers, Tupac Shakur and James Belushi. Director, Jim Kouf. Producers, John Bertolli and Brad Krevoy. Orion Pictures, 1997.
42. ***Hoodlum***. Performers, Laurence Fishburne, Tim Roth, and Queen Latifah. Director, Bill Duke. Producer, Frank Mancuso Jr. United Artists, 1997.
43. *Fakin' Da Funk (1997)*
44. *Squeeze (1997)*
45. *B.A.P.S. (1997)*
46. ***Love Jones***. Performers, Larenz Tate and Nia Long. Director, Theodore Witcher. Producers, Jeremiah Samuels and Nick Wechsler. New Line Cinema, 1997.
47. ***A Thin Line Between Love and Hate***. Performers, Martin Lawrence and Lynn Whitfield. Producers, George Jackson and Douglas McHenry. New Line Cinema, 1997.
48. ***Def Jam's How to Be a Player***. Performers, Bill Bellamy and Natalie Desselle. Director, Lionel C. Martin. Producers, Mark Burg, Preston L. Holmes, and Russell Simmons. Def Pictures, 1997.
49. ***Booty Call***. Performers, Jamie Foxx and Vivica A. Fox. Director, Jeff Pollack. Producer, John Morrisey. Columbia Pictures, 1997.
50. *Sprung (1997)*
51. ***Bulworth***. Performers, Warren Beatty and Halle Berry. Director, Warren Beatty. Producers, Warren Beatty and Peter Jan Brugge. 20th Century Fox, 1998.
52. ***Belly***. Performers, DMX and Nas. Director, Hype Williams. Producers, Larry Meistrich, Ron Rotholz, Robert Salerno, and Hype Williams. Artisan Entertainment, 1998.
53. ***Ride***. Performers, Malik Yoba and Melissa DeSousa. Director, Millicent Shelton. Producers, Reginald Hudlin, Warrington Hudlin, and Ernest Johnson. Miramax, 1998.
54. ***Sphere***. Performers, Dustin Hoffman, Sharon Stone, Samuel L. Jackson, and Queen Latifah. Director, Barry Levinson. Producers, Michael Crichton, Barry Levinson, and Andrew Wald. Warner Bros. Pictures, 1998.
55. ***Living Out Loud***. Performers, Holly Hunter, Danny DeVito, and Queen Latifah. Director, Richard LaGravenese. Producers, Danny

DeVito, Michael Shamberg, and Stacy Sher. New Line Cinema, 1998.

56. *Caught Up (1998)*
57. *I Got the Hook Up (1998)*
58. *He Got Game (1998)*
59. *Belly (1998)*
60. *The Players Club (1998)*
61. **Slam**. Performers, Saul Williams and Sonja Sohn. Director, Marc Levin. Producers, Henri M. Kessler, Marc Levin, and Richard Stratten. Trimark Pictures, 1999.
62. **The Bone Collector**. Performers, Denzel Washington, Angelina Jolie, and Queen Latifah. Director, Phillip Noyce. Producers, Martin Bregman, Michael Bregman, and Louis A. Stroller. Columbia Pictures, 1999.
63. **Black and White**. Performers, Robert Downey Jr., Power, and Allan Houston. Director, James Toback. Producers, Daniel Bigel, Michael Mailer, and Ron Rotholz. Screen Gems, 2000.
64. *Finding Forrester (2000)*
65. *How High (2000)*
66. *Love and Basketball (2000)*
67. **Save the Last Dance**. Performers, Julia Stiles and Sean Patrick Thomas. Director, Thomas Carter. Producers, Robert W. Cort and David Madden. Paramount Pictures, 2001.
68. *Bones (2001)*
69. *Brothers (2001)*
70. *Training Day (2001)*
71. *Baby Boy (2001)*
72. *Two Can Play That Game (2001)*
73. **Brown Sugar**. Performers, Taye Diggs, Sanaa Lathan, Queen Latifah, and Mos Def. Director, Rick Fumuyima. Producer, Peter Heller. Twentieth Century-Fox Film Corporation, 2002.
74. *Drumline (2002)*
75. *Barbershop (2002)*
76. **8 Mile**. Performers, Eminem, Kim Basinger, and Mekhi Phifer. Director, Curtis Hanson. Producers, Brian Grazer, Curtis Hanson, and Jimmy Iovine. Universal Pictures, 2002.
77. **Chicago**. Performers, Renee Zellweger, Catherine Zeta-Jones, and Queen Latifah. Director, Rob Marshall. Producer, Martin Richards. Miramax, 2002.
78. *Biker Boyz (2003)*

79. *Fast and the Furious (2003)*
80. **Bringing Down the House**. Performers, Steve Martin and Queen Latifah. Director, Adam Shankman. Producers, Ashok Amritraj and David Hoberman. Touchstone Pictures, 2003.
81. **Scary Movie 3**. Performers, Regina Hall and Queen Latifah. Director, David Zucker. Producer, Robert K. Weiss. Dimension Films, 2003.
82. **Malibu's Most Wanted**. Performers, Jamie Kennedy, Taye Diggs, and Regina Hall. Director, John Whitesell. Producers, Fax Bahr, Mike Karz, and Adam Small. Warner Bros. Pictures, 2003.
83. *Deliver Us From Eva (2003)*
84. *Love Don't Cost a Thing (2003)*
85. *The LadyKillers (2004)*
86. **Barbershop 2: Back in Business**. Performers, Ice cube, Cedric the Entertainer, and Queen Latifah. Director, Kevin Rodney Sullivan. Producers, Alex Gartner, Robert Teitel, and George Tillman Jr. MGM, 2004.
87. **You Got Served**. Performers, Omarion Grandberry and Marques Houston. Director, Chris Stokes. Producers, Marcus Morton and Billy Pollina. Screen Gems, 2004.
88. **The Cookout**. Performers, Meagan Good, Queen Latifah, and Ja Rule. Director, Lance Rivera. Producers, Shakim Compere and Queen Latifah. Lions Gate Films, 2004.
89. **Taxi.** Performers, Queen Latifah and Jimmy Fallon. Director, Tim Story. Producer, Luc Besson. 20th Century Fox, 2004.
90. **Beauty Shop**. Performers, Queen Latifah and Alicia Silverstone. Director, Bille Woodruff. Producers, David Hoberman, Queen Latifah, Robert Teitel, and George Tillman Jr., MGM, 2005.
91. *Coach Carter (2005)*
92. **Hustle and Flow**. Performers, Terrence Howard, Anthony Anderson, and Ludacris. Director, Craig Brewer. Producers, Stephanie Allain and John Singleton. MTV Films, 2005.
93. **Get Rich or Die Tryin'**. Performers, 50 Cent, Joy Bryant, and Terrence Howard. Director, Jim Sheridan. Producers, Jimmy Iovine, Chris Lighty, Paul Rosenberg, and Jim Sheridan. Paramount Pictures, 2005.

Performers' Filmography

The following is a list of rap artists who appeared in feature-length films by December 2005. This filmography includes films released theatrically, omitting documentaries, straight-to-video vehicles, television movies, and voiceover performances for animation. In some features, the rappers gave cameo appearances as they provided the musical performance for the story line, but the majority of the films included the MCs in fictional roles as major or supporting characters.

The list is as comprehensive as possible, though with some rappers they chose to credit themselves by their birth names, shown in parentheses, or by alternative names which differed from the monikers which made them popular in the hip-hop world. The listing is alphabetically arranged; however, with some performers, such as Tupac Shakur and Marques Houston, the popularity of their first names might place them in the listing accordingly, rather than their last names.

Aaliyah (Aaliyah Haughton)
   Romeo Must Die (2000)
   Queen of the Damned (2002)
Andre 3000 (Andre Benjamin)
   WanSaGo (2001)
   Hollywood Homicide (2003)
   Be Cool (2005)
   Four Brothers (2005)
   Revolver (2005)
Ashanti (Ashanti Douglas)
   Bride and Prejudice (2004)
   Coach Carter (2005)
Erykah Badu (Erica Wright)
   Blues Brothers 2000 (1998)
   The Cider House Rules (1999)
   House of D (2004)
Beyonce (Beyonce Knowles)
   Austin Powers: Goldmember (2002)
   The Fighting Temptations (2003)
Big Daddy Kane
   Posse (1993)
   The Meteor Man (1993)

Biz Markie (Marcel Hall)
 Men in Black II (2002)
Bow Wow (Shad Gregory Moss)
 All About the Benjamins (2002)
 Like Mike (2002)
 Johnson Family Vacation (2004)
 Roll Bounce (2005)
Busta Rhymes (Trevor Smith)
 Who's the Man (1993)
 Strapped (1993)
 Higher Learning (1995)
 Shaft (2000)
 Finding Forrester (2000)
 Narc (2002)
 Halloween: Resurrection (2002)
 Death of a Dynasty (2003)
 Full Clip (2004)
Nick Cannon
 Whatever It Takes (2000)
 Men in Black II (2002)
 Drumline (2002)
 Love Don't Cost a Thing (2003)
 Shall We Dance? (2004)
 The Beltway (2005)
 Underclassman (2005)
 Roll Bounce (2005)
Coolio
 Dear God (1996)
 Batman and Robin (1997)
 An Alan Smithee Film (1997)
 Midnight Mass (1999)
 Tyrone (1999)
 Gangland (2000)
 The Convent (2000)
 Submerged (2000)
 Stealing Candy (2002)
 Storm Watch (2002)
 The Beat (2003)
 Daredevil (2003)

Coolio (cont'd)
    Ravedactyl (2003)
    Exposed (2003)
    Tapped Out (2003)
    Gang Warz (2004)
    Pterodactyl (2005)
Da Brat (Shawntae Harris)
    Kazaam (1996)
    Glitter (2001)
    Civil Brand (2002)
DMX (Earl Simmons)
    Belly (1998)
    Romeo Must Die (2000)
    Boricua's Bond (2000)
    Exit Wounds (2001)
    Cradle 2 the Grave (2003)
    Never Die Alone (2004)
Dr. Dre (Andre Young)
    Coming to America (1988)
    Deep Cover (1994)
    Natural Born Killers (1994)
    Bulworth (1998)
    Wild Wild West (1999)
    Training Day (2001)
    Bones (2001)
    The Wash (2001)
    Hollywood Homicide (2003)
Eminem (Marshall Mathers)
    The Wash (2001)
    8 Mile (2002)
Eve (Eve Jeffers)
    Barbershop (2002)
    xXx (2002)
    The Woodsman (2004)
    Barbershop 2: Back in Business (2004)
    The Cookout (2004)
50 Cent (Curtis Jackson)
    Get Rich or Die Tryin' (2005)
The Fat Boys (Darren Robinson, Damon Wimbley, Mark Morales)
    Krush Groove (1985)

The Fat Boys (cont'd)
    Knights of the City (1986)
    The Disorderlies (1987)
Foxy Brown (Inga Marchaud)
    Woo (1998)
Heavy D (Dwight Myers)
    New Jersey Drive (1995)
    The Deli (1997)
    Life (1999)
    The Cider House Rules (1999)
    Next Afternoon (2000)
    Big Trouble (2002)
    Black Listed (2003)
    Dallas 362 (2003)
    Larceny (2004)
Ice Cube (O'Shea Jackson)
    Boyz N the Hood (1991)
    Trespass (1992)
    The Glass Shield (1994)
    Higher Learning (1994)
    Friday (1995)
    Dangerous Ground (1997)
    Anaconda (1997)
    The Players Club (1998)
    I Got the Hook Up (1998)
    Thicker Than Water (1999)
    Three Kings (1999)
    Next Friday (2000)
    Ghost of Mars (2001)
    All About the Benjamins (2002)
    Barbershop (2002)
    Friday After Next (2002)
    Torque (2004)
    Barbershop 2: Back in Business (2004)
    Are We There Yet? (2005)
    xXx: State of the Union (2005)
Ice-T (Tracy Marrow)
    Breakin' (1984)
    Breakin' 2: Electric Boogaloo (1984)
    New Jack City (1991)

Ice-T (cont'd)
    Ricochet (1991)
    Why Colors? (1992)
    Trespass (1992)
    Who's the Man? (1993)
    Surviving the Game (1994)
    Tank Girl (1995)
    Johnny Mnemonic (1995)
    Mean Guns (1997)
    The Deli (1997)
    Below Utopia (1997)
    Crazy Six (1998)
    Sonic Impact (1999)
    The Wrecking Crew (1999)
    The Heist (1999)
    Frezno Smooth (1999)
    Stealth Fighter (1999)
    Final Voyage (1999)
    Corrupt (1999)
    Guardian (2000)
    Gangland (2000)
    Luck of the Draw (2000)
    The Alternate (2000)
    Kept (2001)
    Crime Partners (2001)
    Stranded (2001)
    3000 Miles to Graceland (2001)
    Point Doom (2001)
    Deadly Rhapsody (2001)
    'RXmas (2001)
    Ticker (2001)
    Out Kold (2001)
    Ablaze (2001)
    On the Edge (2002)
    Tracks (2005)
Janet Jackson
    Poetic Justice (1993)
    Nutty Professor II: The Klumps (2000)
Ja Rule (Jeffrey Atkins)
    Turn It Up (2000)

Ja Rule (cont'd)
  Crime Partners (2001)
  The Fast and the Furious (2001)
  Half Past Dead (2002)
Kid 'N Play
  (**Kid** = Christopher Reid)
  House Party (1990)
  House Party 2 (1991)
  Class Act (1992)
  House Party 3 (1994)
  Pauly Shore Is Dead (2003)
  (**Play** = Christopher Martin)
  House Party (1990)
  House Party 2 (1991)
  Class Act (1992)
  House Party 3 (1994)
  Rising to the Top (1999)
Lil' Kim (Kimberly Jones)
  She's All That (1999)
  Longshot (2000)
  Juwanna Mann (2002)
  Gang of Roses (2003)
  Nora's Hair Salon (2004)
  You Got Served (2004)
LL Cool J (James Todd Smith)
  Wildcats (1986)
  The Hard Way (1991)
  Out-of-Sync (1995)
  Caught Up (1998)
  Woo (1998)
  Halloween H2O (1998)
  Deep Blue Sea (1999)
  In Too Deep (1999)
  Any Given Sunday (1999)
  Charlie's Angels (2000)
  Kingdom Come (2001)
  Rollerball (2002)
  Deliver Us From Eva (2003)
  S.W.A.T. (2003)
  Mindhunters (2004)

LL Cool J (cont'd)
 Slow Burn (2005)
 Edison (2005)
Ludacris (Chris Bridges)
 The Wash (2001)
 2 Fast 2 Furious (2003)
 Crash (2004)
 Hustle and Flow (2005)
Macy Gray (Natalie McIntyre)
 Training Day (2001)
 Gang of Roses (2003)
 Around the World in 80 Days (2004)
 The Crow: Wicked Prayer (2005)
 Shadowboxer (2005)
 Domino (2005)
Marques Houston
 Good Burger (1997)
 You Got Served (2004)
 Fat Albert (2004)
Master P (Percy Miller)
 The Players Club (1998)
 I Got the Hook Up (1998)
 Hot Boyz (1999)
 Foolish (1999)
 No Tomorrow (1999)
 Takedown (2000)
 Gone in Sixty Seconds (2000)
 Lockdown (2000)
 Popcorn Shrimp (2001)
 Undisputed (2002)
 Dark Blue (2002)
 Hollywood Homicide (2003)
 Uncle P (2005)
MC Lyte (Lana Moorer)
 Fly by Night (1993)
 An Alan Smithee Film (1997)
 A Luv Tale (1999)
 Train Ride (2000)
 Civil Brand (2002)
 Playas Ball (2003)

Method Man (Clifford Smith)
Don't Be a Menace While Drinking Your Juice in the Hood (1996)
One Eight Seven (1997)
Cop Land (1997)
Wu-Tang (1998)
Belly (1998)
P.I.G.S. (1999)
Baricua's Bond (2000)
WaSanGo (2001)
How High (2001)
My Baby's Daddy (2004)
Garden State (2004)
Soul Plane (2004)
Venom (2005)
Monica (Monica Denise Arnold)
Boys and Girls (2000)
Mos Def (Dante Terrell Smith)
Ghosts (1997)
Where's Marlowe (1998)
Island of the Dead (2000)
Bamboozled (2000)
Monster's Ball (2001)
Showtime (2002)
Civil Brand (2002)
Brown Sugar (2002)
The Italian Job (2003)
The Woodsman (2004)
Hitchhiker's Guide to the Galaxy (2005)
Mya (Mya Harrison)
In Too Deep (1999)
WaSanGo (2001)
Chicago (2002)
Dirty Dancing: Havana Nights (2004)
Shall We Dance (2004)
Ways of the Flesh (2005)
Cursed (2005)
Nas (Nasir Jones)
Belly (1998)
In Too Deep (1999)

Nas (cont'd)
  Ticker (2001)
  Sacred in the Flesh (2001)
  Uptown Girls (2003)
Nelly (Cornell Haynes Jr.)
  Snipes (2001)
  The Longest Yard (2005)
Omarion (Omarion Grandberry)
  Fat Albert (2004)
  You Got Served (2004)
Queen Latifah (Dana Owens)
  Jungle Fever (1991)
  House Party 2 (1991)
  Juice (1992)
  My Life (1993)
  Set It Off (1996)
  Hoodlum (1997)
  Sphere (1998)
  Living Out Loud (1998)
  The Bone Collector (1999)
  Brown Sugar (2002)
  Chicago (2002)
  Bringing Down the House (2003)
  Scary Movie 3 (2003)
  Barbershop 2 (2004)
  The Cookout (2004)
  Taxi (2004)
  Beauty Shop (2005)
Redman (Reggie Noble)
  P.I.G.S. (1999)
  Colorz of Rage (1999)
  Baricua's Bond (2000)
  How High (2001)
  Thaddeus Fights the Power (2003)
Kelly Rowland
  Beverly Hood (1999)
  Freddy vs. Jason (2003)
  The Seat Filler (2004)
Run-D.M.C. (Joseph Simmons, Darryl McDaniels, Jason Mizell)
  Krush Groove

Run-D.M.C. (cont'd)
> *Tougher Than Leather*

Salt-N-Pepa
> Sandra "**Pepa**" Denton
>> *Stay Tuned* (1992)
>> *Who's the Man?* (1993)
>> *Jason's Lyric* (1994)
>> *Joe's Apartment* (1996)
>> *3 A.M.* (2001)
>> *Love and a Bullet* (2002)
>
> Cheryl "**Salt**" James
>> *Stay Tuned* (1992)
>> *Who's the Man?* (1993)
>> *Raw Nerve* (1999)
>
> Diedre "**Spinderella**" Roper
>> *Stay Tuned* (1992)
>> *Kazaam* (1996)

Schooly-D
> *Scarlet Diva* (2000)
> *Snipes* (2001)

Silkk Tha Shocker (Vyshonne Miller)
> *Hot Boyz* (1999)
> *Corrupt* (1999)
> *Undisputed* (2002)
> *Still 'Bout It* (2004)

Usher (Usher Raymond)
> *The Faculty* (1998)
> *She's All That* (1999)
> *Light It Up* (1999)
> *Texas Rangers* (2001)
> *In the Mix* (2005)

Will Smith
> *Where the Day Takes You* (1992)
> *Six Degrees of Separation* (1993)
> *Bad Boys* (1995)
> *Independence Day* (1996)
> *Men in Black* (1997)
> *Enemy of the State* (1998)
> *Wild Wild West* (1999)

Will Smith (cont'd)
  The Legend of Bagger Vance (2000)
  Ali (2001)
  Men in Black II (2002)
  Bad Boys II (2003)
  I, Robot (2004)
  Hitch (2005)
Snoop Dogg (Cordozar Calvin Broadus)
  Half-Baked (1998)
  Caught Up (1998)
  Ride (1998)
  I Got the Hook Up (1998)
  Urban Menace (1999)
  The Wrecking Crew (1999)
  Eastsidaz (2000)
  Crime Partners (2001)
  Baby Boy (2001)
  Training Day (2001)
  Bones (2001)
  The Wash (2001)
  Malibu's Most Wanted (2003)
  Starsky and Hutch (2004)
  Soul Plane (2004)
T-Boz (Tionne Watkins)
  House Party 3 (1994)
  Belly (1998)
Tone Loc (Anthony Smith)
  The Adventures of Ford Fairlane (1990)
  The Return of Superfly (1990)
  Posse (1993)
  Poetic Justice (1993)
  Surf Ninjas (1993)
  Car 54, Where Are You? (1994)
  Ace Ventura: Pet Detective (1994)
  Blank Check (1994)
  Heat (1995)
  Spy Hard (1996)
  Fakin' Da Funk (1997)
  Freedom Strike (1998)
  Crawlers (2001)

Tone Loc (cont'd)
Deadly Rhapsody (2001)
Storm Watch (2002)
Treach (Anthony Criss)
Juice (1992)
The Meteor Man (1993)
Jason's Lyric (1994)
The Contract (2000)
Boricua's Bond (2000)
3 A.M. (2001)
Face (2002)
Empire (2002)
The Book of Love (2002)
Love and a Bullet (2002)
Playas Ball (2003)
The Orphan King (2005)
Today You Die (2005)
Feast (2005)
Tupac Shakur
Nothing but Trouble (1991)
Juice (1992)
Poetic Justice (1993)
Above the Rim (1994)
Bullet (1996)
Gridlock'd (1997)
Gang Related (1997)
Mark Wahlberg
Renaissance Man (1994)
The Basketball Diaries (1995)
Fear (1996)
Traveller (1997)
Boogie Nights (1997)
The Big Hit (1998)
The Corruptor (1999)
Three Kings (1999)
The Yards (2000)
The Perfect Storm (2000)
Planet of the Apes (2001)
Rock Star (2001)
The Truth About Charlie (2002)

Mark Wahlberg (cont'd)
The Italian Job (2003)
I Love Huckabees (2004)
Four Brothers (2005)

Notes

The abbreviation MHL/MPA indicates materials researched in the Archival Files, Margaret Herrick Library, The Motion Picture Academy, Beverly Hills, CA.

Introduction

1. Sonia Maasik and Jack Solomon, *Signs of Life: Readings on Popular Culture for Writers*, 5th ed. (Boston: Bedford Books, 2006), 220.
2. S. Craig Watkins, *Hip Hop Matters: Politics, Pop Culture, and the Struggle for the Soul of a Movement* (Boston: Beacon Press, 2005), 150.
3. Kermit E. Campbell, *Getting Our Groove On: Rhetoric, Language, and Literacy for the Hip Hop Generation* (Detroit, MI: Wayne State University Press, 2005), 4.

1. Representin' in the Beginnin': The 1980s

1. Ephraim Katz, *The Film Encyclopedia,* 3rd ed. (New York: HarperCollins, 1998), 1110.
2. Internet Movie Database (IMDB), *Purple Rain*.
3. Cristina Veran, "Breaking It All Down," in *The Vibe History of Hip Hop*, ed. Alan Light (New York: Three Rivers Press, 1999), 53.
4. Sally Banes, "Breaking," in *That's the Joint! The Hip-Hop Studies Reader*, eds. Murray Forman and Mark Anthony Neal (New York: Routledge, 2004), 14.
5. Ibid., 19.
6. Craig Castleman, "The Politics of Graffiti," in *That's the Joint!: The Hip-Hop Studies Reader*, eds. Murray Forman and Mark Anthony Neal (New York: Routledge, 2004), 21–29.
7. Jeff Chang, *Can't Stop, Won't Stop: The History of the Hip-Hop Generation* (New York: St. Martin's Press, 2005), 74.
8. Ellin Stein, "Wild Style," *American Film*, November 1983, MHL/MPA.
9. Nelson George, "The Rhythm and the Blues." *Billboard*, October 26, 1986, MHL/MPA.
10. Stein.
11. Clarke Taylor, "Rapping and Breaking in 'Beat Street', *Los Angeles Times*, Sunday Calendar Section, March 15, 1984, MHL/MPA.
12. Ibid.
13. J. Hoberman, "Alphabet City," *Village Voice*, May 15, 1984, MHL/MPA.
14. *Breakin'*, Production Notes, Studio Press Kit, MGM/UA and The Cannon Group, 1984, MHL/MPA.
15. Hoberman.
16. Chang, 193.
17. Jan Cherubin, "Two Street Dancers Breakin' into the Movie Business," *Los Angeles Herald Examiner*, May 29, 1984, MHL/MPA.
18. Banes, 19.
19. "Breakin' 2: Electric Boogaloo," *Box Office*, February 1985, MHL/MPA.
20. Chang, 205.
21. Ibid.
22. "Dancetera: Broadway and Beyond," *Dance Magazine*, August 1984, MHL/MPA.
23. Ibid.

24. Elvis Mitchell, "'Body Rock' Is Gaudy Schlock," *Los Angeles Herald Examiner*, October 12, 1982, MHL/MPA.

25. Melvin Donalson, *Black Directors in Hollywood* (Austin: University of Texas Press, 2003), 41.

26. Arnold Shaw, *Black Popular Music in America* (New York: Schirmer Books, 1986), 292–293.

27. David Samuels, "The Rap on Rap," in *That's the Joint: The Hip Hop Reader*, edited by Murray Forman and Mark Anthony Neal (New York: Routledge, 2004), 148.

28. Ibid., 273.

29. Nelson George, *Buppies, B-Boys, Baps, and Bohos: Notes on Post-Soul Black Culture* (New York: HarperPerennial, 1992), 43–44.

30. Steven Hager, "Afrika Bambaataa's Hip-Hop," in *And It Don't Stop!: The Best American Hip-Hop Journalism in the Last 25 Years*, ed. Raquel Cepeda (New York: Faber and Faber, 2004), 23.

31. Paula J. Massood, *Black City Cinema: African American Urban Experiences in Film* (Philadelphia: Temple University Press, 2003), 122–123.

32. Tricia Rose, *Black Noise: Rap Music and Black Culture in Contemporary America* (Middletown, CT: Wesleyan University Press, 1994), 4.

33. Robert Christgan and Carola Dibbell, "One from the Motormouth," *Village Voice*, November 12, 1985, MHL/MPA.

34. Michael Wilmington, "'Rappin' Hip-Hop Way to Quick Smiles," *Los Angeles Times*, May 10, 1985, MHL/MPA.

35. Janet Maslin, "Film: Timothy Hutton in 'Turk 182!'" *New York Times*, February 15, 1985, MHL/MPA.

36. Castleman, 21–29.

37. "Delivery Boys," *Variety*, July 30, 1986, MHL/MPA.

38. Ibid.

39. Peter Shapiro, *The Rough Guide to Hip-Hop*, 2nd ed. (London: Rough Guides, LTD, 2005), 326–327.

40. Sasha Frere-Jones, "Run-D.M.C.," in *The Vibe History of Hip-Hop*, ed. Alan Light (New York: Three Rivers Press, 1999), 62.

41. Ibid., 63.

42. Robert Hilburn, "Run-D.M.C.: Raising Hell Again in the Movies," *Los Angeles Times*, Sunday Calendar Section, December 14, 1986, MHL/MPA.

43. Ibid.

44. Chris Willman, "Run-DMC's 'Tougher Than Leather,'" *Los Angeles Times*, November 16, 1988, MHL/MPA.

45. Hilburn.

46. Stephen Advocat, "Theaters Yank Run DMC Film After Violence," *Variety*, October 13, 1988, MHL/MPA.

47. Jim Robbins, "Rap Pic Pulled in Long Island," *Variety*, September 15, 1988, MHL/MPA.

48. Hilburn.

49. Ibid.

50. Donald Bogle, *Toms, Coons, Mulattoes, Mammies, and Bucks* (New York: Continuum, 1990), 259.

51. Ed Guerrero, *Framing Blackness: The African American Image in Film* (Philadelphia: Temple University Press, 1993), 148.

52. Massood, 143.

53. Martha Nelson, "Break Dancing—Men Only?" *Ms*, September 1984, MHL/MPA.

2. Chillin' and Killin': Hood Rats and Thugs, 1990–1999

1. Toure, "The Hip-Hop Nation," in *And It Don't Stop!: The Best American Hip-Hop Journalism in the Last 25 Years*, ed. Raquel Cepeda (New York: Faber and Faber, 2004), 274.
2. David P. Szatmary, *Rockin' Time: A Social History of Rock-and-Roll*, 4th ed. (Upper Saddle River, NJ: Prentice-Hall, 2000), 306.
3. Melissa August et al., "Hip Hop Nation: There's More to Rap Than Just Rhythms and Rhymes," in *Common Culture*, 4th ed., eds. Michael Petracca and Madeleine Sorapure (Upper Saddle River, NJ: Prentice-Hall, 2004), 301.
4. Szatmary, 320.
5. Clarence Lusane, "Rap, Race, and Politics," in *That's the Joint: The Hip Hop Reader*, edited by Murray Forman and Mark Anthony Neal (New York: Routledge, 2004), 354–355.
6. John M. Wilson, "Trying to Crash the Party," Sunday Calendar Section, *Los Angeles Times*, March 4, 1990, 88.
7. Lisa Kennedy, "Wack House: House Party Is Business As Usual," *Village Voice*, March 13, 1990, 67.
8. Wilson, 88.
9. Larry A. Stanley, ed., *Rap: The Lyrics* (New York: Penguin Books, 1992), 322.
10. John Leland and Lynda Wright, "Black to the Future," *Newsweek*, May 27, 1991, 58.
11. Chris Willman, "Rap Attack, Take Two," *Los Angeles Times*, Sunday Calendar Section, March 14, 1993, 20.
12. "Fly by Night," *Variety*, February 8, 1993, MHL/MPA.
13. Willman, 20.
14. Peter Shapiro, *The Rough Guide to Hip Hop* (London: Rough Guides, 2005), 41.
15. Bakari Kitwana, *The Rap on Gangsta Rap* (Chicago: Third World Press, 1994), 28–32.
16. Kitwana, 32.
17. Eithne Quinn, *Nuthin' but a "G" Thang* (New York: Columbia University Press, 2005), 10.
18. Robert Marriott, "Gangsta, Gangsta: The Sad Violent Parable of Death Row Records," in *The Vibe History of Hip Hop*, ed. Alan Light (New York: Three Rivers Press, 1999), 321.
19. Imani Perry, *Prophets of the Hood: Politics and Poetics in Hip Hop* (Durham, NC: Duke University Press, 2004), 108–109.
20. Russell Simmons, *Life and Def: Sex, Drugs, Money and God* (New York: Crown Publishers, 2001), 180.
21. Nelson George, *Hip Hop America* (New York: Penguin, 1998), 42.
22. Quinn, 3, 11.
23. Marriott, 320–325.
24. Anthony DeCurtis, "2 Live Crew Trial," in *The Vibe History of Hip Hop*, ed. Alan Light (New York: Three Rivers Press, 1999), 268.
25. Patrick B. Hill, "Deconstructing the Hip-Hop Hype: A Critical Analysis of the *New York Times'* Coverage of African-American Youth Culture," in *Bleep! Censoring Rock and Rap Music*, eds. Betty Houchin Winfield and Sandra Davidson (Westport, CT: Greenwood Press, 1999), 111.

26. Martin Johnson, "'Cop Killer' and Sister Souljah: Hip Hop Under Fire," in *The Vibe History of Hip Hop*, ed. Alan Light (New York: Three Rivers Press, 1999), 288.
27. Ibid.
28. bell hooks, *We Real Cool: Black Men and Masculinity* (New York: Routledge 2004), 27.
29. Ibid.
30. Michael Eric Dyson, *Between God and Gangsta Rap* (New York: Oxford University Press, 1996), 186.
31. Gabriel Alvarez, "Gangsta Rap in the 90s," in *The Vibe History of Hip Hop*, ed. Alan Light (New York: Three Rivers Press, 1999), 291.
32. Barry Michael Cooper, "Teddy Riley's New Jack Swing," in *And It Don't Stop*, ed. Raquel Cepeda (New York: Faber and Faber, 2004), 62–63.
33. Elysa Gardner, "Hip Hop Soul," in *The Vibe History of Hip Hop*, ed. Alan Light (New York: Three Rivers Press, 1999), 307–309.
34. Kristine McKenna, "Ice Cube Melts in Front of the Camera," *New York Times*, July 14, 1991, MHL/MPA.
35. Richard W. Stevenson, "An Anti-Gang Movie Opens to Violence, *New York Times*, July 14, 1991, MHL/MPA.
36. John Leland et al., "New Jack Cinema Enters Screening," *Newsweek*, June 10, 1991, 51–52.
37. *Boyz N the Hood*, Production Notes, Press Kit, Columbia Pictures, 1991, MHL/MPA.
38. Roger Ebert, "Straight Out of Brooklyn," *Chicago Sun-Times*, June 28, 1991, rogerebert.com.
39. Ed Guerrero, *Framing Blackness: The African American Image in Film* (Philadelphia: Temple University Press, 1993), 188–189.
40. Ibid., 189.
41. *Menace II Society*, Production Notes, Press Kit, New Line Cinema, 1993, MHL/MPA.
42. Ibid.
43. Paula J. Massood, *Black City Cinema* (Philadelphia: Temple University Press, 2003), 165.
44. *Menace II Society*, Production Notes, Press Kit, New Line Cinema, 1993, MHL/MPA.
45. Todd Boyd, *The New H.N.I.C.* (New York: New York University Press, 2002), 51.
46. Ibid.
47. Lawrence van Gelder, "For Young Blacks, Decency vs. Crime," *The New York Times Film Review*, November 4, 1998, nytimes.com.
48. Angela Ards, "Organizing the Hip-Hop Generation," in *That's the Joint: The Hip Hop Reader*, eds. Murray Forman and Mark Anthony Neal (New York: Routledge, 2004), 316.
49. *CB4*, Production Notes, Press Kit, Universal Studios, 1993, MHL/MPA.
50. Ibid.
51. Willman, 20.
52. Alex Demyaneko, "N.W.M.H.," *Los Angeles Village View*, June 10–16, 1994, 11, MHL/MPA.
53. Melvin Donalson, *Black Directors in Hollywood* (Austin: University of Texas, 2003), 261.

3. Skimmin' the Phat: Players, Poets, and Professionals, 1996–2005

1. Jeff Chang, *Can't Stop, Won't Stop* (New York: St. Martin's Press, 2005), 446.

2. Ibid.

3. William Van Deburg, *Hoodlums: Black Villains and Social Bandits in America* (Chicago: University of Chicago Press, 2004), 201.

4. Chris Lee, "Hip-Hop Strips Down, Gets Intimate," *Los Angeles Times*, November 8, 2005, E1, E10.

5. Chris Lee, "In Hip-Hop, Beats Do the Talking," *Los Angeles Times*, November 20, 2005, E1, E43.

6. *Rize*, documentary film, directed by David LaChapelle, Lions Gate Entertainment, 2005.

7. Nicola Menzie, "'Krump' Dances into Mainstream," CBS News.com, June 30, 2005.

8. Ibid.

9. Bakari Kitwana, *The Hip Hop Generation: Young Blacks and the Crisis in African-American Culture* (New York: Basic Civitas, 2002), xiii–xiv.

10. Gary Dauphin, "Hip Hop in the Movies," in *The Vibe History of Hip Hop*, ed. Alan Light (New York: Three Rivers Press, 1999), 206.

11. Glenn Whipp, "'Love Jones' Puts Black Filmmaking in New Territory," *The Daily Breeze*, March 16, 1997, MHL/MPA.

12. Ernest Hardy, "A Nouveau Valentine," *Los Angeles Weekly*, March 14, 1997, 47.

13. Andy Klein, "Kickin It," *New Times Los Angeles*, March 13, 1997, MHL/MPA.

14. Melvin Donalson, *Black Directors in Hollywood* (Austin: University of Texas Press, 2003), 271.

15. Kevin Thomas, "'How to Be a Player'—or How to Cheat and Not Get Caught," *Los Angeles Times*, August 8, 1997, F6.

16. Donalson, 272.

17. *Def Jam's How to Be a Player*, Production Notes, Press Kit, Gramercy Pictures, 1997, MHL/MPA.

18. *Variety*, February 24, 1997, MHL/MPA.

19. *Booty Call*, Production Notes, Press Kit, Columbia Pictures, 1997, MHL/MPA.

20. *Brown Sugar*, Production Notes, Press Kit, Fox Searchlight Pictures, 2002, MHL/MPA.

21. Kevin Thomas, "'Brown Sugar': The Hip Hop of Romance," *Los Angeles Times*, October 11, 2002, MHL/MPA.

22. *Brown Sugar*, Production Notes, Press Kit, Columbia Pictures, 1997, MHL/MPA.

23. Allison Samuels, "Minstrels in Baggy Jeans?" *Newsweek*, May 5, 2003, 62.

24. David Denby, "Candid Chimera," *New York Magazine*, May 18, 1998, 51–52.

25. Henry Louis Gates, "The White Negro," *New Yorker*, May 11, 1998, 63.

26. Harry M. Benshoff and Sean Griffin, *America on Film: Representing Race, Class, Gender, and Sexuality at the Movies* (Malden, MA: Blackwell Publishing, 2004), 238.

27. David Ansen, "Shock to the System," *Newsweek*, May 18, 1998, 72.

28. Ernest Hardy, "Pitted Against the Lizard," *Los Angeles Weekly*, May 29, 1998, 35.

29. David Denby, "Opposites Attract," *New Yorker*, April 10, 2000, 100.

30. Stanley Crouch, "Do Blonds Still Have More Fun?" *Talk Magazine*, April 2000, 160.

31. Elvis Mitchell, "Talk the Talk, Then Steal the Life Force," *New York Times*, April 5, 2000, MHL/MPA.

32. *Save the Last Dance*, Production Notes, Press Kit, Paramount Pictures, 2001, MHL/MPA.

33. Ibid.

34. Mark Anthony Neal, *New Black Man* (New York: Routledge, 2005), 29.

35. *Save the Last Dance*, Production Notes, Press Kit, Paramount Pictures, 2001, MHL/MPA.
36. Sean Macaulay, "Trailer Trash Parked Only Eight Miles Away," *The Times London*, November 11, 2002, MHL/MPA.
37. Todd McCarthy, "Slap-Happy House Eyes Crossover Coin," *Variety*, February 24, 2003, 43.
38. Elvis Mitchell, "How Out of It Can You Be? Here's Going All the Way," *New York Times*, March 7, 2003, MHL/MPA.
39. *Malibu's Most Wanted*, Production Notes, Press Kit, Warner Bros., 2003, MHL/MPA.
40. Ibid.
41. Samuels, 62.
42. Bakari Kitwana, *Why White Kids Love Hip Hop* (New York: Basic Civitas, 2005), 113.
43. Samuels, 62.
44. Kitwana, *Why White Kids Love Hip Hop*, 121–122.
45. Ibid., 130.
46. *Ride*, Production Notes, Press Kit, Dimension Films, 1998, MHL/MPA.
47. John Anderson, "A Wild 'Ride' Into the World of the Rap Music Industry," *Los Angeles Times*, April 1, 1998, MHL/MPA.
48. Kelefa Sanneh, "Hip-Hop Conundrum: How Can a Pimp Be a Hero?" *New York Times*, July 28, 2005, MHL/MPA.
49. Erin Aubry Kaplan, "Pimping the Ride," *Los Angeles Weekly*, September 9, 2005, MHL/MPA.
50. Melina Abdullah, personal interview, November 7, 2005.
51. A. O. Scott, "A Pimp with a Heart Follows His Dream," *New York Times*, July 22, 2005, B20.
52. Ibid.
53. Melina Abdullah, personal interview, November 7, 2005.
54. Patrick Goldstein, "Hustling Pays Off," *Los Angeles Times*, January 18, 2005, p. E1.
55. Ibid., E8.
56. Ibid.
57. 50 Cent, *From Pieces to Weight* (New York: Pocket Books, 2005), 165.
58. Ibid., 203–205.
59. Ethan Smith and Merissa Mars, "Will a Rap Star's Violent Messages Play Well on Screen?" *Wall Street Journal*, November 8, 2005, B7.
60. Larry Altman, "Advertising Campaign for Movie Takes a Serious Rap," *The Daily Breeze*, October 28, 2005, MHL/MPA.
61. Dave McNary, "Par Tryin' to Appease Protestors," *Variety*, October 28, 2005, MHL/MPA.
62. Kenneth Turan, "A True to Thug Life Portrait," *Los Angeles Times*, November 9, 2005, E1.
63. Ibid., 198.
64. Paul Cullum, "Black Irish," *V Life Magazine*, October 2005, 18.

4. Tupac Shakur: From Hip-Hop Icon to Screen Idol

1. Elias Stimac, "John Singleton Directs a Well-Versed Cast Towards Poetic Justice," *DramaLogue*, July 29–August 4, 1993, MHL/MPA.

2. Eithne Quinn, *Nuthin' but a "G" Thang* (New York: Columbia University Press, 2005), 174–175.

3. Michael Eric Dyson, *Holler If You Hear Me* (New York: Basic Civitas, 2001), 24–25.

4. Ibid., 36–45.

5. Kevin Powell, "This Thug's Life," in *Vibe: Tupac Shakur*, ed. Alan Light (New York: Three Rivers Press, 1998), 27.

6. Peter Shapiro, *The Rough Guide to Hip Hop* (London: Penguin Books, 2005), 371.

7. S. Craig Watkins, *Hip Hop Matters* (Boston: Beacon Press, 2005), 163.

8. Powell, "This Thug's Life," 129.

9. Ibid., 29–31.

10. *Tupac Resurrection*, documentary film, directed by Lauren Lazin, Paramount Pictures, 2003.

11. Dan White Hodge, personal interview, February 16, 2006.

12. Powell, "This Thug's Life," 25.

13. Andrea M. Duncan, "Interview: Ernest Dickerson," in *Vibe: Tupac Shakur*, ed. Alan Light (New York: Three Rivers Press, 1998), 153.

14. Anitra M. Busch and Andrea King, "Paramount Marketing Plan for 'Juice' Comes Under Fire," *Hollywood Reporter*, January 10, 1992, 1.

15. Ibid., 6, 69.

16. Danyel Smith, "Introduction," in *Vibe: Tupac Shakur*, ed. Alan Light (New York: Three Rivers Press, 1998), 17.

17. John Singleton, "Afterwords," in *Vibe: Tupac Shakur*, ed. Alan Light (New York: Three Rivers Press, 1998), 152.

18. Stimac, 5.

19. Gwendolyn D. Pough, *Check It While I Wreck It: Black Womanhood, Hip Hop Culture, and the Public Sphere* (Boston: Northeastern University Press, 2004), 138–39.

20. Dyson, 223.

21. Ibid., 193.

22. Eric Williams, "Above the Rim," *Boxoffice*, June 1994, MHL/MPA.

23. Kevin Powell, *Who's Gonna Take the Weight? Manhood, Race, and Power in America* (New York: Three Rivers Press, 2003), 120.

24. Alan Light, "Lived Fast, Died Young," in *Vibe: Tupac Shakur*, ed. Alan Light (New York: Three Rivers Press, 1998), 155.

25. Quinn, 177.

26. David Kronke, "Dead Man Acting," *New Times L.A.*, January 30, 1997, MHL/MPA.

27. Ibid.

28. Janet Maslin, "And You Thought Recovery Was Serious Business," *New York Times*, January 29, 1997, MHL/MPA.

29. Joe Morgenstern, "On Film: Vondie Curtis Hall, From Doctor to Director," *Wall Street Journal*, January 30, 1997, A14.

30. Melvin Donalson, *Masculinity in the Interracial Buddy Film* (Jefferson, NC: McFarland, 2006), 130.

31. Todd McCarthy, "Gang Related," *Variety*, October 6, 1997, MHL/MPA.

32. Gary Dauphin, "Casualties of War," *Village Voice*, October 14, 1997, MHL/MPA.

33. Hodge, personal interview.

34. *Tupac Resurrection*, documentary film, Paramount Pictures, directed by Lauren Lazin, 2003.

5. Queen Latifah: From MC to Mainstream Diva

1. Laura Jamison, "Ladies First," in *The Vibe History of Hip Hop*, ed. Alan Light (New York: Three Rivers Press, 1999), 181.
2. Ibid., 178.
3. Gwendolyn O. Pough, *Check It While I Wreck It* (Boston: Northeastern University Press, 2004), 9.
4. Bakari Kitwana, *The Hip Hop Generation* (New York: Basic Civitas, 2002), xiv.
5. Queen Latifah, *Ladies First: Revelations of a Strong Woman* (New York: William Morrow, 1999), 15–18.
6. Ibid., 62.
7. Amy Ruth, *Queen Latifah* (Minneapolis, MN: Lerner Publications, 2001), 25–41.
8. Latifah, 67.
9. Ruth, 45.
10. Jamison, 183.
11. Ruth, 40.
12. Pough, 85.
13. Jamison, 179
14. Ibid., 179–180.
15. Tricia Rose, *Black Noise: Rap Music and Black Culture in Contemporary American* (Middletown, CT: Weslyan University Press, 1994), 163–164.
16. Cheryl L. Keyes, "Empowering Self, Making Choices, Creating Space: Black Female Identity Via Rap Music Performance," in *That's the Joint: The Hip-Hop Studies Reader*, ed. by Murray Forman and Mark Anthony Neal (New York: Routledge, 2004), 267.
17. Latifah, 3–4.
18. Joan Morgan, *When Chickenheads Come Home to Roost* (New York: Simon and Schuster, 1999), 74–75.
19. Ruth, 79.
20. Desson Howe, "Jungle Fever," *Washington Post*, June 7, 1991,http://www.Washington-post.com (accessed May 6, 2006).
21. Ibid.
22. Vincent Canby, "Hip Hop, Hooray, a 'Jammie Jam'to End All Parties," *New York Times*, October 23, 1991, MHL/MPA.
23. Janet Maslin, "Learning About Living, the Hard Way," *New York Times*, November 12, 1993, C17.
24. *My Life*, Production Notes, Press Kit, Columbia Pictures, 1993.
25. Ruth, 79.
26. *Taxi*, Production Notes, Press Kit, Twentieth Century Fox, September 2004, MHL/MPA.
27. Roger Ebert, "A Thriller with a Whole Lot More Than Action," *Long Beach Press-Telegram*, November 6, 1996, MHL/MPA.
28. Melvin Donalson, *Black Directors in Hollywood* (Austin: University of Texas Press, 2003), 317.
29. Amy Taubin, "Live Fast, Die Young," *Village Voice*, November 12, 1996, MHL/MPA.
30. Ruth, 86.
31. Latifah, 123.
32. Ruth, 82–83.
33. Latifah, 125.

34. Todd McCarthy, "Sphere," *Daily Variety*, February 11, 1998, MHL/MPA.
35. *Living Out Loud*, Production Notes, Press Kit, New Line Cinema, September 1998, MHL/MPA.
36. David Ansen, "An Unfinished Woman," *Newsweek*, November 2, 1998, 18.
37. Janet Maslin, "Yada Yada as a Way of Getting Another Life," *New York Times*, October 30, 1998, MHL/MPA.
38. Kenneth Turan, "Stepping Lightly Around Love," *Los Angeles Times*, October 1998, F20.
39. Ruth, 99.
40. "The Queen Latifah Show," CNET Networks Entertainment, TV.com (accessed May 10, 2006).
41. Stephen Holden, "A Taxi Ride to Torture Provokes a Chase," *New York Times*, November 5, 1999, E20.
42. *The Bone Collector*, Production Notes, Press Kit, Universal Studios, September 1999, MHL/MPA.
43. Michael Rechtshaffen, "Brown Sugar," *Hollywood Reporter*, October 7, 2002, 16.
44. Ian Nathan, "Look at My Baby," *The Times London*, December 23, 2002, MHL/MPA.
45. Ibid.
46. Elvis Mitchell, "'Chicago', Bare Legs and All, Makes It to Film," *New York Times*, December 27, 2002, MHL/MPA.
47. *Chicago*, Production Notes, Press Kit, Miramax Films, December 2002, MHL/MPA.
48. Ibid.
49. Kirk Honeycutt, "Taxi," *Hollywood Reporter*, October 6, 2004, MHL/MPA.
50. Dave Kehr, "Stop, Thief! Arrest That Model!" *New York Times*, October 6, 2004, E5.
51. *Beauty Shop*, Production Notes, Press Kit, MGM , 2005, MHL/MPA.
52. Kevin Thomas, "Latifah Rules This Hair Joint," *Los Angeles Times*, March 30, 2005, MHL/MPA.
53. Latifah, 126.

6. Beyond the Reel: Bling, Floss, and Hip Hop

1. Bridget Morris, "Hip Hop Didn't Stop and It's Taking Over," *Sunday Herald (Glasgow, UK)*, June 1, 2003, http://proquest.umi.com.mimas.calstatela.edu (accessed May 22, 2006).
2. Bakari Kitwana, *Why White Kids Love Hip Hop* (New York: Basic Civitas Books, 2005), 177–184.
3. Minya Oh, "'Bling Bling' Added to Oxford English Dictionary," *MTV News*, http://www.mtv.com/news/articles/1471629/20030430/bg.jhtml (accessed July 2, 2006).
4. Melissa August et al., "Hip Hop Nation: There's More to Rap Than Just Rhythms and Rhymes," in *Common Culture: Reading and Writing About American Popular Culture*, 4th ed., ed. Michael Petracca and Madelieine Sorapure (Upper Saddle River, NJ: Pearson, 2004), 303.
5. Uthrie P. Ramsey Jr., "Muzing New Hoods, Making New Identities: Film, Hip-Hop Culture, and Jazz Music," *Callaloo* 25, no. 1 (2002): 312.
6. Nahid Kassabian, *Hearing Film: Tracking Identifications in Contemporary Hollywood Film Music* (New York: Routledge, 2001), 43–44.
7. Uthrie, 313.

8.   Ibid., 314.

9.   Bruce Britt, "From Street to Marquee with Roles in Major Hollywood Films, Rappers Wading into the Mainstream," *Los Angeles Daily News*, March 14, 1991, http://proquest.-umi.com.mimas.calstatela.edu (accessed May 22, 2006).

10. Allister Harry, "Screen: It's a Rap!" *The Guardian (Manchester, UK)*, January 24, 1997, http://proquest.umi.com.mimas.calstatela.edu (accessed May 22, 2006).

11. Jesse Rhines, *Black Film/White Money* (New Brunswick, NJ: Rutgers University Press, 1996), 75.

12. Donald Bogle, *Toms, Coons, Mulattoes, Mammies, and Bucks*, 4th ed. (New York: Continuum, 2001), 343.

13. Guthrie, 311.

14. James Robert Parish, *Today's Black Hollywood* (New York: Pinnacle Books, 1995), 268.

15. Parish, 269.

16. *The Fresh Prince of Bel-Air*, Internet Movie Database.

17. *Variety Box Office Charts, 2001–2006*, Vol. 2, MHL/MPA.

18. Ibid.

19. *Ali*, Production Notes, Press Kit, November 2001, MHL/MPA.

20. Shane Salerno, "The Opposing Corners in Today's 'Ali' Matchup," *Los Angeles Times*, Counterpoint Section, January 7, 2002, MHL/MPA.

21. Jason Ankeny, "Marky Mark," *AOL Music Entertainment Guide*, http://music.aol.com/artist/marky-mark/101905/biography (accessed July 1, 2006).

22. Ibid.

23. *Bogie Nights*, Production Notes, Press Kit, 1997, MHL/MPA.

24. Rebecca Flint, "Mark Wahlberg," *VH1 Movies*, http:www.vh1.com/ movies/person/166-010/bio.jhtml (accessed July 1, 2006).

25. Ankeny.

26. Steve Head, "An Interview with Mark Wahlberg," *IGN Entertainment*, http://filmforce.ign.com/articles/421/421506p1.html (accessed July 1, 2006).

27. Flint.

28. *Variety Box Office Charts, 2001–2006*, Volume 2, MHL/MPA.

29. *Boogie Nights*, Production Notes, Press Kit, 1997, MHL/MPA.

30. Peter Travers, "Sex, Lies, and the Uncensored '70s," *Rolling Stone*, October 16, 1997, MHL/MPA.

31. Jacqui Sadashige, "Boogie Nights," *Magill's Cinema Annual: 1998*, 17th ed. MHL/MPA.

32. Renee Graham, "Singing the Praises of Acting Rappers," *Boston Globe*, May 10, 2005, http://proquest.umi.com.mimas.calstatela.edu (accessed May 22, 2006).

33. Ibid.

34. Vanessa E. Jones, "Hip-Hopping to Hollywood Artists Landing Mainstream Film Roles," *The Plain Dealer*, January 12, 2000, http://proquest.umi.com.mimas. calstatela.edu (accessed May 22, 2006).

35. Patrick Goldstein, "The Big Picture; Hip-Hop Artists Finally Make the Leap to Films," *Angeles Times*, July 24, 2001, http://proquest.umi.com.mimas.calstatela.edu (accessed July 2, 2006).

36. Ibid.

37. Jonathan Cohen, "Three 6 Mafia, Santaolalla Win Musical Oscars," *Billboard News and Reviews*, March 6, 2006, http://proquest.umi.com.mimas.calstatela.edu (accessed July 2, 2006).

38. Robert La Franco, "I Ain't Foolin' Around—I'm Building Assets," *Forbes*, March 22, 1999, 180.
39. Ibid., 186.
40. Toure, "The Book of Jay," *Rolling Stone*, December 15, 2005, 84.
41. Ibid.
42. Ibid., 84–85.
43. Ibid., 85.
44. Emil Wilbekin, "Great Aspirations: Hip Hop and Fashion Dress for Excess and Success," in *The Vibe History of Hip Hop*, ed. Alan Light (New York: Three Rivers Press, 1999), 278.
45. Ibid., 283.
46. Johnnie L. Roberts, "The Rap of Luxury," *Newsweek*, September 2, 2002, 42.
47. Ibid., 44.
48. *Variety Box Office Charts, 2001 –2006*, Vol. 2, MHL/MPA.
49. "Paramount Pictures Corporation," *Hoover's Inc*, http:// www. hoovers. com/paramount-pictures/--ID__103362--/free-co-factsheets.xhtml (accessed July 5, 2006).
50. "Viacom, Inc," *Hoover's Inc*, http://www.hoovers.com/viacom/--ID__143020--/free-co-factsheet.xhtml (accessed July 5, 2006).
51. Ibid.
52. "CBS Corporation," *Hoover's Inc*, http://www.hoovers.com/cbs-corp/--ID__12435--/free-co-factsheet.xhtml (accessed July 5, 2006).
53. Dennis Greene, "Tragically Hip: Hollywood and African-American Cinema," *Cineaste* 20, no. 4 (October 1994), http://wblinks3.epnet.com.mimas.calstatela.edu (accessed May 22, 2006).

Bibliography

The abbreviation MHL/MPA indicates materials researched in the Archival Files, Margaret Herrick Library, The Motion Picture Academy, Beverly Hills, CA.

Abdullah, Melina, personal interview, November 7, 2005.

Advocat, Stephen. "Theaters Yank Run DMC Film After Violence," *Variety*, October 13, 1988, MHL/MPA.

Ali, Production Notes, Studio Press Kit, November 2001, MHL/MPA.

Altman, Larry. "Advertising Campaign for Movie Takes a Serious Rap," *The Daily Breeze* October 28, 2005, MHL/MPA.

Alvarez, Gabriel. "Gangsta Rap in the 90s." In *The Vibe History of Hip Hop*, edited by Alan Light, 285–295. New York: Three Rivers Press, 1999.

Anderson, John. "A Wild 'Ride' Into the World of the Rap Music Industry," *Los Angeles Times*, April 1, 1998, MHL/MPA.

Ansen, David. "An Unfinished Woman," *Newsweek*, November 2, 1998, 18.

———."Shock to the System," *Newsweek*, May 18, 1998, 70, 72.

Ards, Angela. "Organizing the Hip-Hop Generation." In *That's the Joint: The Hip Hop Reader*, edited by Murray Forman and Mark Anthony Neal, 311–323. New York: Routledge, 2004.

August, Melissa , Leslie Everton Brice, Laird Harrison, Todd Murphy, and David E. Thigpen. "Hip Hop Nation: There's More to Rap Than Just Rhythms and Rhymes." In *Common Culture: Reading and Writing About American Popular Culture*, 4th ed., edited by Michael Petracca and Madeleine Sorapure, 300–313. Upper Saddle River, NJ: Prentice Hall, 2004.

Banes, Sally. "Breaking." In *That's the Joint! The Hip-Hop Studies Reader*, edited by Murray Forman and Mark Anthony Neal, 13–20. New York: Routledge, 2004.

Beauty Shop, Production Notes, Studio Press Kit, MGM , 2005, MHL/MPA.

Benshoff, Harry M. and Sean Griffin, *America on Film: Representing Race, Class, Gender, and Sexuality at the Movies*. Malden, MA: Blackwell Publishing, 2004.

Bogle, Donald. *Toms, Coons, Mulattoes, Mammies, and Bucks*. New York: Continuum Books, 1990.

——— . *Toms, Coons, Mulattoes, Mammies, and Bucks*, 4th edition. New York: Continuum, 2001.

The Bone Collector, Production Notes, Studio Press Kit, Universal Studios, September 1999, MHL/MPA.

Boogie Nights, Production Notes, Studio Press Kit, 1997, MHL/MPA.

Booty Call, Production Notes, Studio Press Kit, Columbia Pictures, 1997, MHL/MPA.

Boyd, Todd. *The New H.N.I.C.* New York: New York University Press, 2002.

Boyz N the Hood, Production Notes, Studio Press Kit, Columbia Pictures, 1991, MHL/MPA.

Breakin', Production Notes, Studio Press Kit, MGM/UA and The Cannon Group, 1984,

MHL/MPA.

"Breakin' 2: Electric Boogaloo," *Box Office*, February 1985, MHL/MPA.

Britt, Bruce. "From Street to Marquee with Roles in Major Hollywood Films, Rappers Wading into the Mainstream." *Los Angeles Daily News*, March 14, 1991. http://proquest.umi.com.mimas.calstatela.edu (accessed May 22, 2006).

Brown Sugar, Production Notes, Studio Press Kit, Fox Searchlight Pictures, 2002, MHL/MPA.

Busch, Anitra M. and Andrea King. "Paramount Marketing Plan for 'Juice' Comes Under Fire," *Hollywood Reporter*, January 10, 1992, 1, 6, 69.

Campbell, Kermit E. *Getting Our Groove On: Rhetoric, Language, and Literacy for the Hip Hop Generation*. Detroit, MI: Wayne State University Press, 2005.

Canby, Vincent. "Hip Hop, Hooray, a 'Jammie Jam'to End All Parties," *New York Times*, October 23, 1991, MHL/MPA.

Castleman, Craig. "The Politics of Graffiti." In *That's the Joint!: The Hip-Hop Studies Reader*, edited by Murray Forman and Mark Anthony Neal, 21–29. New York: Routledge, 2004.

CB4, Production Notes, Studio Press Kit, Universal Studios, 1993, MHL/MPA.

"CBS Corporation." *Hoover's Inc*. http://www.hoovers.com/cbs-corp/--ID__ 12435--/free-co-factsheet.xhtml (accessed July 5, 2006).

Chang, Jeff. *Can't Stop, Won't Stop: The History of the Hip-Hop Generation*. New York: St. Martin's Press, 2005.

Cherubin, Jan. "Two Street Dancers Breakin' into the Movie Business." *Los Angeles Herald Examiner*, May 29, 1984, MHL/MPA.

Chicago, Production Notes, Studio Press Kit, Miramax Films, December 2002, MHL/MPA.

Christgan, Robert, and Carola Dibbell. "One from the Motormouth." *Village Voice*, November 12, 1985, MHL/MPA.

Cohen, Jonathan. "Three 6 Mafia, Santaolalla Win Musical Oscars." *Billboard News and Reviews*, March 6, 2006, http://proquest.umi.com.mimas.calstatela.edu (accessed July 2, 2006).

Cooper, Barry Michael. "Teddy Riley's New Jack Swing." In *And It Don't Stop*, edited by Raquel Cepeda, 53–66. New York: Faber and Faber, 2004.

Crouch, Stanley. "Do Blonds Still Have More Fun?" *Talk Magazine*, April 2000, 160–161.

Cullum, Paul. "Black Irish," *V Life Magazine*, October 2005, 18–19.

"Dancetera: Broadway and Beyond," *Dance Magazine*, August 1984, MHL/MPA.

Dauphin, Gary. "Casualties of War," *Village Voice*, October 14, 1997, MHL/MPA.

———. "Hip Hop in the Movies." In *The Vibe History of Hip Hop*, edited by Alan Light, 201–207. New York: Three Rivers Press, 1999.

DeCurtis, Anthony. "2 Live Crew Trial." In *The Vibe History of Hip Hop*, edited by Alan Light, 268. New York: Three Rivers Press, 1999.

Def Jam's How to Be a Player, Production Notes, Studio Press Kit, Gramercy Pictures, 1997, MHL/MPA.

"Delivery Boys," *Variety*, July 30, 1986, MHL/MPA.

Demyaneko, Alex. "N.W.M.H.," *Los Angeles Village View*, June 10–16, 1994, MHL/MPA.

Denby, David. "Candid Chimera," *New York Magazine*, May 18, 1998, 51–52.

———. "Opposites Attract," *New Yorker*, April 10, 2000, 99–100.

Donalson, Melvin. *Black Directors in Hollywood*. Austin: University of Texas Press, 2003.

———. *Masculinity in the Interracial Buddy Film*. Jefferson, NC: McFarland Publishers, 2006.

Duncan, Andrea M. "Interview: Ernest Dickerson." In *Vibe: Tupac Shakur*, edited by Alan Light, 153. New York: Three Rivers Press, 1998.

Dyson, Michael Eric. *Between God and Gangsta Rap*. New York: Oxford University Press, 1996.

———. *Holler If You Hear Me*. New York: Basic Civitas, 2001.

Ebert, Roger. "Straight Out of Brooklyn," *Chicago Sun-Times*, June 28, 1991, rogerebert.com.

———. "A Thriller with a Whole Lot More Than Action," *Long Beach Press-Telegram*, November 6, 1996, MHL/MPA.

50 Cent. *From Pieces to Weight*. New York: Pocket Books, 2005.

Flint, Rebecca. "Mark Wahlberg." *VH1 Movies*. http:www.vh1.com/ movies/person/166010/-bio.jhtml (accessed July 1, 2006).

"Fly by Night," *Variety*, February 8, 1993, MHL/MPA.

Frere-Jones, Sasha. "Run-D.M.C." In *The Vibe History of Hip-Hop*, edited by Alan Light, 61–67. New York: Three Rivers Press, 1999.

The Fresh Prince of Bel-Air, Internet Movie Database.

Gardner, Elysa. "Hip Hop Soul." In *The Vibe History of Hip Hop*, edited by Alan Light, 307–317. New York: Three Rivers Press, 1999.

Gates, Henry Louis. "The White Negro." *New Yorker*, May 11, 1998, 62–65.

George, Nelson. *Buppies, B-Boys, Baps, and Bohos: Notes on Post-Soul Black Culture*. New York: HarperPerennial, 1992.

———. *Hip Hop America*. New York: Penguin, 1998.

———. "The Rhythm and the Blues." *Billboard*, October 26, 1986, MHL/MPA.

Goldstein, Patrick. "The Big Picture; Hip-Hop Artists Finally Make the Leap to Films." *Los Angeles Times*, July 24, 2001, http://proquest.umi.com.mimas.calstatela. edu (accessed July 2, 2006).

———. "Hustling Pays Off," *Los Angeles Times*, January 18, 2005, E1, E8.

Graham, Renee. "Singing the Praises of Acting Rappers." *Boston Globe*, May 10, 2005, http://proquest.umi.com.mimas.calstatela.edu (accessed May 22, 2006).

Greene, Dennis. "Tragically Hip: Hollywood and African-American Cinema." *Cineaste* 20, no. 4 , October 1994, http://wblinks3.epnet.com.mimas.calstatela.edu (accessed May 22, 2006).

Guerrero, Ed. *Framing Blackness: The African American Image in Film*. Philadelphia: Temple University Press, 1993.

Hager, Steven. "Afrika Bambaataa's Hip-Hop." In *And It Don't Stop: The Best American Hip-Hop Journalism in the Last 25 Years*, edited by Raquel Cepeda, 12–26. New York: Faber and Faber, 2004.

Hardy, Ernest. "A Nouveau Valentine." *Los Angeles Weekly*, March 14, 1997, 47.

———. "Pitted Against the Lizard," *Los Angeles Weekly*, May 29, 1998, 34–35.

Harry, Allister. "Screen: It's a Rap!" *The Guardian (Manchester, UK)*, January 24, 1997. http://proquest.umi.com.mimas.calstatela.edu (accessed May 22, 2006).

Head, Steve. "An Interview with Mark Wahlberg." *IGN Entertainment*. http:// Filmforce.ign.com/articles/421/421506p1.html (accessed July1, 2006).

Hilburn, Robert. "Run-D.M.C.: Raising Hell Again in the Movies." *Los Angeles Times*, Sunday Calendar Section, December 14, 1986, MHL/MPA.

Hill, Patrick B. "Deconstructing the Hip-Hop Hype: A Critical Analysis of the *New York Times'* Coverage of African-American Youth Culture." In *Bleep! Censoring Rock and Rap Music*, edited by Betty Houchin Winfield and Sandra Davidson, 104–114. Westport, Conn: Greenwood Press, 1999.

Hoberman, J. "Alphabet City," *Village Voice*, May 15, 1984, MHL/MPA.

Hodge, Dan White, personal interview, February 16, 2006.

Holden, Stephen. "A Taxi Ride to Torture Provokes a Chase." *New York Times*, November 5, 1999, E20.

Honeycutt, Kirk. "Taxi." *Hollywood Reporter*, October 6, 2004, MHL/MPA.

hooks, bell. *We Real Cool: Black Men and Masculinity*. New York: Routledge, 2004.

Howe, Desson. "Jungle Fever." Washington Post, June 7, 1991, http://www.Washington post.com (accessed May 6, 2006).

Jamison, Laura. "Ladies First." In *The Vibe History of Hip Hop*, edited by Alan Light, 177–185. New York: Three Rivers Press, 1999.

Johnson, Martin. "'Cop Killer' and Sister Souljah: Hip Hop Under Fire." In *The Vibe History of Hip Hop*, edited by Alan Light, 288–289. New York: Three Rivers Press, 1999.

Jones, Vanessa E. "Hip-Hopping to Hollywood Artists Landing Mainstream Film Roles." *The Plain Dealer*, January 12, 2000, http:// proquest.umi.com.mimas. calstatela.edu (accessed May 22, 2006).

Kaplan, Erin Aubry. "Pimping the Ride." *Los Angeles Weekly*, September 9, 2005, MHL/MPA.

Kassabian, Anahid. *Hearing Film: Tracking Identifications in Contemporary Hollywood Film Music*. New York: Routledge, 2001.

Katz, Ephraim. *The Film Encyclopedia*, 3rd ed. New York: HarperCollins, 1998.

Kehr, Dave. "Stop, Thief! Arrest That Model!" *New York Times*, October 6, 2004, E5.

Kennedy, Lisa. "Wack House: House Party Is Business As Usual." *Village Voice*, March 13, 1990, 67.

Keyes, Cheryl L. "Empowering Self, Making Choices, Creating Space: Black Female

Identity Via Rap Music Performance." In *That's the Joint: The Hip-Hop Studies Reader*, edited by Murray Forman and Mark Anthony Neal, 265–276. New York: Routledge, 2004.

Kitwana, Bakari. *The Hip Hop Generation: Young Blacks and the Crisis in African-American Culture*. New York: Basic Civitas, 2002.

———. *The Rap on Gangsta Rap*. Chicago: Third World Press, 1994.

———. *Why White Kids Love Hip Hop*. New York: Basic Civitas, 2005.

Klein, Andy. "Kickin It." *New Times Los Angeles*, March 13, 1997, MHL/MPA.

Kronke, David. "Dead Man Acting." *New Times L.A.*, January 30, 1997, MHL/MPA.

La Franco, Robert. "I Ain't Foolin' Around—I'm Building Assets." *Forbes*, March 22, 1999, 180–185.

Lee, Chris. "Hip-Hop Strips Down, Gets Intimate," *Los Angeles Times*, November 8, 2005, E1, E10.

———. "In Hip-Hop, Beats Do the Talking," *Los Angeles Times*, November 20, 2005, E1, E43.

Leland, John. "New Jack Cinema Enters Screening," *Newsweek*, June 10, 1991, 51–52.

Leland, John and Lynda Wright, "Black to the Future," *Newsweek*, May 27, 1991, 58.

Light, Alan. "Lived Fast, Died Young." In *Vibe: Tupac Shakur*, edited by Alan Light, 154–155. New York: Three Rivers Press, 1998.

Living Out Loud, Production Notes, Studio Press Kit, New Line Cinema, September 1998, MHL/MPA.

Lusane, Clarence. "Rap, Race, and Politics." In *That's The Joint: The Hip Hop Reader*, edited by Murray Forman and Mark Anthony Neal, 351–362. New York: Routledge, 2004.

Maasik, Sonia, and Jack Solomon. *Signs of Life: Readings on Popular Culture for Writers*, 5th ed. Boston: Bedford Books, 2006.

Macaulay, Sean. "Trailer Trash Parked Only Eight Miles Away," *The Times London*, November 11, 2002, MHL/MPA.

Malibu's Most Wanted, Production Notes, Studio Press Kit, Warner Bros., 2003, MHL/MPA.

Marriott, Robert. "Gangsta, Gangsta: The Sad Violent Parable of Death Row Records." In *The Vibe History of Hip Hop*, edited by Alan Light, 319–325. New York: Three Rivers Press, 1999).

Maslin, Janet. "And You Thought Recovery Was Serious Business," *New York Times*, January 29, 1997, MHL/MPA.

———. "Film: Timothy Hutton in 'Turk 182!'" *The New York Times*, February 15, 1985, MHL/MPA.

———. "Learning About Living, the Hard Way." *New York Times*, November 12, 1993, C17.

———. "Yada Yada as a Way of Getting Another Life." *New York Times*, October 30, 1998, MHL/MPA.

Massood, Paula J. *Black City Cinema: African American Urban Experiences in Film*. Philadelphia: Temple University Press, 2003.

McCarthy, Todd. "Gang Related." *Variety*, October 6, 1997, MHL/MPA.

———. "Slap-Happy House Eyes Crossover Coin." *Variety*, February 24, 2003, 43, 51.

———. "Sphere," *Daily Variety*, February 11, 1998, MHL/MPA.

McKenna, Kristine. "Ice Cube Melts in Front of the Camera." *New York Times*, July 14, 1991, MHL/MPA.

McNary, Dave. "Par Tryin' to Appease Protestors." *Variety*, October 28, 2005, MHL/MPA.

Menace II Society, Production Notes, Studio Press Kit, New Line Cinema, 1993, MHL/MPA.

Menzie, Nicola. "'Krump' Dances into Mainstream." CBS News.com, June 30, 2005.

Mitchell, Elvis. "'Body Rock' Is Gaudy Schlock." *Los Angeles Herald Examiner*, October 12, 1982, MHL/MPA.

———. "'Chicago', Bare Legs and All, Makes It to Film." *New York Times*, December 27, 2002, MHL/MPA.

———. "How Out of It Can You Be? Here's Going All the Way." *New York Times*, March 7, 2003, MHL/MPA.

———. "Talk the Talk, Then Steal the Life Force." *New York Times*, April 5, 2000, MHL/MPA.

Morgan, Joan. *When Chickenheads Come Home to Roost*. New York: Simon and Schuster, 1999.

Morgenstern, Joe. "On Film: Vondie Curtis Hall, From Doctor to Director," *Wall Street Journal*, January 30, 1997, A14.

Morris, Bridget. "Hip Hop Didn't Stop and It's Taking Over." *Sunday Herald (Glasgow, UK)*, June 1, 2003. http://proquest.umi.com.mimas.calstatela.edu (accessed May 22, 2006).

My Life, Production Notes, Studio Press Kit, Columbia Pictures, 1993.

Nathan, Ian. "Look at My Baby." *The Times London*, December 23, 2002, MHL/MPA.

Neal, Mark Anthony. *New Black Man*. New York: Routledge, 2005.

Nelson, Martha. "Break Dancing—Men Only?" *Ms*, September 1984, MHL/MPA.

Oh, Minya. "'Bling Bling' Added to Oxford English Dictionary." *MTV News*, http://www.mtv.com/news/articles/1471629/20030430/bg.jhtml (accessed July 2, 2006).

"Paramount Pictures Corporation." *Hoover's Inc.* http:// www. hoovers.com/paramount-pictures/--ID__103362--/free-cofactsheets.xhtml (accessed July 5, 2006).

Parish, James Robert. *Today's Black Hollywood*. New York: Pinnacle Books, 1995.

Perry, Imani. *Prophets of the Hood: Politics and Poetics in Hip Hop*. Durham, NC: Duke University Press, 2004.

Pough, Gwendolyn D. *Check It While I Wreck It: Black Womanhood, Hip Hop Culture, and the Public Sphere*. Boston: Northeastern University Press, 2004.

Powell, Kevin. "This Thug's Life." In *Vibe: Tupac Shakur*, edited by Alan Light, 21–31. New York: Three Rivers Press, 1998.

———. *Who's Gonna Take the Weight? Manhood, Race, and Power in America*. New York: Three Rivers Press, 2003.

Purple Rain. Internet Movie Database .

Queen Latifah. *Ladies First: Revelations of a Strong Woman*. New York: William Morrow, 1999.

"The Queen Latifah Show." CNET Networks Entertainment, TV.com (accessed May 10, 2006.

Quinn, Eithne. *Nuthin' but a "G" Thang*. New York: Columbia University Press, 2005.

Ramsey, Guthrie P. Jr. "Muzing New Hoods, Making New Identities: Film, Hip-Hop Culture, and Jazz Music." *Callaloo* 25, no. 1 (2002): 309–320.

Rechtshaffen, Michael. "Brown Sugar," *Hollywood Reporter*, October 7, 2002, 10, 16.

Rhines, Jesse. *Black Film/White Money*. New Brunswick, NJ: Rutgers University Press, 1996.

Ride, Production Notes, Studio Press Kit, Dimension Films, 1998, MHL/MPA.

Rize, documentary film, directed by David LaChapelle, Lions Gate Entertainment, 2005.

Robbins, Jim. "Rap Pic Pulled in Long Island." *Variety*, September 15, 1988, MHL/MPA.

Roberts, Johnnie L. "The Rap of Luxury." *Newsweek*, September 2, 2002, 42–44.

Rose, Tricia. *Black Noise: Rap Music and Black Culture in Contemporary America*. Middletown, CT: Wesleyan University Press, 1994.

Ruth, Amy. *Queen Latifah*. Minneapolis, MN: Lerner Publications, 2001.

Sadashige, Jacqui. "Boogie Nights." In *Magill's Cinema Annual: 1998*, 17th ed., edited by Beth A. Fhaner, 62–64. Detroit, MI: Gale, 1998.

Salerno, Shane. "The Opposing Corners in Today's 'Ali' Matchup." *Los Angeles Times*, Counterpoint Section, January 7, 2002, MHL/MPA.

Samuels, Allison. "Minstrels in Baggy Jeans?" *Newsweek*, May 5, 2003, 62.

Samuels, David. "The Rap on Rap." In *That's the Joint: The Hip-Hop Studies Reader,* edited by Murray Forman and Mark Anthony Neal, 147–153 . New York: Routledge, 2004.

Sanneh, Kelefa. "Hip-Hop Conundrum: How Can a Pimp Be a Hero?" *New York Times*, July 28, 2005, MHL/MPA.

Save the Last Dance, Production Notes, Studio Press Kit, Paramount Pictures, 2001, MHL/MPA.

Scott, A. O. "A Pimp with a Heart Follows His Dream." *New York Times*, July 22, 2005, B1, B20.

Shapiro, Peter. *The Rough Guide to Hip-Hop*, 2nd ed. London: Rough Guides, 2005.

Shaw, Arnold. *Black Popular Music in America*. New York: Schirmer Books, 1986.

Simmons, Russell. *Life and Def: Sex, Drugs, Money and God*. New York: Crown Publishers, 2001.

Singleton, John. "Afterword." In *Vibe: Tupac Shakur*, edited by Alan Light, 152. New York: Three Rivers Press, 1998.

Smith, Danyel. "Introduction." In *Vibe: Tupac Shakur*, edited by Alan Light, 15–16. New York: Three Rivers Press, 1998.

Smith, Ethan, and Merissa Mars. "Will a Rap Star's Violent Messages Play Well on Screen?" *Wall Street Journal*, November 8, 2005, B1, B7.

Stanley, Larry A., ed. *Rap: The Lyrics*. New York: Penguin Books, 1992.

Stein, Ellin. "Wild Style." *American Film*, November 1983, MHL/MPA.

Stevenson, Richard W. "An Anti-Gang Movie Opens to Violence." *New York Times*, July 14, 1991, MHL/MPA.

Stimac, Elias. "John Singleton Directs a Well-Versed Cast Towards Poetic Justice." *Drama-Logue*, July 29-August 4, 1993, MHL/MPA.

Szatmary, David P. *Rockin' Time: A Social History of Rock-and-Roll*, 4th ed. Upper Saddle River, NJ: Prentice-Hall, 2000.

Taubin, Amy. "Live Fast, Die Young." *Village Voice*, November 12, 1996, MHL/MPA.

Taxi, Production Notes, Studio Press Kit, Twentieth Century Fox, September 2004, MHL/MPA.

Taylor, Clark. "Rapping and Breaking in 'Beat Street.'" *Los Angeles Times*, Sunday Calendar Section, March 15, 1984, MHL/MPA.

Thomas, Kevin. "'Brown Sugar': The Hip Hop of Romance," *Los Angeles Times*, October 11, 2002, MHL/MPA.

———. "'How to Be a Player'—or How to Cheat and Not Get Caught," *Los Angeles Times*, August 8, 1997, F6.

———. "Latifah Rules This Hair Joint." *Los Angeles Times*, March 30, 2005, MHL/MPA.

Toure, "The Book of Jay," *Rolling Stone*, December 15, 2005, 81–94, 167.

———. "The Hip-Hop Nation." *And It Don't Stop!: The Best American Hip-Hop Journalism in the Last 25 Years*, edited by Raquel Cepeda, 272–278. New York: Faber and Faber, 2004.

Travers, Peter. "Sex, Lies, and the Uncensored '70s." *Rolling Stone*, October 16, 1997, MHL/MPA.

Tupac Resurrection, documentary film, Paramount Pictures, directed by Lauren Lazin, 2003.

Turan, Kenneth. "A True to Thug Life Portrait," *Los Angeles Times*, November 9, 2005, E1, E4.

———. "Stepping Lightly Around Love." *Los Angeles Times*, October 1998, F20.

Van Deburg, William. *Hoodlums: Black Villains and Social Bandits in America.* Chicago: University of Chicago Press, 2004.

van Gelder, Lawrence. "For Young Blacks, Decency vs. Crime." *The New York Times,* Film Review, November 4, 1998, nytimes.com.

Variety, February 24, 1997, MHL/MPA.

Variety Box Office Charts, 2001–2006, Vol. 2, MHL/MPA.

Veran, Cristina. "Breaking It All Down." In *The Vibe History of Hip Hop*, edited by Alan Light, 53–59. New York: Three Rivers Press, 1999.

"Viacom, Inc." *Hoover's Inc.* http://www.hoovers.com/viacom/--ID__143020--/free-co factsheet.xhtml (accessed July 5, 2006).

Watkins, S. Craig. *Hip Hop Matters: Politics, Pop Culture, and the Struggle for the Soul of a Movement.* Boston: Beacon Press, 2005.

Whipp, Glenn. "'Love Jones' Puts Black Filmmaking in New Territory." *The Daily Breeze*, March 16, 1997, MHL/MPA.

Wilbekin, Emil. "Great Aspirations: Hip Hop and Fashion Dress for Excess and Success." In *The Vibe History of Hip Hop*, edited by Alan Light, 277–283. New York: Three Rivers Press, 1999.

Williams, Eric. "Above the Rim." *Boxoffice*, June 1994, MHL/MPA.

Willman, Chris. "Rap Attack, Take Two." *Los Angeles Times*, Sunday Calendar Section, March 14, 1993, 3, 20.

———— . "Run-DMC's 'Tougher Than Leather.'" *Los Angeles Times*, November 16, 1988, MHL/MPA.

Wilmington, Michael. "'Rappin' Hip-Hop Way to Quick Smiles." *Los Angeles Times*, May 10, 1985, MHL/MPA.

Wilson, John M. "Trying to Crash the Party." *Los Angeles Times*, Sunday Calendar Section, March 4, 1990, 88.

Index

-H-